The Russians Are Coming!
The Russians Are Coming!

An armed guard controls entrance to the theatre in Mosinee, Wisconsin, where "Communists" seized power on May 1, 1950, in the most dramatic of America's Cold War pageants.

The Russians Are Coming!
The Russians Are Coming!

Pageantry and Patriotism in Cold-War America

Richard M. Fried

New York   Oxford
OXFORD UNIVERSITY PRESS
1998

Oxford University Press

Oxford   New York
Athens   Auckland   Bangkok   Bogotá   Bombay
Buenos Aires   Calcutta   Cape Town   Dar es Salaam
Delhi   Florence   Hong Kong   Istanbul   Karachi
Kuala Lumpur   Madras   Madrid   Melbourne
Mexico City   Nairobi   Paris   Singapore
Taipei   Tokyo   Toronto   Warsaw

associated companies in
Berlin   Ibadan

Library of Congress Cataloging-in-Publication Data
Fried, Richard M., 1941–
The Russians are coming! The Russians are coming! :
pageantry and patriotism in Cold-War America /
Richard M. Fried.
p. cm.
Includes bibliographic references and index.
ISBN 1–19–507020–8
1. Cold War—Social aspects—United States.
2. Political culture—United States—History—20th century.
3. Patriotism—United States—History—20th century.
4. Pageants—United States—History—20th century.
5. Anti-communist movements—United States—History.
6. United States—Civilization—1945–
I. Title.
E169.12.F736 1998   973.92—dc21   98–12913

Frontispiece reproduced courtesy of the *Milwaukee Journal Sentinel*

1 3 5 7 9 8 6 4 2
Printed in the United States of America
on acid-free paper

To my wife
Barbara Brachman Fried

Contents

Preface

This book is about some of the ways Americans sought to nerve fellow-citizens for the long struggle against communism abroad and at home. We know much about the "hard" side of the cold-war political culture—the anti-communism expressed in calls to answer the question "Are you now or have you ever been...," the lists of suspects and victims famous and obscure, the checklists of traits by which Communists betrayed themselves, and the ways anti-communism crept into facets of culture such as entertainment and intellectual discourse.

We know less about Cold War America's "soft" side, about the diurnal aspects of life in the period. School children did not "Duck and Cover" from atomic attack every school day. Adults may have worried more about car payments than Bolshevism—though doubtless many would have liked this priority reversed. How did anti-communism settle into people's lives at times HUAC or McCarthy or lesser imitators were not in the news? We remember volcanic eruptions, but what of the fine dust? We need to know what was in the Metro or Women's sections as well as on the front page. How did Americans, when not consumed by Alger Hiss or Stalin or Korea, articulate their concern about communism and translate it into patriotism?

It is important to discover how we expressed broader fears about what it was that communism menaced and how we articulated what made communism's target—ourselves—so vulnerable and, indeed, so laggard in response to danger. There were psychological theories about where Commies came from (McCarthy's "bright young men ... born with silver spoons in their mouths" or the twisted women in Hollywood's version of communism). But anti-communist activists also elaborated marketing plans to "sell" the American Way to the public and a sociology to explain the latter's sometime torpor.

Much documentation for these worries and this activism has lain at hand for years in presidential and other archives, seeming dross intermingled with the "important" correspondence among political leaders and memos strategizing the communist issue; similar gems lay buried in the inside pages of newspapers. In past forays I often shuffled past materials treating the milder, didactic side of anti-communism and the archival remains of civic and patriotic pageantry. The quainter items include a boy's request that President Truman design an ensign for his newly founded "Freedom Club" and solicitations of a presidential greeting from American Legion women's auxiliaries, an old shirt to be raffled by another group, or an inspiring message for a publication or anniversary. Presidential papers afford better entree into social history than one might suspect. Even gaseous chamber of commerce and Kiwanis speeches had something to say.

I similarly discounted as secondary phenomena the common and concrete manifestations of the "soft" side of anti-communism, patriotism, cold-war civic activism. Patriotic rallies, loyalty parades and pageants, Know Your America Weeks, "Rededication" Weeks, and flag presentations, while interesting, seemed more like anti-communism's punctuation than its grammar. But the profuse variety of cold-war pageantry prompted reconsideration.

Such activities do not necessarily give access to "bottom-up" social history: too many of the actors belonged to the elite, and too many of the target audiences's responses evade measure. But some episodes do provide a whiff of the grassroots. Moreover, "elite" is an expansive term. The *creme de la creme* launched some initiatives: the Freedom Train was organized by leaders of the federal government, Wall Street, Madison Avenue and the media. But Americanism Days and Freedom Weeks, though sometimes with guidance from national authorities, depended on the energies of local civic groups.

The fetes and rituals of anti-communism, patriotism, and civic education do reveal much about the attitudes of those who masterminded them. The basic conundrum was: if communism was so patently evil and the American Way so obviously superior, why did plain facts apparently not convince enough *others* to assume the level of alert citizenship and Americanism that the danger dictated? For many activists doubted that their cause would be heeded.

This book attempts to answer that question and to plumb the way citizenship activists struggled to define what it was we had to defend and then to convey the message to others. Their varied efforts to do so consumed huge amounts of energy and, whether profoundly or lightly, touched many American lives. Sponsors of the Freedom Train claimed that forty million people took part in associated "rededication" activities. Each year the Veterans of Foreign Wars toted up several million participants and onlookers at Loyalty Day parades. The American Heritage Foundation sent recordings of the National Anthem to every school in the country. To get a sense of the impact of campaigns to play "The Star-Spangled Banner" at every public and athletic event, we need to multiply the years by the number of games on the schedule by the attendance at each.

We tend to assume that the patriotic practices now second nature to us grew up with the Republic, but they are of more recent vintage. A good many entered usage during the Cold War or in the longer period that included the anxious years prior to American entry into World War II, the war itself, *and* the Cold War. In fact, mobilizing the American public to meet the challenges of the Cold War was a task analogous to promoting the home-front war effort during World War II. Many of the calls to action and methods and even some of the personnel of Cold War morale-building demonstrate carryover from the fondly-remembered days of the "good war" of 1941–45. Many of the practices of nationhood date from this long period of concern with foreign dangers and influences.

Acknowledgments

In writing this book I have incurred many debts. Archivists have provided crucial help. Several, after being briefly taken aback by the odd nature of my interests, thought of topics that expanded my notions of civic and patriotic pageants. The list of manuscript sources at the end of the book suggests some of the places that have assisted me. I owe particular gratitude to Dennis Bilger, Phil Lagerquist and Irwin Mueller of the Truman Library, James Leyerzapf at the Eisenhower Library, Fred Klose of NARA at Laguna Niguel, Karl Kabelac of the University of Rochester, James Gregory Bradsher at the National Archives in Washington, Marian Smith at the Immigration and Naturalization Service Research Library, and Grace O'Connor of Mosinee High School. My thanks go also to George Johnson, Elly Vajda Seng and Clinton W. Kanaga, Jr., for access to materials in their possession, and to those kind enough to let me interview them.

I received much assistance at the Richard J. Daley Library of the University of Illinois at Chicago, notably from Kathleen Kilian of Interlibrary Loan. The involvement of Dr. Stephen E. Wiberley, Jr., in this book was nearly conspiratorial. The staffs of the Glen Ellyn Public Library and the College of DuPage also provided much help.

Many fellow-historians have aided me. They gave me documents or information about sources, commentary on conference papers, opportunities to impose my ideas on their students and colleagues, and useful reminiscences. My debts extend to James L. Baughman, Debra Beil, Mary C. Brennan, Don E. Carleton, John Lewis Gaddis, Alonzo L. Hamby, Paul

Hass, John O. Holzheuter, Masahiro Hosoya, Harold Josephson, James J. Lorence, R. Alton Lee, Charles H. McCormick, Michael Mayer, Donald J. Mrozek, David M. Oshinsky, Gary W. Reichard, Leo P. Ribuffo, Gregory L. Schneider, Robert D. Schulzinger, William Vandercook, Stephen Vaughn, Allan Winkler, and Allen Weinstein. William E. Leuchtenburg provided ideas and inspiration on several levels over many years.

For advice, stimulation and indulgence of my obsessions, I have relied on colleagues at the University of Illinois at Chicago, including but not limited to Marion Miller, Carolyn Edie, Ed Thaden, Burt Bledstein, Richard Jensen, Perry Duis, Mary Kay Vaughan, Jim Cracraft, Bob Messer, Peg Strobel, Dan Smith, John Kulczycki, Mildred Schwartz, and Jim Sack. As director of the UIC Humanities Institute, Gene Ruoff established a productive environment for work on this project, as did assistant administrator Linda Vavra and the other fellows of the 1988–89 Institute.

Several institutions gave me essential support. A year's fellowship at the UIC Humanities Institute and a University of Illinois sabbatical afforded crucial time for research and conceptualization. The Humanities Institute and UIC's Campus Research Board provided valuable travel funds. I am also grateful for short-term research grants from the John F. Kennedy Library Foundation, the Rockefeller Archive Center, and the National Endowment for the Humanities. As UIC Honors College undergraduate research assistants, Amish Desai and Ted Ebersold ably tracked down valuable and fugitive materials.

Many people at Oxford University Press provided valuable assistance. As editors Nancy Lane made possible the inception of this book, and Thomas LeBien and Helen B. Mules ably guided it to completion.

Some obligations fall under the heading of "family values." Rocky and Gail, and now their spouses Lycia and Kevin, have provided encouragement and been tolerant of numerous paternal quirks, including visits disrupted by research binges. Duffy, Bingo and Daisy have also provided dogged support.

Cannon salutes, huzzahs and strewn flowers are noisy, messy, and uncommon among historians. Even so, they would not be out of place to recognize the role played by my wife in this long project. By comparison a dedication page seems meagre pageantry indeed. Nevertheless, this book is lovingly dedicated to my wife, Barbara Brachman Fried.

Glen Ellyn, Illinois   R.M.F.
October 1997

The Russians Are Coming!
The Russians Are Coming!

Introduction

Patriotic Pageantry in America

"**K**eep, ancient lands, your storied pomp." So begins the final verse of Emma Lazarus's "The New Colossus." Though less often recited than her paean to the golden door, these words sound a powerful theme of national identity. Americans reject the pomp and pageantry of the tired, monarchical, militaristic, oppressive Old World. They do not "stand on ceremony." During World War I, President Woodrow Wilson defined the enemy as "Governments clothed with the strange trappings and primitive authority of an age that is altogether alien and hostile to our own."[1] Negative political repercussions befall those who forget the egalitarian folklore, from John Adams to Richard M. Nixon, who garbed White House police in uniforms befitting an operetta set in Mitteleuropa.

Yet despite the democratic ethos, Americans do cherish ceremony. Absent ancient knightly orders, we join civic and fraternal organizations with comparable titles and regalia.[2] Lacking royal family or palaces, we make do with presidents, their families and the White House. Much of John F. Kennedy's appeal was the storybook glamor with which he and Jackie enlivened the White House. Aiming to demystify the imperial presidency, Jimmy Carter carried his own garment bag and heard fewer renditions of "Hail to the Chief," gestures that did little for his political standing. We denigrate pomp but have never been without it, and as patriotic activists became a growing presence in American life, they insisted that patriotism was best instilled through pomp and ceremony.[3]

As a young nation lacking ruined abbeys or royal houses, we have strained to create history out of whatever comes to hand. We are a people

of anniversaries. Twenty years after the break-in at the office of the Democratic National Committee, surviving members of the Senate Watergate
Committee and its staff held a reunion. Even disasters are marked. Johns-
town, Pennsylvania, celebrated the centennial of the 1889 flood that killed
2,209 of its citizens. Nor is triviality a hurdle. Spectators at the 1988
Purdue-Ohio State football game paid homage to the Buckeye national
champs of twenty years earlier. In 1995 the thirty-fifth anniversary of the
Barbie Doll was duly noted.[4]

America's pageantry did not originate from a single source, and it over-
simplifies even to chart two points of origin. Show, ceremony, parades and
ritual could arise from many places, but in general they came either from
the relatively prosperous, who laid claim to being society's proper leaders,
or from those of lesser stature who devised symbolic means to contest the
hegemony of the "better sort." Some public observances were planned in
elegant drawing rooms or atheneums; others were improvised in taverns.
Often a dialogue developed between these competing modes of representation.[5]

Near the turn of the twentieth century, America acquired a taste for
pageantry. Older towns had important anniversaries—or at least long his-
tories—to mark. As their inhabitants sensed the inroads of industrializa-
tion on rural life, the nationalizing of the culture and the economy, and
the exodus of their children, the dominant note was nostalgia. In this,
American pageant creators shared the attitude of fellow-enthusiasts in
England who, inspired by the arts and crafts movement, cherished a sim-
pler, innocent past. Sponsors of town pageants aimed to reestablish the
authority of the older elites and build civic pride and cohesion in a time
when change was scouring away the societal landscape on which the old
way of life had been built.[6]

Such a pageant marked the 150th anniversary of the founding of Thetford, Vermont, in 1911. The background of its initiator, William Chauncy
Langdon, included social services in New York City, work in educational
reform, an enthusiasm for the Country Life movement, and training in
history, literature, and theater. The pageant linked Thetford's early years,
much idealized, through struggles of a more recent vintage to a future
beckoning with hope. It aimed to forge a spirit of community based on a
common past to meet the challenges of that future. "The pageant," said
Langdon, "brings people together and kindles the spirit of enthusiastic
unanimity as does nothing else." Though pageants would evolve beyond

the forms adopted in Thetford and other locales in the early twentieth century, sponsors of later varieties could agree fully with Langdon's rationale.

Pageants were not confined to small towns. Progressive-era educational and playground reformers had discovered the value of play and of history taught through play as means with which to inculcate the democratic spirit. Their efforts and those of activists in the movement for a Safe and Sane Fourth of July led, in 1908, to a parade in Springfield, Massachusetts, which included floats illustrating historical events meaningful to a wide variety of racial and ethnic inhabitants of the city. In 1910 Bostonians attended "From Cave Life to City Life: The Pageant of a Perfect City." The genre reached a peak in the 1914 Pageant and Masque of Saint Louis. Commemorating the city's sesquicentennial, this elaborate performance had a purpose beyond entertainment. Prior to it, the muckraker Lincoln Steffens had held the city government of St. Louis up to national opprobrium; shortly after it, St. Louis civic leaders won passage of a charter reform.[7]

These early twentieth-century pageants became a focus of professionalization. Founded in 1913, the American Pageant Association attempted to establish standards for the genre. The APA enjoyed its greatest influence in that decade. However, commercial firms soon assumed a growing role. After World War I, for-profit pageant-masters outstripped the influence of the reformists. For instance, the John B. Rogers Producing Company, founded in 1903, sold its skills after 1918 as a business that provided celebrating communities "a complete service . . . from money-raising campaign to final production." By 1947, they boasted having put on the Will Rogers Memorial Celebration, the North Dakota Golden Jubilee, the Lodi Grape and Wine Festival, the Wapello County Iowa State Centennial, and countless other events. The future lay with businessmen, not reformers, and more with events like Macy's Thanksgiving Day Parade and Pasadena's Tournament of Roses than with Thetford or even St. Louis. The APA closed its doors in 1930.[8]

This profusion of pageantry was primarily local. In a federal republic with a history of decentralization, the sinews of nationhood were often loose and undeveloped, the Jeffersonian ideal of localism and states rights and the Madisonian concept of pluralism persisted. The onset of and American entry into World War I did much, however, to stimulate efforts to promote patriotism and to nationalize celebration.

The United States had not lacked patriotic exercises in its early years. In 1777 the Fourth of July[9] was celebrated in three cities. John Adams had expected July 2, when the Continental Congress voted for independence, to be marked with "solemn acts of devotion to God Almighty" and "pomp and parade, with shows, games, sports, guns, bells, bonfires, and illuminations, from one end of this continent to the other, from this time forward, forevermore." However, it was July 4, when the Declaration was formally approved (but not signed by most delegates), that Americans swiftly made the occasion for festivity.

Washington's Birthday also garnered patriotic salutes. The first celebration seems to have occurred in 1779 in Milton, Massachusetts. Yet neither of these two observances was, strictly speaking, a national holiday. July Fourth was widely celebrated but entirely dependent on local initiative. As sectional strife began to unravel the nation, both occasions fell into disuse in the South. Indeed, it was national news that Vicksburg, Mississippi, resumed celebrating the Fourth in 1945—a "spiritual return to the Union" after an eighty-two-year hiatus begun while General U. S. Grant laid siege to the town.[10]

Several locales claimed to have first celebrated Memorial Day (or Decoration Day), including Boalsburg, Pennsylvania, and Waterloo, New York. The occasion also had roots as a day of homage to the Confederate dead. When the women of Columbus, Mississippi, also honored the Union dead in their graveyard, their kindness worked itself into the mythology of sectional reconciliation and recommended itself as a national institution. The Grand Army of the Republic adopted Memorial Day in 1868. In 1873 New York became the first state to celebrate it. By 1891, every northern state did so. It did not for some time become a nationwide observance, as Southern states continued to celebrate Confederate Memorial Day.[11]

The emergence of an industrialized, multi-ethnic urban society prompted Americans who fretted over these trends to seek appropriate rituals to domesticate alien influences. In the 1890s patriotic consciousness and activism quickened.[12] The phrase "The New Nationalism," Teddy Roosevelt's 1912 presidential campaign theme, captioned a number of currents of concern to Progressives. Pageantry offered one way to teach citizens of an increasingly complex urban world their expanded civic duties. *Century Magazine* editorialized that "nothing is more likely to cement the sympathies of our people and to accentuate our homogeneity than a cultivation of pageants."[13]

Foreign challenges heightened the felt need to reinforce cohesion. Two world wars and their preliminaries, and threats, both real and imagined, from alien sources, stimulated self-appointed guardians of American nationality to act. The menace of drastic social change also energized keepers of tradition on numerous occasions. Red scares accelerated patriotic work. That of 1919–20 comprised not only the Palmer raids but efforts to inspire greater patriotic devotion. In the late 1930s, the conservative reaction to the New Deal and a more general response to the perceived menace of alien "isms" produced a similar patriotic renewal. Often Americans scarcely differentiated between German fascism and Soviet communism; during the Hitler-Stalin pact, such distinctions seemed vacant.

Flag Day was a patriotic byproduct of World War I. The date had enjoyed spotty local celebration prior to 1916. On June 14, 1861, the anniversary of the Continental Congress's adoption of the nation's banner, citizens of Hartford, Connecticut, flew the flag to attest support for the Union. In 1877 Congress recognized the flag's hundredth anniversary. Schools began to mark Flag Day. In 1893 it was celebrated for the first time at Philadelphia's Betsy Ross House.[14] Woodrow Wilson issued the first presidential proclamation of Flag Day in 1916, at a time both he and the nation wavered between belligerence and pacifism. Thanks to the preparedness movement, in support of which Wilson marched in a parade with an American flag draped around his torso, patriotism had entered a boom period. In 1918, the nation now fully engaged in the conflict, Flag Day opened a period of wartime patriotic activity called Loyalty Week.[15]

Wilson innovated in other forms of patriotic endeavor. In a time when massive immigration stirred unease, his administration took special interest in assimilating newcomers into American life. Various agencies worked to make immigrants literate in English, impress on them the virtues of the American system and attach them more firmly to it. Such activists deemed it crucial to prepare immigrants for citizenship, encourage them to seek it, and devise meaningful ceremonies to mark its attainment.

On May 10, 1915, President Wilson addressed 5,000 new citizens and 12,000 observers at a naturalization ceremony in Philadelphia. He declared America "too proud to fight" in the war but, more pertinently, gave an artfully balanced assessment of the immigrant's presence. On one hand, immigration made the United States "the only country in the world which experiences this constant and repeated rebirth." While love of one's country of birth was "very sacred," Wilson warned: "You cannot become thorough Americans if you think of yourselves in groups. America does not consist of groups." [16]

The Philadelphia ceremony inspired "a wave of patriotic sentiment." On July 4, 1916, Americanization Day celebrations were held in some 150 cities. In 1916, at a Washington, D.C., Citizenship Convention, Wilson spoke, but with a sharper edge than he had in Philadelphia, reflecting a rising concern about divisions at home aggravated by the war. He warned that "Certain men,—I have never believed a great number,—born in other lands, have in recent months thought more of those lands than they have of the honor and interest of the government under which they are now living." Such a pattern "is absolutely incompatible with the fundamental idea of loyalty." [17]

The war spurred such programs. A high point was July Fourth of 1918, rechristened Loyalty Day, on which Americanizers and ethnic organizations put on a nationwide array of pageants, parades and ceremonies to demonstrate loyalty. In New York City, over forty nationality groups mounted a "parade pageant" with floats dramatizing their pasts. Some questioned the project. Viewing it as proof of "incomplete" assimilation, the *New York Times* would rather see "that it has progressed to the point where the several groups of which we are composed think of themselves as undifferentiated Americans."

The preliminaries bore out such misgivings. Italians lit into Hungarian plans to display the Hungarian flag and Magyar dress. They ought not wear the garb nor vaunt the history of an enemy land, but rather, a critic insisted, "let them come draped in mourning with ashes on their heads, and their floats covered with black veils." Others whose homelands had felt the Hungarian boot also expressed anger. One float's boast that Magyars had withstood Turkish hordes for centuries was belittled by a spokesman for Slovaks and Bohemians, who charged that they had "betrayed Christian civilization to the Turks in this war" and in the past. After heated negotiations and threats of boycott, the Hungarians agreed to forego native attire.

The spectacle succeeded, as 110,000 marchers paraded up Fifth Avenue for ten hours. Military aircraft flew over the route, and a dirigible rained down copies of "The Star-Spangled Banner." A mounted woman clad as

Joan of Arc, followed by a Spirit of '76 tableau, heralded the parade's foreign-born section, which was led by a lone Zoroastrian Parsee. Then came floats depicting Armenia's struggles, Albanians hailing President Wilson, "protector of small nationalities," the Chinese led by a baseball team, Spanish toreadors, Lithuanian knights, Swiss Guards, and Bolivian llamas. Parade authorities strictly scrutinized the messages on all floats and banners. Other locales marked the day. Washingtonians watched the pageant "Democracy Triumphant," and Wilson welcomed the diplomatic corps and delegates from thirty-three nationalities to rites at Washington's tomb.[18]

The war and ensuing Red Scare heightened concerns with Americanization. However, budgetary stringencies forced the federal government to cut back its activities in the 1920s, so that Americanization efforts had to rely mostly on state and local efforts and the energies of schools, civic organizations and patriotic groups. The Bureau of Naturalization remained the sole federal entity active in Americanization.[19]

During the Red Scare, Constitution-worship came into vogue. Localities, especially Philadelphia, had previously marked Constitution Day on September 17, when the document had been signed. For the Constitution's centennial, that city hosted a half-million visitors for a three-day observance that included parades and a speech by President Grover Cleveland. Other localities began to celebrate, and, at the time of World War I, the occasion was adopted as a cause by the National Security League, a virile guardian of Americanism; the American Bar Association; and the Sons of the American Revolution.

In troubled 1919, patriotic organizations mounted emphatic observances, and some twenty-two states and scores of cities marked Constitution Day. In 1923, the American Bar Association and National Education Association made it the anchor of their Constitution Week observance. In 1920, the original Constitution and Declaration were removed from basement storage and displayed at the State Department, presumably in hope that their totemic power would be felt in that frightsome time. In 1921 the documents were exhibited at the Library of Congress. President Coolidge dedicated the bronze and glass "Shrine" in 1924.

Still, Constitution Day remained a secondary observance except during the sesquicentennial of the Constitution. That three-year period overlapped the controversy stirred by FDR's futile 1937 effort to pack the Supreme Court. Anti-New Dealers had often seized the cloak of patriotism. As plans for the sesquicentennial developed, Roosevelt and the critics of his court bill were contesting symbolic custody of the sacred document, and the tug-of-war gave particular poignance to traditionalist reverence for the old constitutional order.[20]

In the 1920s and '30s, various groups sought to instill reverence for ancient traditions, mark historic events and spread patriotic observance. Continuing fears of radicalism, concern with the effects of deep-running social forces upon customs and morals, and later, sometimes apoplectic reactions to the New Deal caused guardians of American tradition to redouble their efforts. Sponsored by the four-year-old American Legion, a National Flag Conference convened in 1923 to decide proper flag etiquette. Under the stress of war and depression, the government took a growing, if sometimes fitful, role in fostering patriotism. Despite the overall nationalizing tendency, in the commemorative events of the period after World War I, according to John Bodnar, there remained room for vernacular, local and personal themes of celebration (such as homage to the "pioneers").[21]

What is remarkable about such efforts to inculcate a sense of nationhood is less their variety and strength than the difficulty activists seemed to encounter. Just as the power to govern was dispersed under the federal system, so the elaboration of rituals of nationhood was a decentralized process subject often to local influence (or apathy) in the absence of firm national direction. Between the wars "the Nation," according to Barry Karl, "was an abstraction, a distant idea."[22] The New Deal would bring greater national focus to government and economic regulation as well as to celebrating nationhood, but progress was not always steady.

A few episodes illustrate the point. In 1932, the national commission to celebrate the bicentennial of George Washington's birth did so by erecting no edifice and holding no fair. Led by ex-impresario, then Congressman Sol Bloom of New York, the George Washington Bicentennial Commission busied itself chiefly with a "media barrage." The deepening depression militated against lavish display or spending and would have made an observance that emphasized the nation's progress bitterly ironic. There were pamphlets, homilies, artistic renderings and speeches under the bicentennial aegis, and plenty of Washingtoniana for those who had money to buy.[23] But in seeking to encourage private and local groups to celebrate and operating primarily through exhortation, the commission was pursuing an essentially federal model, one which would shape subsequent celebrations.

Flag Day also shows how spotty and contingent was federal government guidance of patriotic observance. Although Wilson had decreed it in 1916, after the war the day languished. Subsequent proclamations were not automatic. Thus, responding in 1934 to one of Flag Day's putative founders, an aide stated President Roosevelt's hope that there would be "special patriotic exercises," but since Wilson's 1916 proclamation applied to all subsequent Flag Days, another was unneeded. It was "the responsibility of the people to see that the anniversary is fittingly observed." In 1941 another aide explained that while Flag Day was indeed "a national custom," FDR was powerless to proclaim it a national holiday.[24]

Change was at hand. In the late 1930s, the federal government took up the task of building patriotism. The Great Depression, the New Deal, and the accompanying political culture sharpened the focus on the nation and its capital.[25] While FDR riveted attention through the mass media upon the White House as never before and while New Deal arts projects engaged in production of what might be termed a national culture (though regional as well), in the realm of patriotic observance the general rule of "limited government" still was in force.

The approach and conduct of another war and the persisting tensions of the ensuing Cold War would bring dramatic change. During the preliminaries to World War II the federal government created a new patriotic occasion (in response, admittedly, to local initiatives and predecessor celebrations). During the war itself techniques for consolidating homefront citizens into the war effort were honed and would provide precedent and personnel for similar campaigns to make citizens an integral part of the Cold War. Indeed, World War II and the (sometimes imagined) social solidarity that accompanied it became models for the commitment that the nation's leaders sought from citizens for the perduring struggle that the Cold War quickly seemed to impose.

I

Wake Up, America

Origins of Modern Patriotism

The coming of World War II reenergized patriotic activity as Americans fretted over the rise of jackbooted dictatorships abroad and the threat of "fifth-column" techniques of subversion at home. These fears stimulated efforts across the political spectrum to inculcate patriotism, animating liberals as well as conservatives.

The New Deal moved many conservatives to warn that American liberties, too, might vanish. They accused FDR of straying down the "road to communism." In 1938 Martin Dies's committee began to seek out un-American activities, which the Texas congressman ascribed mostly to Communists in New Deal agencies or CIO unions. FDR's court packing scheme further piqued conservative fears. The 1937–39 sesquicentennial of the Constitution coincided with the war's approach; that document became a rampart behind which both foes and adherents of FDR's foreign policies rallied.[1]

Amid nightmares of dictatorship and subversion, the flag's totemic power grew. Against the "turmoil" of 1938 and menace of "communistic, nazistic and fascistic forces," Colonel James A. Moss, leader of the United States Flag Association, urged "loyal Americans" to hoist the Stars and Stripes. In June 1940, as German panzers tore across France, buyers reported "an extreme shortage of American flags." By July 4, brisk sales laid to "the increased emphasis on national defense and the campaign against subversive forces" had stripped some New Jersey stores of flags.[2]

Pledging allegiance to the flag, a rite dating from the 1890s, became contested symbolism. In many places children began the Pledge with hands over hearts, then (at the word "flag") raised arms stiffly toward the banner, palms down. In 1936 New York's state commissioner of education wished to replace the current gesture, which resembled a military salute, by having students start with hand on heart, then extend it palm upward. His circular triggered confusion and dismay. He denied wanting to ape fascist ways, yet some principals reported that students of German or Italian birth confounded the gesture with old-country practices. The palm up/palm down distinction was too arcane for eight-year-olds. The head of New York City's Principals Association called the change "un-American." At length the board of education opted for the older version.

Salute mechanics stirred ripples of controversy. In 1940, a River Edge, New Jersey, school moved to have students keep hands over hearts throughout the Pledge. In 1941, District of Columbia schools replaced the arm-aloft gesture with an Army salute to avoid mimicking the Nazis. In 1942, West Virginia dropped the stiff-armed salute as "too much like Hitler's." In 1943 even the previously resistant DAR yielded, calling for hand to be held over heart during the Pledge. These fine points of patriotic etiquette may have eluded many students; those pictured saluting at a Milwaukee high school in 1939 had their hands palms up, palms down, and everywhere in-between.[3]

Americans grew prickly about the flag. Jehovah's Witnesses, who acknowledged no secular symbol, became targets of wrath. In 1940, the Supreme Court held that they could be forced to salute the flag. Wrote Justice Felix Frankfurter: "national unity is the basis of national security" and was "fostered by the symbols we live by." Witnesses faced ostracism and violence. By 1943, over 2,000 had been expelled from schools. In Nebraska a Witness was castrated. In September 1942, twenty men disrupted a gathering in Arkansas, shooting two Witnesses and hurting others; a mob of a thousand burst into an Oregon meeting; after several were injured, Witnesses at an Illinois convention grudgingly saluted a flag brandished by a deputy sheriff. Such events helped prompt the Court to reverse its stand in 1943.[4]

More trivial episodes evidenced a hypertension over the flag. A news account of a Long Island gas station burglary noted that the yeggs had ripped down and trampled a flag. A couple who painted a flag on their car to advertise a business were charged with desecrating the symbol. A New Jersey union leader was arrested for "mutilating and defiling" the flag at a strike meeting by draping it over a table and hitting it with a gavel. Westchester County American Legionnaires voiced opposition to use of the national symbol by strikers. The U.S. House Judiciary Committee approved a bill to criminalize flag desecration.[5]

Flag Day became a lightning rod. In 1938, Colonel Moss of the United States Flag Association commended Flag Day as a reply to "the challenge of the communistic, Naziistic and fascistic forces." "Political, social and economic forces are combating one another," warned the Elks. "Never in our history have we had greater need for the qualities for which our flag stands." At a Manhattan Flag Day rally of the Sons of the American Revolution, a speaker declared Americans "about ready to clamp down on these mobs of fanatics, whether foreign or domestic, whose open and avowed purpose is to destroy our government."

Politicians now paid heed to Flag Day. As for those "who don't like our flag," the president of the Borough of Queens declared: "My advice to them is to get out." Jersey City Mayor Frank Hague's anti-communist exertions made him the unofficial hero of Flag Day 1938. In contrast, Mayor Fiorello La Guardia earned the censure of Colonel Moss and his association for not, like mayors of "other leading cities," proclaiming Flag Day in Gotham. By 1941, Flag Day had such status that FDR, hitherto uninterested, issued a call for faith in American ideals "when the principles of unity and freedom symbolized by Old Glory are under attack."[6]

The American Legion became the preeminent arbiter of flag etiquette and achieved several patriotic goals in these tense times. It won status for Armistice Day as a national holiday in 1938. It strove to sacralize Memorial Day, but the incursions of sport and entertainment activities continued to profane the day. In 1942, Congress wrote much of the Legion's flag code into law.[7]

The Immigration and Naturalization Service maintained its interest in the training and recognition of new citizens. Though its role contracted in the 1920s, in the 1930s demand for its skills and lore renewed, especially as war neared. Under the New Deal its approach grew more pluralistic and less normative. As an official recalled, World War I had stimulated "a desire to make everyone a 100 percent American." Newcomers were to discard "old-world cultural traditions, customs, and habits." But later, they were taught to cherish facets of their cultures "that would make a real contribution to the American way of living." [8]

I Am An American Day, a new *fete*, meshed nicely with these New Dealish aims. Aside from Armistice Day, it was the chief interwar addition to the patriotic calendar. Though this annual exercise at its peak attracted over a million citizens to New York's Central Park, it has faded from historical memory. Conceived on the cusp between the demise of the New Deal and America's entry into World War II, I Am An American Day accommodated both conservative and liberal persuasions.

This new rite had many would-be parents, all of whom feared that citizenship had been devalued. Some credited the American Legion or National Education Association (NEA).[9] Benjamin Edwards Neal, creator of the "I Am An American" Foundation, claimed he founded I Am An American Day, holding the first such event in the Hollywood Bowl on June 12, 1939. With a "ritual committee," he designed an "'I Am An American' Panegyric" to elevate twenty-one-year-olds to voting status in a ceremony worthy of other transitions such as school graduation or marriage.[10] The Helios Foundation asserted that *its* 1938 I Am An American Day at the Long Island home of Mr. and Mrs. Paul d'Otrenge Seghers was the first.[11]

The event had even hoarier, if less official precedents. Highland Park, Michigan, had held an annual "welcome to new citizens" since 1926.[12] In 1930, Clara Vajda founded the Americanization League of America in Milwaukee. A refugee from Hungary's Communist revolution, Mrs. Vajda worked to help other immigrants win naturalization, providing the sort of citizenship education she had found lacking in her own years as a newcomer. In 1931, the League held the first of what became annual mass meetings to honor new citizens. By the late 1930s, the event filled Milwaukee's Auditorium, and thousands were turned away.[13]

San Diego's Sons of the American Revolution also claimed authorship. In 1937 they pondered launching a new holiday to recognize all first-time voters. For the "widespread apathy" implicit in low voter turnouts, one speaker blamed "the apathy of the government in receiving citizens." The San Diegans also warned of "'sullen discontent' among the poor youth of the nation and 'selfish apathy' among the rich." Their proposal received encouraging responses from other SAR chapters. San Diego's SARs mounted the first such observance on September 17, 1938.[14]

Another initiative arose in Manitowoc County, Wisconsin, where in May 1939 under the guidance of the state university extension division a Citizenship Day ceremony took place. It culminated a five-month program in which rising twenty-one-year-olds met to discuss the rights and duties of citizens. The legislature enacted a law to mandate that schools provide similar programs and to reserve May's third Sunday as Citizenship Day. "The Manitowoc idea" won praise from the *New York Times* and William Randolph Hearst and calls for imitation.[15]

Moved by similar concerns, the federal government, too, sought to create a meaningful national rite of passage. The New Deal thus managed to coopt Americanization, at least in part, from its usually conservative constituency. In 1939, Secretary of Labor Frances Perkins called for local New Citizens Day exercises to welcome new adults and the newly naturalized. Over 200 hastily planned programs occurred (mostly on June 1). In New York City there were speeches, music and folk dancing. Participants were urged to "forget the traditional enmities of the countries from which you came." In Chicago, 60,000 saw new Americans take the oath of citizenship and then vanish into a large "melting pot." At Washington's costumed "pageant of naturalization," Secretary Perkins read FDR's message of "warm welcome." The day was marked in WPA naturalization classes.[16]

Led by New York Democratic Senator James Mead and Wisconsin Republican Congressman Joshua L. Johns, Congress mandated the day in 1940. Debate mainly pitted rival schemes from Wisconsin and California. Mead called for a National Youth Citizenship Day every April 19. Another bill would make the last Sunday in May Citizenship Recognition Day. The House Judiciary Committee altered the date to the third Sunday in May and the name to Citizenship Day. The Senate opted for the label "I Am An American Citizenship Day" and, after some vacillation, concurred in the choice of the third Sunday in May.

The Senate's views prevailed in conference, and FDR signed the bill on May 3. The end result was murky: the third Sunday of May was to be "Citizenship Day" and the President was to proclaim it each year to recognize "all who, by coming of age or naturalization, have attained the status of citizenship, and the day shall be designated as 'I Am An American Day.'" INS district offices, state education departments and county agricultural agents would take the lead in organizing ceremonies.[17]

I Am An American Day focused on naturalized Americans and native-born young adults, but the first group received primary emphasis. Both elements were deemed vulnerable to alien "isms," but especially the former. Martin Dies termed aliens "the backbone of communism and fascism."[18] The growing global crisis raised consciousness of the "fifth-column" threat.

I Am An American Day was widely celebrated. New citizens in Elyria, Ohio, traded banners of their homelands for American flags. In Washington, D.C., a pageant was staged and clergy gave special sermons. In New York City, 15,000 recently naturalized citizens assembled in Central Park. Orators invoked the European crisis, one warning: "the world is too small for us to protect ourselves by simply saying, 'I am an American,' .... We must stand ready to make sacrifices to preserve our freedom." [19]

The 1940 I Am An American Day came on short notice—not even three weeks after FDR signed the measure. In 1941 celebrations grew more energetic, particularly in Fiorello La Guardia's New York. He named over 1,000 people to a planning committee, including three former presidential candidates, prominent clerics, and show biz figures Kate Smith, Eddie Cantor and George M. Cohan. La Guardia was a dynamo. He mobilized students, "civic workers" and welfare agencies to collect signed pledges of support for the May 18 rally; they collected 4.5 million. At the festivities, he spoke, emceed and even led the band.

The result was an extravaganza. Planners expected 100,000 to attend. Whether it was the worrisome times, Fiorello's salesmanship or the entertainment by Kate Smith, Marian Anderson, Eddie Cantor and others, some 750,000 turned out in Central Park, "the greatest patriotic gathering the city has ever seen." The message was double-edged—plenty of star-studded clowning, but admonitions too that "we live in dangerous times." A reporter favorably contrasted the paucity of marching, the genial indiscipline and "fun" with goose-stepping Nazi precision. Other cities also celebrated. In Chicago, 100,000 citizens filled Soldier Field. In Washington, the vice president, attorney general and Speaker of the House orated; the common theme was opposition to isolationism and "defeatism." [20]

After Pearl Harbor, I Am An American Day joined the war effort. For 1942 FDR termed it "even more essential" that Americans comprehend "the form and genius of their government and the responsibilities of citizenship." With planning more intense and entertainment more lavish than in 1941, La Guardia engineered a turnout of 1,250,000. This "largest crowd ... ever assembled at a single point anywhere in the world" heard a radio greeting from Free French leader Charles de Gaulle and Lily Pons rendering the "Marseillaise." For the finale of "God Bless America," La Guardia conducted the band as Irving Berlin led the singing.[21]

By 1943, the city and its mayor had settled into successful routine. Vice President Henry A. Wallace's speech was broadcast throughout the hemisphere. In 1944, 1,400,000 heard Senator Robert F. Wagner call for an international peace-keeping body. In 1945 an equally large crowd heard La Guardia read a message from President Harry S. Truman.[22]

I Am An American Day was not confined to big cities. The Agriculture Department mobilized county agents to stimulate rural celebrations. Besides the INS, sponsors included the American Legion and VFW, the NEA, state education departments, schools, fraternal, patriotic and civic groups and religious bodies. Some locales held "I Am An American" Weeks. In 1943, 420 communities marked the day. In a celebration broadcast on radio, the Liberty Bell received thirteen taps. In 1944, almost 800 communities conducted programs; in 1945, over 1000 did so, with nearly three million people taking part.[23]

Americans fondly recall World War II as the last time of unity, shared burdens and a sense of civic commonality. Many leaders feared that something good ended on V-J Day, that harmful new trends were afoot in the land. They cited such lapses as intolerance, civic apathy, crime and juvenile delinquency, and whoring after strange doctrines. They saw an America afflicted by a personal and group selfishness frustrating to the common weal. On I Am An American Day in 1946, the *New York Times* editorialized that Americans lived "in an age of intense loyalties," some so parochial "that they are used to disunite us and break us down." We must "put the common welfare above our private or group squabbles." The flaw had national security implications: "Our internal dissensions have encouraged those who do not believe in the democratic system."[24]

However excessive its nostalgia, the nation had convinced itself that the pluralistic yet united devotion to common cause attested at I Am An American Day and other wartime festivals was the real McCoy. If illusory, it seemed real, and so did the widely remarked letdown in morale and discipline after the war.

Postwar I Am An American Days lost some allure. New York City's 1946 observance drew only 150,000 people. The 1947 celebration was expected to attract a million people, but the police estimate was only 300,000. Rain cut the audience to 15,000 in 1948. The 1949 program, with better weather, assertedly drew 1,250,000 New Yorkers into Central Park.

The 1950 assemblage was described as encompassing "thousands." In 1951, only 50,000 attended.[25]

The tone changed too. Liberal themes persisted but emphasis shifted. In 1946 New York Mayor William O'Dwyer warned that citizens should "guard against the forces of intolerance and bigotry" but also that "liberty does not grant the right to intrigue" nor "encourage . . . the fostering of strange ideologies." A year later, his call to celebrate invoked a world "beset" and urged people to "declare publicly their faith in the stability and permanence" of their government and institutions. In 1947, Attorney General Tom C. Clark enjoined an I Am An American Day gathering to beware of subversives. In 1948, the governor of Illinois cautioned against "communist threats abroad and communist propaganda at home." [26]

I Am An American Day's glory years were over. Despite the early successes, guardians of public morale came to sense that a single observance on the third Sunday in May would not cure the malady. The postwar years saw an ongoing search for occasions and media by which to shore up patriotism and good citizenship.

One effort, launched in 1946, would add professionalism to the day's amateur gregariousness. Scheduled for I Am an American Day, the National Conference on Citizenship met in Philadelphia, sponsored by the INS, Justice Department and NEA. Organizers saw a pressing need for it. Peace had opened "a dangerous period in our history" with "clear signs of growing disunity, of increasing intolerance, of suspicion of leaders and of organizations, and of apparent lack of personal and group responsibility for our national welfare." Patriotic and civic groups sent delegates to what became an annual event that founders hoped would be "a source of inspiration and enlightenment on civic and social matters; a common ground where all schools of thought, all classes and creeds may meet" to fortify citizenship.[27]

Varied views were voiced, but the compass needle flicked to the right. While Georgia's liberal Governor Ellis Arnall urged abolishing the poll tax, a corporate chief rumbled on against "the spread of doctrines that are utterly subversive." Senator Joseph H. Ball complained that unions abused power just like "industrial tycoons of the past century." Tom Clark rebuked "organized bigotry" (meaning the Ku Klux Klan) and the "habit . . . of tagging people with names." While it was wrong to "impute un-American activity to groups which are merely liberal," we must "be vigilant that un-American thinkers do not gain control of organizations which *are* liberal and use them as a cloak." [28]

As much as any American, Tom C. Clark fretted over civism's demise. As attorney general, he helped initiate or encourage some of the most important efforts to combat this trend. Even after 1949, as a supreme court justice, he continued, albeit less actively, to promote citizenship. In launching the Freedom Train, his signature contribution, he was disturbed by postwar unrest, a rise in crime and juvenile delinquency, the challenge posed by the growing global crisis, and subversion at home.

He addressed some of these evils by more direct methods. He was a, if not the, major instigator of government anti-communist actions, including the 1947 federal loyalty program and the prosecution of Communist Party leaders. He took several executive actions to combat juvenile delinquency.[29] He strongly supported the annual National Conference on Citizenship.

President Truman echoed Clark's concern with the weakened civic fabric. In greeting a fraternal conclave he declared: "We live in a time sadly in need of discipline, particularly self-discipline, that quality of personal responsibility so essential in the individual called to discharge the duties of citizenship in a democracy." The far too many "who do not exercise their rights, particularly the right to vote, are among the least worthy of our citizens." Addressing the 1952 National Citizenship Conference, he issued a similar warning about the "ignorance and apathy" of the many *blasé* Americans.[30]

Anti-communists especially bemoaned public apathy. FBI Director J. Edgar Hoover felt driven in 1946 to launch a program of leaks to friendly politicians and journalists to convey the CPUSA's "basically Russian nature." In 1945 the U. S. Chamber of Commerce began publishing monitory anti-communist pamphlets. At 1947 House Un-American Activities Committee hearings on communism in Hollywood, Congressman Richard Vail lamented the public's underdeveloped awareness. During 1948's "spy" revelations, the Hearst papers lamented that, despite their years of sounding the tocsin, too many Americans belittled the Red menace.[31]

Yet to most doom-criers softness on communism was only part of a broader civic laxity. In 1951 the secretary of the navy warned, "the most serious danger" was not communism but "growing national disunity." Leaders convened the National Citizenship Conference in 1946 "because of the grave evidences of disunity spreading throughout our land." The

American Legion's national commander opined that "un-American philosophies" flourished because "too many Americans" were ignorant of their government and the benefits of free enterprise. Martin Dies, the pioneering congressional anti-communist, laid the nation's "greatest danger" on that front to "indifference and selfishness." [32]

Many critics of postwar society levied blame on liberalism and the New Deal. They feared socialism around the next turn. Though "collectivists" had suffered some setbacks after the war, these, said National Association of Manufacturers spokesmen, had prodded them to greater efforts —"they are busier than ever." [33] Conservatives inveighed against the spinelessness of citizens seduced from American ways by welfare-state siren songs.

Civic worriers gauged moral declension by the standard of the late war. Virtually from V-J Day, nostalgia bloomed and actuated restorative efforts. One lawmaker characterized the postwar as a time "when we are trying to reinspire our people with patriotic fervor." A citizenship activist fondly recalled wartime, when "a spirit of unity prevails among people." They "stand for the great values of life, protect the things they love and defend the things they cherish." Convenors of the National Conference on Citizenship identified a postwar "reaction" that led to "a lessening of the high interest in active citizenship and patriotic service strongly marked during a time of crisis." [34]

Business groups alarmed by a loss of leverage under the New Deal also worried. They built new or revitalized old associations well enough to gain paramount influence on the nation's postwar political culture.[35] By 1942, leaders in advertising had become convinced that attacks on their trade by New Dealers, intellectuals, and a rudimentary consumers movement threatened its viability. It was a time, an adman recalled, when businessmen were highly "suspect." They therefore founded the War Advertising Council, later renamed the Advertising Council. The Ad Council led public service campaigns for the war effort and, later, other causes, cooperating with the federal government and demonstrating the industry's public spiritedness.[36]

Impelled by similar fears after the war, two ad industry associations set up a Joint Committee on Economic Education for the Nation charged with mounting a crusade to publicize capitalism's virtues. Kenneth D. Wells, Jr., hired to direct the campaign, had led a varied career, including stints as a roustabout in the oil industry, director of an oil company's program in training and safety, and officer of the National Association of Foremen.

Wearying differences within the Joint Committee moved Wells, adman Don Belding, business leader E. F. Hutton, and General Dwight D. Eisenhower to create Freedoms Foundation of Valley Forge. It launched a program of awards of money and medals to those whose speeches, writings and other endeavors enhanced the American way of life, thus harnessing "the incentive idea to preserve and maintain the incentive system." Hutton hoped the awards might some day rank with the Nobel Peace Prize. Freedoms Foundation strove to end "national apathy" on "vital issues of the American Constitutional enterprise system" and to recruit a "vast articulate, creative army of ministers, teachers, professional people, students, men and women from the farm and factory" who revere and defend "the American Way." [37] Winners of the first awards, for 1949, included a housewife for her "Freedom cookies" and "recipe for freedom." [38]

While Freedoms Foundation advocated flinty economic conservatism, the American Heritage Foundation (AHF), founded in 1947, preached civic activism in a more generic idiom. The "panacea of state control" troubled AHF leaders too, but so did a host of other symptoms of postwar malaise, such as "lawlessness and cynicism" and "voices of discord" made raucous by "the grave trials of postwar economic readjustment." [39]

The efforts of such new groups found reinforcement in the activities of many older ones, including the American Legion, the Chamber of Commerce, Junior Chamber of Commerce and scores of civic, fraternal, patriotic, veterans and business groups. Local chapters of these and other groups also teamed up to promote community-level projects with the same general purposes.

These activities took place in a clear political context. They followed a tumultuous era in which the state's role in managing the economy had expanded, union power had grown, and the clout of at least some corporate leaders had suffered. Worried by these inroads and fearful of more to come, the latter launched campaigns using varied media to educate the public in the virtues of capitalism and in the next two decades achieved the "intellectual reconquest of America." [40]

The economic interests of many initiators of patriotic and civic pageantry may suggest the term "cultural hegemony" to describe their activities. While a concern with citizenship afflicted leaders outside the corporations too, this, it might be argued, merely proves that cultural hegemony's potency.[41] Yet the language and motives which gave expression to that concern entailed a definition of desirable citizenship traits which went beyond service as dutiful minions of capitalism.

Unless all such rhetoric is dismissed as mere eyewash, the economic goals of some activists must be seen as only part of a broader galaxy of values. While we associate the term "participatory democracy" with the 1960s Left, conservative civic activists of the 1940s and 50s espoused a similar ideal. Though that parallel should not surprise us in a society in which democracy is a core value, it is still striking.

While fraying civic fiber was seen as a national problem, action often occurred locally. In 1947, the National Association of Manufacturers announced a public relations campaign that was to include "a local-action program to help industry and business in its own community" to build "greater understanding and active good-will for Enterprise." In 1948 the U.S. Chamber of Commerce devised "A Program for Community Anti-Communist Action." [42]

Local campaigns proliferated. "America the Beautiful," in Washington, D.C., ran from Washington's to Lincoln's birthday in 1954. Aligning the two icons on the side of America's economic system, it aimed to show Washingtonians "that the wellsprings of their community strength are those people who *earn, save, invest* and *share* the community's wealth" and to create a model "for a renewal of community consciousness throughout the nation." [43] "America the Beautiful" exemplified countless *ad-hoc* local efforts to inspire citizens to cherish and defend the American Way of Life.

Civic and patriotic pageantry flourished *con brio* in postwar Los Angeles—no surprise given Hollywood's nearby talent and the city's long habit of boosterism. Even so, Mayor Fletcher M. Bowron gave a place to pageantry rivaled only by La Guardia. Through such ceremonies Bowron could address his diverse constituency about unity and civic duty amid the social problems of a booming, modern city in flux.[44]

World War II heightened both the problems and Bowron's zeal for pageantry. Los Angeles faced a transient population, a war boom that overtaxed housing and other facilities, and rising intergroup friction. Clashes between men in uniform and local Anglos on one side and Mexican-Americans on the other, notably the zoot-suit riots, shook the city. Bowron also fretted that the expanding black population seemed vulnerable to Communist agitation. Toward war's end, with the impending return of newly-released Japanese-Americans, Bowron feared that that group would once more face hostility, and, with their housing now taken by war-workers, especially blacks, the possibility of race riots beckoned.[45]

With such undercurrents licking at his city's cohesion, Bowron turned to unifying civic ceremony as a means of keeping the parts lashed together. The war's triumphal closing months and their aftermath provided numerous opportunities.

In March 1945 Bowron invited Edward R. Stettinius to come to a "civic demonstration" en route to the United Nations Conference soon to open in San Francisco. Angelenos, he told the secretary of state, wanted to show "confidence in our government and its foreign policy." Coming eleven days after FDR's death, the quickly adjusted "Franklin Delano Roosevelt Memorial and United Nations Rededication Program" would also avow support for Harry Truman and dedication to FDR's "unfinished task." Stettinius did not attend, but a constellation of stars like Ingrid Bergman, Frank Sinatra and Eddie Cantor made it a gala event at which a tone of "religious and patriotic fervor" prevailed.[46]

Like other cities, Los Angeles hosted returning heroes after V-E Day. On June 9, 1945, Generals George C. Patton and James H. Doolittle paid a triumphal visit. Some 1.5 million watched the parade, and Jack Benny emceed a lavish show in their honor at the Coliseum. Bowron also arranged a star-studded welcome-home banquet for Admiral William "Bull" Halsey.[47]

Bowron was loathe to let martial display lapse with the war. He planned a Victory Celebration, combined with Navy Day, that included a lavish "spectacle." The October 27 event featured parading units galore (perhaps the city's last time to "get the thrill of seeing marching armed forces," Bowron suspected). Thirteen docked Navy ships welcomed visitors. The spectacle offered simulations of a carrier attack, the Marines at Iwo Jima, and the Japanese surrender ceremony. B-29s roared over the Coliseum as the firebombing of Tokyo and the atomic destruction of Hiroshima were dramatized with sound, light, and explosives; and miniature kamikaze planes smashed into ship mockups.[48]

Pageantry continued to thrive. In August 1946, Los Angeles marked the centennial of the raising of the American flag over the city. Festivities mixed recent with ancient history and showbiz with boosterism. The Navy gave the city a Japanese fighter plane; Frank Sinatra and "Hollywood's best" put on a nationally broadcast show at city hall; the flag-raising was reenacted. The simultaneous arrival of an ox-cart and jet plane was meant to demonstrate progress. One aim of the celebration was to "advertise to the Nation and to the World the Great growth of a sleepy pueblo into the greatest City of Western America." In 1947 Bowron threw a 166th birthday party for Los Angeles to accent its status as the nation's third largest city.[49]

Hardly a ribbon went unsnipped or a date or group unheralded in Bowron's town. At a September 1945 Filipino Fiesta, he warned that "recently some sinister outside influences have come into our state . . . to stir up race bigotry and religious hatreds" but took heart that most Californians "repudiate these fascist doctrines." Before the leftist Mobilization for Democracy, he stated, "we do not subscribe to the principles of Communism any more than Fascism" but he reminded them that Hitler and Mussolini "effectively used the red scare device as a road to power."[50]

Anti-communism soon edged anti-fascism from Bowron's rhetoric. At the centennial, he warned: "There is too much agitation, foreign ideologies are given too much attention by some of our people." He sounded the same note at a November 1946 Americanization rally whose guest of honor was boxer Joe Louis. Of the champ's virtues, he stressed "above all, [his] good Americanism." With Naziism and Fascism beaten, Communism was now "our greatest menace" and evident in "the restlessness of the people, discord, disharmony, efforts to disrupt and set class against class, divide our people into groups. There should be no groups. . . . We are all Americans."[51]

Bowron feared a general slackening of citizenship. He hoped 1947's I Am An American Day might help erase "the defeatism, the confusion, the cynicism, and the moral anarchy which is being thrust at the impressionable new citizens today."[52] His concerns were not unique. In the late 1940s, others fretted about and worked to counter communism's impudent omnipresence and the apathy and civic laxity of so many of those it targeted.

In September 1948, for example, Kansas City, Missouri's Junior Chamber of Commerce mounted Democracy Beats Communism Week. The program was the brainchild of Clinton W. Kanaga, Jr., insurance man, World War II vet and Jaycee. Alarmed by a speech of ex-Vice President Wallace that endorsed "nationalizing everything," he conceived the idea of a week-long, city-wide comparison of the American and Soviet systems. Fellow Jaycees took up the idea with gusto, aware that "one of the major threats to the Democratic institutions of this country is the failure of many of its citizens to understand the basic principles underlying democracies" or the "antagonistic philosophies" which threaten them.[53]

The Jaycees prepared with care. They won media backing; got permission to send speakers into every high school in the city; and scheduled programs for any group that would listen. They convinced Democratic politicians leery of the communist issue that the focus was nonpartisan. (Kanaga and many other Jaycees were Democrats themselves.) For six months they buried themselves in comparative study of the Soviet and American systems. They assembled an elaborate speaker's manual covering such topics as labor, education, religion and civil liberties. They drafted model speeches for varied audiences.

The speakers' syllabus emphasized freedom's total absence from Soviet life: labor unions had no autonomy; students learned under "an extraordinarily severe" and politicized state-imposed regimen; freedom of religion was a sham. But the Jaycees found most compelling the evidence dramatizing the material advantages of capitalism—or "democracy" as it was usually termed. Comparisons of how long American and Soviet citizens had to work to afford everything from milk to cars were eloquent. An average American Joe earned the price of a loaf of bread in 7 minutes; Ivan took ten times as long. For a radio, the respective figures were 21 and 225 hours' work. Jaycees also highlighted the relative availability of consumer items. There was a phone for every 5 Americans, one for every 188 Soviets; a car for every 4 Americans but one for every 252 Russians. Some Soviet claims and ideals were treated positively, but, said the speaker's manual: "Theory is one thing, practice is another." [54]

Oratory pervaded DBC Week. Ninety-five Jaycees spoke to high schools, unions and service clubs, and on twenty-nine radio programs. Churches heard sermons. The Jaycees also held a banquet and a week-ending "Torch of Freedom Parade" through every neighborhood by over a hundred cars, each fitted with two smudge pots to create the effect of a modern "torchlight parade." There were sound trucks, bands, marching units; a searchlight served as a "beacon of liberty." [55]

The underlying premise held that communism had at least some Siren-like appeal. "Idealists or lunatic-fringe intellectuals" seized on its "so-called advantages" but ignored its drawbacks. The week's slogan was: "An American Won't Buy Communism If He Knows What He's Getting." Jaycees felt driven to combat "the vast amount of ignorance and listlessness on the subject of Communism." There was no doubt as to democracy's superiority, only that not all were aware of it.[56]

DBC Week won plaudits for its cerebral tone. It was no "witch hunt," the Jaycees' president asserted, "and we are not simply a group of Red-baiters." Nor was the program allowed to become a right-tilting debate over "socialism." A luncheon skit stressed the reasoned approach. Lights went out; the Jaycees' president declared, "Comrades, let us stand"; a spotlight picked out a Soviet flag as Soviet music played. When an angry member tried to tear down the banner, the speaker remonstrated, "That method will accomplish nothing." Missouri Congressman Richard Bolling praised DBC Week for presenting not "bitter denunciation" or "flag-waving," but "all the facts on both sides." [57]

Kansas City's Jaycees anticipated wide interest and perhaps imitation. National Jaycee President John Ben Shepperd endorsed the program. It was not broadly emulated, but Gladewater, Texas, Shepperd's home town, borrowed the name for its 1949 Democracy Beats Communism Week.[58] The event differed from Kansas City's.[59] It began with a Sunday "go-to-church campaign"; on Monday came "Citizenship Day," with meetings of civic groups, a luncheon and a "Freedom parade"; Tuesday was Local Government Day; Wednesday focused on the schools; Thursday's programs included "Negro Day"; and so on.[60]

Some locales had addressed similar concerns even before the Cold War. Since 1930, the Women's Auxiliary of the Massachusetts VFW had mounted an annual "May Day Patriotic Rally" on Boston Common. From 1932, Jersey City had held each year an Americanization Day—assertedly "the largest demonstration of its kind in America," with 20,000 marchers. The American Legion of Uniontown, Pennsylvania, had celebrated Americanism Day since 1934, its parades serving as antidotes to May Day.[61]

Other communities held longer but single-shot programs. In 1950, Weirton, West Virginia, conducted Americanism Week. A how-to manual for imitators suggested starting with Rededication Day, then Americanism Sunday, Bill of Rights Day, Fight Socialism-Communism Day, Citizenship Responsibilities Day, Freedom of Opportunity Day and climaxing on July 4. Weirton's planners touted the value of comparing costs of living and work hours needed to obtain consumer items; merchants should put two tags on their goods, the American price and the cost "under Socialism—either the British or the Russian type." [62]

Erie, Pennsylvania, held a Loyalty Week in 1951 for Erieites to "demonstrate to all communistic [forces] that the in[it]iative and resourcefulness of our forefathers in founding the United States of America has [*sic*] not been wasted." Events included school activities, a concert, Civil Defense Day, "programs keynoting the loyalty of the American Workers," and Loyalty Sabbath. It culminated on May 1, Loyalty Day, with a parade and patriotic ceremony aimed at preempting the day from the Communists. [63]

Milwaukee, Wisconsin's still more elaborate Freedom Week of December 7–17, 1951, ran from the tenth anniversary of Pearl Harbor to the 160th of adoption of the Bill of Rights. Forty-nine community organizations took part. The days had themes such as Freedom of Worship, Choice, Education, Opportunity and Liberty Under Law. Events included a freedom letters contest and a puppet show for kids. A meeting of the All American Conference to Combat Communism brought in noted anticommunist speakers, including Soviet-bloc escapees. A play dealt with the Bill of Rights. The spectrum of anti-communism was fairly broad. On one panel, a liberal Democrat and conservative Republican congressman debated. One speaker rued the "blemishes on human rights in our society" in the realm of race; another decried the federal loyalty program's chilling effect on expression. While one participant urged Americans to purge libraries of pro-communist books, another retorted that no one was qualified to make such a determination. [64]

In May 1952 in Muskegon, Michigan, over two hundred organizations led by the Chamber of Commerce celebrated Freedom Week. It opened with Rededication Day, followed by Americanism Sunday (also Mother's Day), Bill of Rights Day with a "Unity-Strength-Freedom Parade," Citizenship Responsibilities Day, Freedom of Opportunity Day and two Fight Communism Days. The latter featured panels about life in the USSR as presented by Soviet escapees. Sponsors claimed that 62,000 out of the area's population of 100,000 took part. [65]

How many programs like these occurred is hard to guess—not to mention all the less elaborate community activities—or the failures. Such efforts faced many hurdles. Knights of Pythias wished to hold an educational patriotic program in Granite City, Illinois, but the town had too few "prominent people" to pull it off. Might President Truman lend his "great name and influence" and suggest citizens of nearby St. Louis who might help? Then again, at exercises to honor Washington and Lincoln in 1949, Boston Mayor James M. Curley indignantly complained to

26 participants and 43 spectators that in Roxbury a simultaneous Communist meeting had drawn "fully 1,500 people." The Elks of Honolulu slated a "Wake Up America" rally in May 1950 but cancelled it "because of lack of attendance." [66]

Local initiatives sprouted in hundreds of communities; visible for a week, they often popped up in similar guise but perhaps different sponsorship elsewhere. The All-American Conference to Combat Communism, founded in 1950, fostered Know Your America Week observances. Soon such weeks sprang up under varied auspices—the Galveston Chamber of Commerce in 1956, the Arlington-Fairfax Elks Lodge in 1963 and the Elks of Phoenix in 1965.[67] Freedom Weeks (a favorite of Sertomans), flag pageants, Fly Your Flag Weeks and presentations of Freedom Shrines to schools also proliferated. Exchange Clubs, Civitan, Altrusa, schools, local committees and other bodies got into the act.

Successful or not, these local endeavors bespoke a concern over communism on one hand and, on the other, the broader malady of flaccid citizenship. Such worries beset people on Main Street —and on Wall Street and Pennsylvania Avenue too. Americans were seen to suffer from varied sorts of malaise, and the perception undergirded a malaise on the part of observers.

Such concerns affected conservatives but also moderates and liberals. The grandest effort at cold-war pageantry, the Freedom Train, would coalesce members of these groups and meld national government and elite initiatives with the local energies in a way that would serve for years as a model for those who sought to elevate American patriotism and Cold War consciousness.

2

Precious Freight

The Freedom Train

Attorney General Tom Clark was a worried man. The nation's chief law enforcement officer from 1945 to 1949, he confronted the problems of war's aftermath. Similar concerns had eroded the patience and tweaked, then mocked, the political ambitions of A. Mitchell Palmer, Wilson's attorney general. Like Palmer, Clark served in a time of tumult that included labor militancy, a perceived decline in law and order, consumer shortages and inflation, and Communist agitation given poignancy by threats emergent in the Soviet Union—all in a context of clamorous interest-group politics and a plummeting civic consciousness.

Clark often stated his fears. He noted the global struggle between "one form of 'state-ism' and another. Whether it's fascism, communism, or the various degrees of socialism—it's not the American brand of democracy as we know it." Perils lurked at home too. "Dynamic forces, aided by economic and political dissentions, may well seek to undermine and discredit our system of government." War had fused the people into one, but peace brought "the disintegration of much of our American unity."

Symptoms lay all about. Idealism gave way to "the practical philosophy of 'each man for himself.'" "Characteristic cynicism, disillusionment, and lawlessness" marred the peace. Juveniles were delinquent. Clark decried the "disruption of reconversion and disregard for the rights of others." "Professional bigots" and "alien id[e]ologies" fed on "economic stress." Then, too, "we have too many Old World rivalries and hatreds being reenacted in this country." While cultural pluralism was a strength, "we must impress upon all our citizens their primary obligation to the best interests of our own country." "Unrest" was rampant.[1]

Sometimes Clark vented a conservative fretfulness about the self-seeking of interest groups. Yet the Texan couched some of his sermons in populist and even liberal terms. Warning in 1945 of "intolerance" and "bigotry"—especially the Ku Klux Klan's—he suggested that "a small but vile group of greedy men, present in our land in these periods of unrest and reconstruction, prey upon the gullible and incite hate to further their powers and their profits." In 1947 he termed "prejudice" the gravest national threat.[2] But generally he was probing at what he saw as the ignorance, apathy and privatism of average Americans. Their citizenship needed a fillip.

An aide's lunch-hour ramble inspired a solution. Assistant Director of Justice's Division of Public Information, William A. Coblenz had the duty of perusing "the most fantastic splurge of lunatic fringe literature that has probably ever afflicted this country . . . a literary spectrum of subversion" ranging from right to left. At noon, Coblenz sometimes strolled through a display of Nazi documents at the National Archives. Why not, it struck him in April 1946, let all Americans see these vestiges of tyranny? His boss heartily endorsed the idea of putting the documents on tour together with contrasting charters of American freedom. Coblenz suggested a specially fitted railroad car mounted with pictures and documents of the Third Reich on one side of the aisle and "the American Way" on the other. The display could inferentially indict "Communist despotism" through criticism of "government by secret police."

The idea swiftly won backing. The Archivist of the United States gave support. The Association of American Railroads offered logistical aid. Some resistance materialized inside the Justice Department, but Clark's zeal and President Truman's support more than counterbalanced it. To fund the exhibit, Clark sought help from friends, particularly in the film industry.[3]

The program grew and ramified. Clark and his aides had first had in mind a "civil liberties exhibit" mounted by his department with the aid of the railroads, the American Legion, the NEA and U. S. attorneys in each city visited. At one point the project title was "Liberty on Wheels." Then it became "Bill of Rights Exhibit" and briefly "Liberty Train." Clark had envisioned a single railroad car, but the train eventually grew to three refitted exhibit cars plus four others.

Clark had hoped to launch the tour in the fall of 1946 but decided to wait until after November's elections— "a good idea," thought Elizabeth Hamer of the National Archives, given Justice's initial insistence on putting Truman's and Clark's pictures in the accompanying booklet. Indeed, as first planned the exhibit's umbrella of nonpartisanship would have leaked. While filmed speeches by some eminent Republicans would be screened, Coblenz noted that "naturally" the exhibit would "have a preponderance of the photographs and utterances of the notables of this administration," including Truman, Clark and FDR's pictures.[4]

It was not just Clark who sought a civic reawakening; the Advertising Council was casting about for a comparable cure. On November 15, 1946, as directors mulled a suggestion by Thomas d'Arcy Brophy, president of the Kenyon & Eckhardt agency, for "a campaign to sell America to the Americans," they also learned of Clark's "train proposal." It struck a responsive chord. The advertising industry had effectively spurred war bond sales. In 1945, the Ad Council had promoted a bond drive by dispatching six Victory Loan trains to forty states to show off Japanese and German surrender documents (facsimiles in five cases) plus weapons and such war booty as Hitler's silverware.[5] Indeed, the idea of a train-borne exhibit of historic documents was not exactly new. Librarian of Congress Archibald MacLeish suggested such a scheme before the war. Professor Peter Odegard proposed a similar train tour to sell war bonds. The idea, recalled Librarian of Congress Luther Evans, had been "kicking around Washington" for years.[6]

Momentum gathered. On December 10, 1946, Clark put his idea to forty-two leaders of the mass media gathered in his office. Guests included Barney Balaban, President of Paramount Pictures; songwriter Irving Berlin; Thomas D'Arcy Brophy; presidents of the Motion Picture Association of America, the Advertising Council, CBS and NBC, the American Bar Association, the National Association of Broadcasters and the American Society of Newspaper Editors; and representatives of wire services, newspapers and other media. Clark explained that the enthusiasm his idea had received had prompted a more ambitious approach. It required a full media blitz and the talents of those present to reach the millions who would never board the train.[7]

Most of these leaders plus representatives of the Chamber of Commerce, NAM and other prime business groups met again. In January, they moved to incorporate a non-profit foundation to carry out the project: the American Heritage Foundation. Winthrop W. Aldrich, chairman of the Chase National Bank, headed the AHF's Board of Trustees; Thomas d'Arcy Brophy was president; and Louis Novins, Barney Balaban's assistant at Paramount, was vice president. Brophy had run public relations for the National War Fund and the USO. J. Edward Shugrue, who had handled publicity for the Treasury Department's Victory Train campaign, served as national director of the AHF. Members of the American Association of Railroads agreed to move the train.[8]

The Ad Council and the AHF expanded the project's scope far beyond Clark's early vision. The idea of a special train, a foundation to run it, many of the publicity activities and publications enhancing it, and the elaborate Rededication Weeks heralding each train visit originated with those whose help Clark had sought.[9] From an initial base in the ad industry and the media, the AHF expanded its membership. It drew in AFL and CIO chieftains, numerous business leaders and a smattering of other prominent figures like John Foster Dulles and Reinhold Niebuhr.

The project was formally unveiled on May 27, 1947, at a White House pep talk for sponsors. Clark once more decried "shocking evidence of disloyalty to our Government," breaches of civil liberties, and acts by "professional bigots and other disrupters of American unity." What dictated action, said AHF President Brophy, was "the increasing complexity of our lives, the increased economic dependency of one group upon other groups, and of each individual upon all individuals, the attacks upon the basic principles of democracy by governments abroad and subversive groups" at home as well as "serious class conflicts" stirred by "stresses and strains of postwar economic readjustment." Winthrop Aldrich sensed "that same wonderful kind of unity which we always show in time of war." Walter White of the National Association for the Advancement of Colored People struck the only off note. Citing a jury's recent refusal to convict a southern lynch mob, he said that foreign isms worried him less than domestic conditions. Even White endorsed the campaign, and cheerleading far overshadowed discussion.[10]

Control of the Freedom Train now passed to the AHF, with Justice retaining only the power of "approval or veto" and the task of train security. Yet the AHF's diagnosis of conditions echoed Clark's. Postwar hardships made many nations veer toward "the panacea of state control"; democratically ruled territory was now "perceptibly shrinking." "Voices of discord" clamored at home amid "the grave trials of postwar economic readjustment." "Lawlessness and cynicism," "subversive forces," and "demagogues and bigots" walked the land. Since Americans took their system for granted, a "comprehensive program of education in the ideals and practices of American democracy" was essential.[11]

Though many points of the social compass were embossed on the foundation's letterhead, the needle generally pointed to Wall Street and Madison Avenue. Yet the Freedom Train did not encapsulate just one point of view. More than "corporate hegemony," as Stuart J. Little has argued, it manifested "the conflicting forces and languages within the political culture that were attempting to define citizenship and Americanism." Definitions of freedoms "were malleable ideas in the postwar years." Whatever the initiators' "vision of freedom . . . , the program's abstractions were contested terrain."[12]

Little is correct: the train became the focus of disputed meanings. Indeed, the notion radiated plural meanings even as it took shape in Tom Clark's brain. It had the liberal aim of curbing right wing bigotry, the conservative goal of combatting left wing ideologies, and rather neutral targets like juvenile delinquency. Noting charges of "our failure to protect 'minority rights' etc.," Clark claimed his scheme was meant "to counteract such propaganda" and might buffer the administration from leftist political pressures. He also hoped the Freedom Train would preempt suggestions by members of the President's Committee on Civil Rights that the administration follow up on its report with a broad "educational civil rights campaign."[13]

The very choice of documents for the train pointed to rival definitions of "freedom." Though the AHF shared Clark's diagnosis of the American ailment, its involvement reshaped the project. An early casualty was the idea of a display contrasting Nazi and American documents, which was discarded in favor of a more "positive" emphasis on "the American way-of-life."[14]

Skirmishes flared over document selection. With a liberal vision for the exhibit, National Archives personnel proposed to use pictures and posters showing contributions by immigrants, evidence of "America's Liberal

Imperialism," documents like the Wagner Act and the order creating the Fair Employment Practices Committee, and other expressions of liberalism. The AHF thought not. Elizabeth Hamer of the Archives queried Louis Novins whether AHF decisions were not altering the exhibit's "fundamental character" away from civil liberties. She got "no satisfactory answer." Both Novins and Coblenz of Justice avowed an unwavering civil-liberties focus but stressed that Clark had been offered other documents "of such historical character that people would expect to find them in an exhibit." Hamer resisted displaying extraneous items such as General Robert E. Lee's letter resigning his U.S. commission prior to joining the Confederacy. Novins, she claimed, rejected "items relating to Jews" as creating "controversy." "I told him they were all a bunch of reactionaries. . . ." [15]

The American Heritage Foundation concentrated less on civil liberties, still less on modern liberal causes, and more on a sort of American Century triumphalism. The end result was an exhibit with no reference to current controversies over civil liberties or rights or New Deal-era economic issues. Important rights were indeed documented—the ending of slavery, women's suffrage, religious freedom in the colonial period—but such themes were balanced, if not outweighted, by items which vaunted national expansion and battlefield victories.

The lengthy selection process elicited much carping from the sidelines. The conservative New York Congressman Ralph W. Gwinn saw red on reading an early list of documents that included a program of an "'American mass meeting to celebrate the triumph of Russian Democracy,' New York, March 25, 1917." Knowing Clark's anti-communism, Gwinn was "at a loss" to understand such a choice. Clark replied that the program announced a meeting of supporters of the Kerensky regime; while "not a communistic document," it had been eliminated "under a policy of avoiding any political atmosphere in connection with the train." [16]

Liberals quibbled too. Congressman Adolph Sabath complained of the Wagner Act's absence. When the American Council on Race Relations queried omission of the report of Truman's Committee on Civil Rights, Executive Vice President Novins cited an AHF tenet "that no document should be carried on the Freedom Train which is the subject of current legislative consideration." [17]

The train's contents were in flux up to its departure. Just before embarkation, new sections were added. "Fight for Freedom—World War II" included documents related to feats of General Eisenhower and Admiral Chester W. Nimitz; the section "Freedom Triumphs" showed off German surrender articles and Japan's submission recorded in the log of the USS *Missouri*. Further additions depicted the "Inspiration of American Freedom to Other Peoples." The resulting collation of 130 documents and flags had a common denominator of democracy triumphant. The banners, treaties and surrender instruments showed that, however daunting the present challenge, freedom had a long winning streak. The AHF disavowed aiming to stimulate "chauvinistic nationalism," but the Freedom Train struck a note heavy in triumphalism.[18]

Some on the right assailed not just the documents but the train itself. Michigan Congressman Clare Hoffman took offense. Sneering at a "deathbed concern for the Constitution by the New Dealers who have flaunted [*sic*] it for fourteen years," the Republican suspected that the Freedom Train, carrying a freight of pro-Truman propaganda, was highballing straight into the 1948 campaign.[19] Hoffman haled Clark before his Committee on Expenditures in the Executive Departments to testify about the train's funding and legal basis. Clark defended his progeny as "a spontaneous citizens' movement." Hoffman finally clambered aboard, but with an alternate destination in mind: the train should visit "every city where strikes and mass picketing are depriving Americans of their constitutional rights."[20]

The *Chicago Tribune* scented partisan motives too, scoffing that Democrats "discovered" the Constitution and Declaration only after their 1946 election defeat and their borrowing of "the 'me, too' doctrine" of Wendell Willkie and Thomas E. Dewey. The train was a ploy to conceal that Truman's regime still employed Reds even as it tried to seize the anticommunist high ground with its "fraudulent Greco-Turkish aid plan." Far better, said the *Trib*, "to load that train with the New Dealers of both parties and send them out to see America and be seen by the Americans. They might become imbued with the republicanism of the west."[21]

Others espied a liberal plot. One citizen protested that early lists of documents slighted Alexander Hamilton "while Thomas Jefferson's name appeared again and again." Conservative pundit George Sokolsky assailed the AHF's "Freedom Pledge" for declaring its taker "Free to oppose what I believe wrong." But "no American is free to be a fifth columnist for a foreign Power." Columnist John O'Donnell scented "the same war psychology buildup" Wilson and FDR had used in manipulating foreign threats.[22]

Farther right even wilder accusations arose. The National Blue Star Mothers of America wrote J. Edgar Hoover to excoriate the Freedom Train's "Banker-Big-Business sponsors" and the scheme to remove "precious documents from their sacred resting place and jeopardize their safety." They suspected the "pompous traveling display" was part of a "sinister plan of a WORLD STATE GOVERNMENT" and doubted "the so-called 'Freedom Train' will ever return . . . with *the original* records which it now bears." [23]

A few on the left also dissented. Henry Wallace said that viewing the train's documents "in air-conditioned showcases is not enough." The day must come when Southern blacks leaving the Freedom Train "won't step forth into the reality of jimcrowism," or government employees to life under the federal loyalty order, or workers to the Taft-Hartley Act. [24] Antiwar groups were also drawn to the Freedom Train. At ceremonies in Philadelphia conscientious objectors leafleting against compulsory military service were arrested. Later, near the Freedom Train in New York, pacifists held a "poster walk" to demand amnesty for draft violators. The train carried amnesties granted by eight presidents, but Truman, they noted, had done nothing comparable for foes of World War II. In the ensuing melee, twenty protestors were arrested. [25]

The Communist Party chimed in too. Its district education directors were told to greet the train with campaigns "for the rights of labor and the people, and exposing the aims of its big business backers" for whom the Freedom Train was "'democratic' camouflage behind which they will also intensify Wall Street's anti-Communist and anti-democratic imperialist drive." [26]

Criticism from the fringes confirmed the AHF's claim to the broad middle. The group insisted that its focus was resolutely nonpartisan; it avowed a civic activism that transcended seamier definitions of politics. The cure for problems under the current system lay not in radical change but in broader participation.

Good Citizen epitomized the AHF's message. The seventy-two-page pamphlet drafted by adman Leo Burnett outlined the civic virtues for which the Freedom Train stood, illustrating them with pithy vignettes, poetry and noble sayings. Good citizens voted and took part in the political process, welcomed jury service, paid taxes willingly if not joyfully, served the nation in arms, shunned intolerance and prejudice, supported the schools, and knew that religion, while never compulsory, was a good thing. The booklet also sought to demystify details of the political system—what were legal and illegal voter's marks, how did juries function, what was a lobby, where did taxes go?

Though *Good Citizen* urged readers not just to gripe but to cooperate for political change, the system it depicted already seemed to work nicely. The pamphlet highlighted that Americans owned 72 per cent of the world's motor vehicles and 61 per cent of its phones. It proudly detailed the profusion of churches, schools, hospitals, libraries and cultural institutions. About the economic system that produced such wonders, the booklet was remarkably coy. The term "property" appeared sparingly, and only in a brief enumeration of constitutional rights. There was no rhapsody to "free enterprise"—only to "democracy."

Good Citizen upheld the AHF's commitment to nonpartisanship. The party system earned praise for bringing workability and discipline to politics, but its specifics were left murky. Burnett even removed a reference to the two-party system lest it offend third-party advocates. He reserved a page for Norman Rockwell's "Four Freedoms" magazine cover, hoping the artist's prestige would offset the outrage of any "Roosevelt haters," but the AHF Executive Committee had decided not to include the paintings on the Freedom Train. (Eventually, two Freedoms, Worship and Speech, survived in *Good Citizen*; Want and Fear succumbed to nonpartisanship.)[27]

While a desire not to offend suffused the pamphlet, pointed if veiled commentary crept in. A section on education stressed that the planet waited on "the humanitarian leadership and know-how of young America" to make atomic energy "an instrument for the betterment of all mankind." A photo of a mushroom cloud dominated the page. Without irony, it was captioned: "Made in America."

Women's role drew comment too. A page on the home as cradle of republican virtue expressed unease about social trends and modern women. While society's complexity put strain on the family and the women who held it together, such women "don't want *out* of the home," the excerpt assured. "They want *men back in the home.* . . ." Other Freedom Train materials touched on this theme. A radio spot alluded to the song "She's only a bird in a gilded cage" and a woman's natural temptation at times to have someone else take over shopping and diapers. "But she doesn't really mean it," for she would then lose "her most priceless possession"—freedom to run her home and raise her children as she wished.

Other spots noted her right to marry or not as she chose, contrasting Princess Elizabeth's need to have Parliament approve her bans. "Can you imagine any American girl having to ask permission to fall in love?" America boasted "the most envied women in the world!" [28]

However, the challenge of threats from abroad gave the enterprise its poignancy, and the train's boosters often alluded to the current global struggle. At the Philadelphia opening ceremonies, one speaker tasked the train with bringing home "the fact that there are other camps in the world manned by people whose whole experience and philosophy make them antagonistic to our thinking and our way of life." Tom Clark warned: "Unless we Americans share our freedom with our neighbors and with the world, in the end we shall have none for ourselves." Speaker of the House Joe Martin called for unity "to stop the march of despotism across the world." One of Clark's aides used a subsequent Freedom Train event to summon the nation to "aid a long-range recovery program for Western Europe." [29]

Yet Freedom Train rhetoric usually stressed the propagation of American values through emulation rather than enforcement. If Americans demonstrated their freedoms day by day, they would spread. Truman's message when the train departed emphasized less foreign policy than right behavior. "Our world will be won or lost in our homes, our churches, our schools, our union halls." Therein lay the crux of the AHF's "rededication" campaign. [30]

This theme that America must (again) be as a city upon a hill occasioned the AHF's deepest plunge into current politics. That body sought to avoid controversy, but in one case it could not just take things as it found them. To maintain the premise that American freedoms were universal required ongoing negotiation and accommodation with some groups. As issues of race muscled their way into the postwar political agenda, civil rights advocates scrutinized Freedom Train practices. The patent on freedom claimed for the nation gave them leverage.

Moderate civil-rights leaders lobbied heavily. The NAACP's Walter White and Urban League's Lester Granger, both present at the May 1947 White House conference, pointed out the need to ensure bias-free access to the train. White emphasized the gap between rhetoric and racial realities. However, AHF staff hesitated to move too rapidly. When one activist suggested that Clark write every mayor on the route to stress the need to forbid segregation at the train, the proposal was rejected as "a political football." But the issue would not recede.[31]

Langston Hughes's poem "Freedom Train" cast the issue most profoundly. The AHF had already decided to bypass towns that barred desegregated viewing, but Hughes remained skeptical. He hoped the train carried no Jim Crow car, doubted a black engineer could be more than a porter on it, and wondered whether the "Greenville lynchers" and the jury that acquitted them would heed the train's message in South Carolina. Seconding Hughes, Paul Robeson asserted that "it will take much more than a Freedom Train," especially one sponsored by an attorney general "who has failed to end lynchings and terror against Negroes," to "make Negroes believe that freedom for them is more than a word."[32]

The AHF won support from mainstream civil rights groups, but policy required ongoing review. In July, the executive committee resolved that Freedom Train showings must be unsegregated. Later, Chairman Aldrich stated a "firm determination" that the train "be an instrumentality for strengthening the freedoms and liberties of all Americans, regardless of race, creed or color." Its public relations director was instructed to "make hourly inspections of the railroad station and the line-up of the public" to insure nondiscrimination. If any occurred, he was to close the exhibit. Trustees stated privately, however, that AHF responsibility was not to "extend beyond the doors of the train."

Headquarters puzzled over the variations in segregation. If whites and blacks were held in separate waiting rooms and fed into separate lines, "these lines must be merged before reaching the train door." If groups of, say, a hundred of each race were alternately merged, that would be "regulation," but if the line of blacks was "held up any extended period that is segregation." Two Georgia towns formed segregated lines and let them into the train in alternate blocks of twenty-five, but they emerged "mixed up." Policy was made more stringent: a "single line leading to the Freedom Train must be open to all and must extend [the] length of train and through exhibition area."[33]

Two cities were lifted from the itinerary. When the mayor of Memphis insisted on segregation, proposing separate but equal viewing times, his city was bypassed. In Birmingham, Alabama, AHF staff negotiated amicably with one city commissioner, but the other two ordered separate lines to join only at the train door. Birmingham, too, received no visit. The

Washington Post labeled these responses "a moral victory with implications far beyond the immediate event." Things went smoothly elsewhere in the South. A Roanoke paper applauded its city's decision for an integrated showing. "Any American should be proud to stand in line with any other American" to see these "immortal documents." In Jackson, Mississippi, mixed crowds entered the train. Noting that the races mingled in line to "pay taxes, buy groceries and make bank deposits," the mayor saw no reason to make an issue. Other towns offered to replace Memphis and Birmingham.[34]

The Freedom Train received reverential welcome everywhere. Chicago's neo-gothic Tribune Tower was the chief exception. *Tribune* coverage was grudging. It trumpeted the American Legion's Fourth of July *fete* at Soldier Field and as an aside added that the fireworks were to honor the nearby Freedom Train. A report on a welcoming parade for the train was buried in the comics. An editorial noted the "happy coincidence" of the train's presence on July 4 but regretted that the mere 60,000 people who could board it would barely be able to make out a few lines in the documents. News stories also stressed how rapidly visitors were herded through.[35]

The *Tribune* hit on a painful shortcoming: the unbridgeable gap between the public's enthusiasm, stirred by so much media hooplah, and the train's limited capacity. An average of 8,500 people entered the train daily. (The peak figure was 14,615.) As a result many—up to eleven of twelve would-be visitors—could not be accommodated. In Charlotte, North Carolina, some 100,000 citizens came to the exhibit but only 8,416 got in. In Los Angeles, 400,000 lined up but fewer than 30,000 got aboard. The line snaked back through New York's Grand Central Station concourse and along the streets for fifteen blocks. While the crowds added to the train's mystique, at times a bitter taste lingered. In Pasadena, California, kids dazzled by advance publicity were crestfallen to learn that only two per school would actually go on the train. When a Marine guard cut off the waiting line in Bangor, Maine, as the closing hour approached, "there were some words one does not associate with freedom of speech."[36]

The AHF had always known that only a fraction of Americans could actually visit the train. Therefore, President Brophy had stated, "we must surround the train in each locality with all the activities and instrumentalities of the Week of Rededication," necessitating a "crusade" by community leaders. The train was a powerful symbol to stimulate "rededication." The AHF took pride in the 3½ million people who walked through the train, but more important were the over forty million who took part in the varied Rededication Week activities.[37]

Complaints were drowned in thunderous acclaim. The train was freighted with potent symbolism. It shared its cargo's aura and tapped the romance and power reserved in American culture for the rails— "high iron." "It all seemed to fit appropriately together," said a reporter: "the great train, symbol of American[s'] will to move and to 'go places' and the venerable documents which guarantee a man's right to chart his own route, write his own ticket and take off at full speed for a destination of his own choosing." Tour's end inspired one newsman to vaulting metaphor: "An idea that crystallized into a red, white and blue iron horse burdened with the documentary wealth of a Nation is breathing what may be the last two days of its life." [38]

The train took on totemic attributes. One mother asked if her sightless son might touch it. Feeling the sleek locomotive, he exclaimed, "Mamma, I can see the Freedom Train now, and just think it belongs to me and all the other kids." A tendency to drop the definite article from its title gave "Freedom Train" mystical qualities. Its sponsors saw it as "a moving shrine," and so it became. Irving Berlin's song "The Freedom Train" declared that inside it "you'll find a precious freight."

An advance man caught the spiritual overtones: some perhaps arrived "in a holiday mood, but ... when they stepped off ... it was as though they had been to the church of their choice!" One reporter observed parents hushing their children and little boys doffing their caps unbidden. Another heard the "low, guarded tones used by tourists in ancient cathedrals." Newsman Edward R. Murrow saw a gaggle of Brooklyn school children enter the train "as though they were going to a circus" but exit "as though they had been to church." An evaluator declared, "In a very real sense it was a tremendous revival meeting." [39]

The Freedom Train crystalized a folklore and tall tales. In Brooklyn, its red, white and blue striping suddenly became just red and blue. According to a reporter, as several thousand high-school girls waited in line, one "impulsively kissed the train." Others, heavily lipsticked, imitated her, crimsoning the mouth-level white stripe. The Freedom Train achieved celebrity status in the popular culture. In the comics, the character "L'il

Abner" greeted the train: "Oh happy day!! Hyar it come!!" The train also appeared in "Joe Palooka" and received the attention of Captain Marvel.[40]

The AHF put the arm on corporations and wealthy benefactors for funds, held drives en route, and put a collection box at the train. It strove to crimp private profiteering, but hawkers flocked to every stop. One entrepreneur proposed to sell "Bill of Rights" and "Constitution" hankies on the train with the slogan: "Every time you blow your nose, why not blow it into the Constitution or the Bill of Rights." Another wrote a song he wanted to sing for money. (Irving Berlin donated the royalties from his Freedom Train song. Bing Crosby and the Andrews Sisters recorded it.) One individual inquired about selling advertising at ends of the cars.[41]

More typical was patriotic behavior that thrilled sponsors. Everywhere throngs waited for hours and still risked being turned away. They braved drenching rains in New Jersey, sleet in New Rochelle. In Boston the line stretched four abreast over a mile. Visitors took prodigious pains. A Polish-born Manhattan shoe repairman rose at 2 a.m. to be first in line. The millionth viewer, an Oklahoma teen, drove classmates sixty miles through a blizzard. A motherless thirteen-year-old first taken for a runaway biked across pre-dawn Los Angeles to see the train.[42]

News reports depicted diverse and good-natured crowds. The *New York Post* saw democracy "working at full blast in Grand Central Terminal . . . white and black, Nordic, Slav and Oriental, native and immigrant, bobby-soxer and barrister. . . . In the line bandanna mingled with fancy chapeau." The *Times* sketched a "melting pot" composed of "the battered and the triumphant, the befurred and the ragged, all races, colors and creeds." There were touching visits. At one stop, a 108-year-old waited hours to board the train. "I just wanted to see Mr. Lincoln's papers before I died," she explained. "You see, I was born a slave." Over documents on women's suffrage, a mother whispered with pride to her daughter: "Your grandmother, sweetie pie, was one of the women who worked very hard to get that." [43]

The Freedom Train sparked imitation. In Albany, impressed by the vast crowds turned away, a state library administrator mounted an exhibit of duplicates of items on the train and others showing "New York State's contribution to the growth of freedom." It toured the state by train in 1949 and 1950. A "Kentucky Freedom Train"—a single car with documents of local import—was exhibited beside the Freedom Train in that state. Bypassed by the train, Montclair, New Jersey, got up a Freedom

Truck from an old bus and documents of local import. Some towns off route held rededication weeks coinciding with the train's nearest stop.[44]

If the train was the caviar, Rededication Week constituted the meat and potatoes. The AHF put greatest emphasis on what happened beyond station concourses. Rededication Weeks required elaborate planning. Freedom Train area representatives visited each town eight weeks ahead of the train, met with the mayor and got him to appoint a Rededication Week Committee, then continued to monitor progress. They supplied promotional materials—mats for newspapers, radio spots, a documentary for movie theatres, cards for buses and window displays for stores. They worked with local government and schools, civic and veterans groups.

Rededication Weeks comprised events like Veterans Day, Labor and Industry Day, Schools Day, Youth Day, Women's Day and Inter-Faith Day. They accentuated public ceremonies at which the Freedom Pledge was taken and other patriotic activities took place. Some communities had Freedom of Enterprise, Merchants', Civil Liberties, or Bench and Bar Days. Greensboro, North Carolina, devoted a month to rededication. Joint and amicable labor-management activities such as rallies received emphasis, and in some cities Rededication Week occasioned efforts to promote racial and religious tolerance.[45]

Local variation flourished. Iowa City's Women's Day included a set of tableaux: Betsy Ross, Uncle Tom's Cabin, Susan B. Anthony, the melting pot, scenes of racial tolerance and religious freedom. Bakersfield, California, held a Freedom Pageant and a Farmer's Street Banquet; women in Stockton held a Freedom Tea. Baton Rouge had a Freedom Train Dance. Ann Arbor sent a Freedom Pilgrimage motorcade to Ypsilanti. A Cincinnati women's club staged a "'Stop the Bigot' demonstration" and that city's Freedom Train committee spread a message of toleration.[46]

Local effort levels varied. In Montana, the AHF Area Rep met resistance from chambers of commerce which stemmed, he suspected, from a jealous state president's having been bypassed. In another place a bibulous local leader impeded progress. In Wisconsin there was competition from the state's centennial. Madison was so balky that the AHF advance man was tempted to ask that it be skipped.[47]

Still, virtually everyone agreed that the Freedom Train was a monumental triumph. The throngs it drew gave "a heartening indication of the virility of the democratic idea," said the *Washington Post*. Yet its impact proved hard to measure. Poetic conviction often occluded prosaic facts. It got credit for some upsurges in voting. Columnist Bob Considine claimed it raised voter registration in its wake—by 400 per cent in Los Angeles County and double in Butte, Montana. Kenosha, Wisconsin, and Ann Arbor, Michigan, scored dramatic rises in registration. A Provo, Utah, poll found that a more detailed knowledge of citizenly rights and duties and a more societal, less individual, conception of them emerged after the train's visit.[48]

The train's success plus the importunings of towns omitted from its itinerary prompted proposals to extend its tour. The AHF demurred. It would be "anticlimactic" to return to once-visited cities. A second trip would include smaller towns which could not support it financially. The railroads also wanted back their equipment. The AHF preferred to end the tour after 1948 but granted the Democrats' wish to have the train in Washington for Inaugural Week, adding a short supplemental tour en route.[49]

Tom Clark and his aide William A. Coblenz strongly backed a new trip. Coblenz would include smaller towns "because they show the highest degree of sincerity, larger cities having too many competing entertainments." A second tour might also focus on school children. He knew no "better answer educationally to communism, communist hysteria and the rest of it." [50]

Many in Congress agreed. Leaders in both parties backed a bill authorizing the National Archivist, advised by a Freedom Train Commission, to keep the train rolling until mid-1951. The House debate became an anticommunist pep rally aimed against urban America. Noting plans to visit smaller towns, one solon claimed: "you will find the spirit of freedom, liberty, and genuine patriotism running pretty high in the so-called hinterlands," unlike the cities. Another said it was not "the boys and girls from the forks of the creek and . . . the hill country" but New York and the East, "where Communists are running at large," which most needed—and so should pay for—the train.[51] The Budget Bureau's cool response to the $2½ million price tag apparently sidetracked the Freedom Train. Both houses easily passed an authorization bill, but when funds were omitted from an appropriation bill, the project died. In September 1949 most of the Freedom Train documents went on display at the National Archives; that exhibit ended in late 1950.[52]

The Freedom Train inspired thoughts of variations. The idea that a traveling display could manifest America's essence persistently intrigued those who sought to convey the virtues of the American experiment. One senator hoped to send the train abroad. For some, Mexico and Canada beckoned. The challenges of operating on foreign soil and the AHF's desire to end the tour seem to have been controlling. In 1951 American Airlines contemplated a Freedom Plane but the cost deterred it.[53]

In 1948, *Collier's Magazine* floated the spectacular scheme of author Pat Frank to nestle a miniature American town on an aircraft carrier's hangar deck, where it could impress visitors—including Soviet subjects—with the virtues of American life. Guests could inspect "a slice of America"—homes and stores illustrating consumer abundance, a schoolroom, a library, a church. The ship's "secret weapon," truth, was "the equivalent of the atomic bomb." [54]

Assiduously lobbied, President Truman and his chief of naval operations seem to have "tentatively approved" the idea. The Navy saw virtues, but also pitfalls. It lacked funds; the hangar deck's low clearance posed "structural problems"; posting female personnel aboard was problematic. The State Department policy planning staff also pondered "Operation Flattop." Though aware that things made better messengers than words, it too had doubts. The plan looked too propagandistic. Too much dazzle might engender "disbelief," "envy" or "resentment," and a carrier's hard-to-disguise arrival might occasion criticism. A memo by George Kennan, the intellectual sire of "containment," rejected the scheme, and it received a quiet manila burial.[55] In 1956, the United States Information Agency considered reconfiguring the project by outfitting a carrier with a Cinerama theatre. The initiative again failed to escape the talking stage.[56]

The Freedom Train remained so deeply etched in memory that soon the AHF pondered another tour. A 1957 rerun was proposed but tabled amid speculation that television, barely a presence in 1947, might be a more effective medium.[57] In 1962 the idea briefly resurfaced in Congress. In the tumultuous mid-60s, some saw it as a pathway back to spiritual bedrock, but the train did not roll then either.[58]

Part of the difficulty lay in social changes which reduced the salience of any public education program geared to trains. The Freedom Train toured in the twilight period of the decline of the railroads. The iron horse still retained its grip on the nation's psyche.[59] Over time, however, in growing reaches of the American landscape the train simply did not run.

Indeed, the next major effort to raise public consciousness with a traveling exhibit used different logistics. In the grim winter of 1950–51, as UN forces in Korea reeled before China's armies, the U.S. government,

alarmed at the nation's vulnerability to atomic attack, created the Federal
Civil Defense Agency. The FCDA approached Freedoms Foundation to
mount a campaign to educate citizens in their nuclear-age duties.
Kenneth D. Wells, that group's president, thought it wiser that a separate
organization conduct the effort, and so in 1951 the Valley Forge Foundation was established, with Wells in charge.

Alert America, the campaign to raise civil defense awareness, used the
Freedom Train as a model. The designer of the Freedom Train exhibit also
worked on Alert America. One AHF executive became vice president of
the Valley Forge Foundation. The Ad Council, as for the Freedom Train,
produced kits promoting Alert America. The three identical Alert America displays traveled not by rail but in ten-truck convoys. As with visitors
to the Freedom Train, observers noted a palpable mood change among
those who trooped through the civil defense exhibit. Attendees at the
Washington, D.C. preview, came out "somber faced and noticeably lacking in small talk." [60]

Though it left a lighter imprint on national memory than the Freedom
Train, Alert America was successful. In eight months of 1952, over a million people visited displays in eighty-two of what staff referred to as
"principal target cities." Like the Freedom Train, Alert America aimed to
catalyze community action. Convoy visits highlighted "Alert America"
Weeks similar to Rededication Weeks. Weeks under "Plan I" included days
linked to freedom of worship, women, youth, veterans, labor and manage-
ment and so on. "Plan II" showcased more pragmatic civil defense functions like First Aid Day and "Give Your Blood" Day.[61]

Civil defense was a subset of broader efforts to revitalize citizenship.
Both required long-term, active commitment; both entailed defense of a
physical, but also a moral and ideological entity; each cherished a comforting past while confronting a dire future.[62] President Truman rooted
civil defense in "the American tradition, dating back to the frontier days"
when every family member "had a task to do in defending their homes
and their stockades from marauding savages." Civil defense also showed
how short Americans fell in their commitment. After a year of civil defense, Truman lauded the two million "patriotic citizens" who had volun-
teered but noted that fifteen million more were needed. Too many
Americans, said Federal Civil Defense Administrator Millard Caldwell,
were "willing to let George do it." [63]

As the Freedom Train neared journey's end, the AHF took stock and determined to continue its work. It had developed effective methods of civic mobilization; a system of mayor's committees was in place in cities the train had visited. It had a $400,000 surplus. But more compelling than current assets were current challenges. Flabby citizenship would require continued attention. The public also needed tutoring in the workings of the U.S. economic system and how it was linked to political liberties. In March 1949, the AHF trustees agreed to pursue further citizenship and community activities.[64]

The AHF strove to build broader political participation. Working with the Ad Council and through various national organizations, it directed a "Get Out the Vote" drive which, it claimed, helped raise the 1950 off-year vote by over five million.[65] Since low turnout and political apathy afflicted every election, such campaigns became an ongoing task.

The AHF's nonpartisanship proved convincing enough that leaders of all persuasions endorsed its programs. Both the NAM and CIO cooperated with its 1952 Register and Vote campaign. Yet as its nonpartisan arrows arced into the ether, there was a subtle gravitational tug rightward. While a series of Freedom Train car cards had depicted men in working-class garb, some with ethnic surnames, to point up the ballot's efficacy, the AHF's emphasis on "informed" voting gave preference to responsible, individualist suffrage over class-based bloc voting. AHF officials believed that "merely getting people to vote without encouraging them to vote intelligently and on an informed basis is not necessarily a good thing."

They conveyed this theme to potential donors who might fear such drives only mobilized those favoring "left wing programs." Winthrop Aldrich once had such qualms, but not after Eisenhower's victories. Some GOP activists thought AHF efforts turned out "millions" of normally nonvoting independents for Ike. In 1952, in soliciting John D. Rockefeller, Jr., the AHF accented its nonpartisanship, but Aldrich suggested that Ike might profit from a larger vote, and Rockefeller agreed to a donation if it "gives promise of being helpful" to him.[66]

Yet as the AHF plumbed the causes of low vote turnout, it also confronted the obstacles erected by Southern states against voting by blacks. A 1960 press release decried "poll taxes, rigged literacy tests and various social pressures on minority groups." The AHF endorsed mild—very mild—reforms: literacy tests that were "objective, discrimination-proof and corrected according to answer-key" and tax-free voter registration.

Whatever the implications of such efforts, at the operational level, close political calculation dissolved amid efforts to make voting a sacrament. In 1958, an AHF-produced film, "See You At the Polls," starred Bing Crosby, Bob Hope, Jimmy Durante and Groucho Marx. A "Lassie" TV episode dramatized how one vote helped elect "the best man for dog-catcher." Pure Oil gave a gallon of gas to every "first voter." Wausau, Wisconsin, held a contest to become the "votingest city in the U.S.A." In 1956 the AHF publicized a leading cleric's message that voting was a "sacred duty" to be done "prayerfully." [67]

In the ongoing battle with "national apathy and citizen deficiency" which called the AHF into being, its task seemed "without visible end." The Cold War's indeterminate duration challenged efforts to keep up civic muscle tone. There was "grave danger," said an AHF official, that it might become, as General Omar Bradley put it, an endless "war of boredom." Even in the depths of the Korean crisis, most Americans appeared "apathetic." Five years later, AHF leaders warned that "the problem of indifference will always be with us." [68]

To build civic-mindedness, the AHF strove to bulk up the ideological content of holidays. It put out "Rededication" guides for Thanksgiving, Labor Day, Washington's Birthday, July 4, Memorial Day and New Year's Day. Its "Mid-Century Manual" suggested that communities hold Weeks of Rededication like those for the Freedom Train. [69] Allentown sought the AHF's advice for its 1950 *fete* honoring attainment of 100,000 population and Milwaukee, for its 1951 Freedom Week. The AHF also did much of the work of marking the 175th Independence Day in 1951. [70]

President Eisenhower asked the AHF to take over the public campaign for the Crusade for Freedom. Since 1950, Crusade for Freedom had financed the National Committee for a Free Europe (and thus Radio Free Europe) and the Committee for a Free Asia. Beginning in 1953, the AHF devoted much of its energy over the next several years to the crusade. [71]

The crusade elicited grassroots Cold War activism in ways reminiscent of the Freedom Train. A radio ad asked citizens to ward off "the dread mushroom cloud" and "World War III" with "Truth Dollars" for Radio Free Europe. The 1954 Crusade for Freedom sponsored the cross-country tour of a trailer-drawn "Freedom Tank," an armored car which eight "plucky Czechs" had rammed through the Iron Curtain. Now it was a "Piggy Bank for Freedom." With it went "Freedom Scrolls" for Americans to sign. A model radio transmitting tower was erected in Times Square to punctuate the crusade's fund drive.[72] The Crusade for Freedom was the AHF's last single riveting program.

The American Heritage Foundation had stature as the leading initiator of programs to bolster American citizenship. Its endeavors won wide praise as innovative and nonpartisan. Despite such accolades, the AHF would never again reach the level of *éclat* it achieved with the Freedom Train. That project would become the ideal against which its own and anyone else's efforts at patriotic education would come to be measured.

3

Capturing the Streets for Loyalty

A parade can be an ambiguous sociopolitical construct. It enables those who rule to impress their sense of right order upon an audience in a linear, moving ceremony full of symbol, protocol and ornament. Yet groups with differing interests can offer competitive dramaturgy of their own. When one aspires to seize ceremonial space and time and to dictate proper appearance and behavior, any opposition element may well assert its own claim to such public commodities. Like its brute cousin the riot, a parade is a show of power. During the Cold War, having or lacking power often dictated who might parade and who might not.[1]

Not surprisingly, contests over the right to mount public display, and its timing and location, embroiled the Left and its foes during the Cold War. Since the Bolshevik Revolution—and even before—it had galled conservatives to see radicals claim public areas to celebrate and instruct through sociodramas of their own devising. The right-wing American Defense Society deemed it scandalous that, during the 1926 Passaic furriers strike, kids were led by the Communist Young Pioneers of America in playground games like "Strikers and Scabs."[2]

In the Cold War era, anti-communists witnessed numerous leftist demonstrations, all of which offended them. When eleven Communist

Party leaders went to trial under the Smith Act in 1949, their well-wishers picketed the federal courthouse in Manhattan's Foley Square, chanting and carrying signs. During the travail of Julius and Ethel Rosenberg, especially near the end, protesters as well as advocates of their execution demonstrated near the White House.

Sometimes those who contested the legitimacy of the Left's public ceremonies used force. In 1919, when left-wing demonstrators emboldened by the October Revolution met hostile mobs, riots erupted in several cities. Occasional violence also marked the anxious opening years of the Cold War. In 1948, there were several mobbings. In Columbus, Ohio, a CP leader's house was destroyed. In Rochester, New York, veterans broke up a Communist meeting, hustled the speakers off the stage, beat several Communists and burned publications. A Henry A. Wallace speech in Evansville, Indiana, was disrupted. The riots punctuating Paul Robeson's 1949 concert in Peekskill, New York were the most egregious outrage.[3]

While some anti-communist activists condoned such methods, others deplored them. A U.S. Chamber of Commerce memorandum noted that while "direct approaches" such as denying or picketing Communist venues were "understandable," by making "martyrs" of their targets they might "backfire."[4] Anti-communists who sought more pacific techniques of preemptive counterdemonstration would find Loyalty Day to be their most sustained and successful ceremonial program against communism.

On May 1, 1948, that Communist day of days, Veterans of Foreign Wars in Manhattan and Brooklyn found an effective way to grasp control of public space, a means by which Americans might "take a positive stand rather than the usual defensive position." With Loyalty Day, the VFW met Communist marchers on their own terms, if not turf. This VFW-sponsored observance soon spread across the country. It remains surprisingly ill-chronicled, given the VFW's many years of success in mobilizing millions of people on May Day or the nearest convenient weekend day.[5]

The essential tactic of Loyalty Day predated 1948. Between the wars, New York City Veterans of Foreign Wars had demonstrated against "Red soap-box orators . . . spewing forth their communist poison in Union Square." After 1920, local VFW posts celebrated Americanization Day on or about April 27, a date which came just before May 1 and was General Ulysses S. Grant's birthday. The national VFW termed Americanism Day a means of "competing with the Reds for public attention by demonstrating that loyal Americans were equally willing to parade in much larger

ing that loyal Americans were equally willing to parade in much larger numbers than the communists could mobilize." Programs included rallies, radio shows, a ceremony at Grant's Tomb, and an essay contest. The VFW also encouraged celebrations of Americanization Week in the days prior to May 1.[6]

In 1930, a Manhattan VFW leader proposed a large patriotic counter-celebration on May Day; forty-two groups agreed to take part. City Hall lent support: city workers would be paid while marching and a permit was granted to end the program in Union Square. Denied use of Madison Square Garden and halls reserved by the Socialists, the Communists had no meeting site. Workers, they vowed, "will fight for the use of the streets in Union Square." At length, the police commissioner allowed them to parade to Union Square once their foes had left. Though they could now gather, the Communists had paid a price. By seeking a permit from the "Cossack" police, they had retreated from earlier boasts that they would enforce their claim against the ban.

The rival processions came off peacefully. The Communists' assemblage outnumbered the VFW-led coalition, but their turf had been sullied. The rival parade chairman exulted that "for forty-four years the foreign-controlled Communist party has used this historic American open space to celebrate anarchy, chaos, revolt, sabotage and atheism." Now the VFW disputed "the right of any alien party to dedicate any day in the year" to such doctrines. VFW posts elsewhere elaborated similar techniques to preempt May Day. From 1930 on, the VFW Women's Auxiliary sponsored annual May Day patriotic rallies on Boston Common.[7]

However, these observances had largely local carry. May Day continued to affront patriots until Loyalty Day's advent. In 1950, New York Governor Thomas E. Dewey lamented that May 1, long "pre-empted by subversive groups," had become "virtually disloyalty day." Loyalty Day, said a VFW leader, aimed "to usurp the parade routes of our big cities" with patriotic processions "and thus shunt to the side streets, alleys and underground, where they belong," the Communists' activities. He declared May Day now cured "of its Communistic ulcer of the twenties."[8]

For Loyalty Day, New York City became a Free World focal point. Brooklyn and Manhattan's Loyalty Day celebrations, coming on an upswell of Cold War tensions, captured wide notice. As Loyalty Day became a fixture of the 1950s, the 1948 observance acquired official status as the inaugural Loyalty Day. It was the first to receive national attention.[9] The 1948 event also stimulated formation of a National Loyalty Day Parade Committee headed by Secretary of Labor Maurice J. Tobin.[10]

Local lore had it that Benjamin Lippsett, a Brooklyn mailman and VFW leader, conceived of Loyalty Day in its modern form. However, according to a variant version, two VFW members, James Mackin and former King's County Commander Joseph M. Aimee, while observing the 1947 May Day parade, were stunned to see uniformed veterans parading, including one of Mackin's former men who he knew was no Communist. Bemoaning such vets as "victims of insidious subversive propaganda," the two straightway began planning Brooklyn's 1948 Loyalty Day observance.[11]

The purpose was blunt: to capture the May Day streets from the Left. A photo caption referred to Loyalty Day preparations as a plan to "eclipse Commie Day celebration." "We will compete with them in time, spirit and ideologies," said an organizer. Indeed, the parade was rescheduled to coincide directly with the Communists' procession, a shift a May Day spokesman termed "provocative." A Republican city council member even sought, unsuccessfully, to bar the Left's May Day march, avowing that it "amounts to an open invasion by the Communists of our streets." The *Daily Worker* counterinsinuated that the Catholic Church might be "plotting May Day violence." Granted use of Fifth Avenue from 95th to 62nd Street, Loyalty Day had much the choicer itinerary. May Day celebrants followed their traditional route: south on Eighth Avenue from 56th Street, then east on 17th to Union Square.[12]

Loyalty Day won city hall backing. Mayor William O'Dwyer signed on as honorary chairman. Initially scheduled to be on vacation, instead he showed up at the reviewing stand, joined by Attorney General Clark. The city council ordained that city employees receive paid leave to march in the parade. Communists protested the city's partiality. Communist City Council member Benjamin J. Davis, Jr., scolded the mayor for letting the city's Veterans Service Center serve "as a mobilization point for inciting violence and Hitlerite ideology." Likening the paid leave granted to marchers to U.S. meddling in Italy's elections, a May Day parade leader compared it to the Marshall Plan, "with the city playing the role of the Truman Government." [13]

Though Loyalty Day aspired to transcend politics, there was partisan elbowing backstage. James Mackin, Brooklyn's Loyalty Day chairman, reported pressure in veteran groups to schedule a speech by GOP presidential hopeful Harold Stassen. Sensing the Democratic National Committee's failure to see the danger, Mackin maneuvered deftly. He fended off Stassenites with claims that he had a cabinet officer committed to speak—then implored Tom Clark to do so. Having first declined, ten days before the rally the attorney general consented to speak.[14]

As marchers stepped off, U.S.-Soviet tensions were deepening. The VFW's New York County commander deemed it time to tell the USSR that its surge to dominance in Europe had ended. Four exiled leaders of Iron Curtain nations agreed to review the parade. The *New York Times* ran parallel columns on preparations for May Day locally and across the Atlantic. "Nervous Europeans" reportedly anticipated demonstrations that might turn violent; the Soviet Armed Forces minister was quoted ordering his troops to be ready for "intrigues of international reaction." (In fact, Greece's minister of justice was assassinated on May Day.)

Many organizations followed the VFW's lead. Participating veterans groups included the American Legion, Catholic and Jewish War Veterans. Loyalty Day ranks were also augmented by members of anti-communist unions and nationality groups (especially from Iron Curtain countries). Marchers from the Democratic and Republican parties also filled out the ranks. The Catholic diocese of Brooklyn "ordered" parochial schools to participate, adding 20,000 school children to the line of march.[15]

Left and Right each viewed their own procession as a form of ritual cleansing, their rivals' as ceremonial pollution. A *Daily Worker* column asserted that "a six or eight-hour parade of tens of thousands of banner-carrying workers through the heart of New York clears much of the poisoned atmosphere that accumulates through the year." More than "a mobilization of progressive strength," the parade "provides powerful education for hundreds of thousands of less advanced onlookers."[16]

Both sides competed in numbers. May Day leaders expected over 100,000 marchers, "the largest May Day parade in New York City's history"; Loyalty Day organizers predicted first 50,000, then 75,000 paraders. Anti-communists clearly won the contest if newspaper accounts are credited, though crowd estimates have always proven imprecise and prey to political purposes. The Left mobilized 20,000 marchers, while 30,000 to 40,000, by police estimate (with one exuberant guess of 70,000), walked for Loyalty Day. Loyalty Day had the bigger audience: a crowd pegged at 750,000, to May Day's 50,000. Manhattan's VFW commander

boasted that his side had "walked them off the streets." In Brooklyn perhaps 60,000 paraded for Loyalty Day.

Loyalty Day's claim to pedestrian hegemony did not go unanswered. A
"press fairy tale," sniffed the *Daily Worker*, one of whose writers counted
fewer than 8,000 marchers on Fifth Avenue. He ridiculed one paper's
claim of a million viewers, calculating that that would require over sixty
per front foot along the parade route; the true total lay closer to 25,000.
Claiming that 85,000 marched on Eighth Avenue, the *Worker* declared:
"only the capitalist press could figure out how a parade of ninety minutes
[sic] could be bigger than one of five hours and ten minutes."

Comparisons of the two parades extended beyond numbers. Loyalty
Day was less noisy than May Day, but the quiet, said a *New York Times* reporter, befitted its mood of "defiance." "In every countenance one could
read determination to accept the challenge of the rival marchers and hurl
it back." The *Daily Worker* drew a different contrast. May Day had "youth,
students, children, color, song, a myriad of banners and dramatic floats";
Loyalty Day's "muffled march . . . testified to little but hatred and obscur-
antism." It pronounced the effort to "steal May Day and turn it into a
demonstration of war hysteria" a failure.[17]

In 1949 the VFW strove to expand Loyalty Day in New York and nationally. Manhattan's parade emphasized showcasing labor's loyalty. Top
AFL and CIO leaders endorsed the event. Secretary of Labor (and grand
marshal) Maurice J. Tobin urged a big union turnout. Interior Secretary
Julius A. Krug and ex-Postmaster General James A. Farley added Democratic eminence to the reviewing stand, and Vice President Alben Barkley
spoke at a Loyalty Day event sponsored by the Catholic Archdiocese.
Francis Cardinal Spellman led a strong Catholic push to swell numbers.
In the first of many Loyalty Days in which he figured prominently, he
marched at the fore, then reviewed the parade.

Loyalty Day organizers aimed to mass 150,000 paraders, with fifteen
bands, twenty fife-and-drum corps, and Boy Scouts toting the flags of
every state. The parade encompassed veterans plus their auxiliary units,
unions, ethnic societies, political organizations (now including the Liberal Party), students from two Catholic colleges and city employees. In
Brooklyn, school children marched. Boston, Trenton, Los Angeles, and
other cities also planned parades.[18]

Evidently stung by the challenge, May Day parade organizers shifted it
to Saturday, April 30 to "show up" their competitors, who chose that date

because May Day fell on Sunday. Belittling the Right's effort to add labor coloration, the May Day committee director declared that "the working class will be in our parade" and promised to outdraw Loyalty Day by "at least ten to one, as we did last year." To rid themselves of the "slander" of alleged disloyalty, the left-wing group also proposed that their marchers take en masse "an anti-Fascist loyalty pledge." [19]

VFW sponsors declared that "the eyes of the world are on the Fifth Avenue Loyalty demonstration to see how it outdraws and by how much—the Eighth Avenue May Day crowd." They again "dwarfed" May Day, they boasted. A police official guessed that "more than a million" viewers watched 117,000 paraders on Fifth Avenue, but "independent estimates" put the number at 50,000. Planned for six hours, the procession took a bit less than four. By police count, 8,100 walked for May Day, but others assayed the number at twice that. Terming the cops' figure a "despicable, contemptible falsehood," the May Day committee claimed 85,000 marchers, but a West Side business group with counting machines tracked only 13,462. Police gauged the audience at ten to twenty thousand—"the thinnest May Day crowd in years," said one inspector.

Although the left boasted far more floats than usual, the Loyalty Day procession offered numerous attractions: Chinese dragon dancers accompanied by cymbals and drums, kilted Scots and Irish with bagpipes, and other ethnics in national garb. Greek girls robed in white adorned a float bearing ruins of an ancient Hellenic temple and the legend, "Communism Spells Destruction." One bedraggled marcher carried a placard: "Just Arrived From the Red Paradise." Telephone operators held banners that read: "We Don't Like Stalin's Party Line." [20]

In 1950 Loyalty Day became truly national, as the VFW sought to rouse its 10,000 posts. It claimed over 400 parades involving five million people in Chicago, Boston, Cleveland, Pittsburgh, Salt Lake City, New Orleans, San Francisco, Los Angeles and elsewhere. In 1951 it boasted of 7,500,000 celebrants of Loyalty Day. By 1952 it found the day observed in forty-four states.

No larks, Loyalty Day manifestations of morale were needed to undeceive enemies, outsiders and doubters, to show before the world that Americans rejected communism. The march "is every New Yorker's answer," said a VFW official, "to those among us who can only see red." Another deemed it crucial to warn "would-be traitors and fellow travelers" that "the great mass of American people are loyal to the principles of

Americanism." A national parade committee member termed the project a way to "show the world" that May Day efforts of subversives "do not reflect the sympathies of the American people." New York's Legislature passed a 1949 Loyalty Day resolution imploring people at home and abroad to "be not deceived" by May Day and to "understand that the vast majority" of New Yorkers were loyal.[21]

Though Loyalty Day remained linked to May Day, it soon developed a rhythm of its own. The Left celebrated May 1 by the calendar, but Loyalty Day 1950 took place on Saturday, April 29. (By 1952 Loyalty Day was observed on whatever day of the week bracketing May 1 was locally most convenient.) In Manhattan the weekend date allowed broader participation and interfered less with Fifth Avenue businesses. Though it thinned the crowd of onlookers, cold, rainy weather did not prevent the parade from outdoing its predecessors. This time Gothamites could glimpse U.S. House and Senate leaders of both parties marching in the section of the parade for local political clubs. Ethnic groups included horsemen in Cossack garb, whose passage a band incongruously marked with "Swanee River." Communists dismissed the marchers as parochial school kids carrying dummy rifles, city employees, postal workers, vets, displaced persons, and a paltry sixteen unionists—a "clerical military demonstration of hatred against the Soviet Union and progressive American thought." [22]

Thus, by the early 1950s the VFW had established a pattern. Though there were local variations, Loyalty Day typically included a parade and perhaps a rally and speechmaking. Veterans, government agencies, Catholic groups, scouts and other school children, and ethnic groups, especially from Iron Curtain nations, filled out the marching ranks.

Loyalty Day became an occasion whose attendance by public officials was mandatory. State governors and mayors proclaimed the day; along with national functionaries, they (especially mayors) took part in parades. Loyalty Day organizers had managed to plant their event on the civic calendar, competing for the attention and time of politicians. Its rapid ascent owed much to national political leaders, notably the Secretary of Labor and Attorney General, but theirs was not the primary impetus. Though the story that a Brooklyn mailman originated the event made alluring folklore, the birth of Loyalty Day was neither so simple a process nor one so closely connected to the grassroots.

Public memory emerges dialectically from a colloquy between "official" and "vernacular" cultures, according to John Bodnar.[23] Loyalty Day's principals would seem to belong among guardians of the official culture. A glance at the event's leading exponents confirms such an estimate. They included the U.S. secretary of labor, VFW potentates, and, in New York, the general manager of the *New York Times*, Democratic Party leader and ex-Postmaster General James Farley, Cardinal Spellman, and Charles Silver, a vice president of the American Woolen Company who chaired the Citizens Committee for the parade. The *Daily Worker* described Loyalty Day's provenance more grumpily: "war-minded cliques" and "professional 'vets'" serving big corporate interests "itching for war contracts and war profits" plus "high-paid swivel-chair" labor leaders, "notorious stooges of Big Money" and "quisling-fascist splinter groups in the foreign-language field." [24]

But mostly Loyalty Day occupied a middle range. Its leaders could enforce their agenda on such as the Boy Scouts, schoolkids, Catholic groups, government workers, union members, ethnics—and veterans. [25] Within limits, they also compelled the attention of local, state, and second-echelon national political leaders. No president seems ever to have attended Loyalty Day—nor secretary of state or defense. The relationship between Loyalty Day's organizers and the mighty was less a mingling of peers than a kind of tugging by the former on the latters' lapels. In the ability of VFW leaders and their allies to put their annual rite on the calendar of political feast days lay an important element of the power transactions which operated on Loyalty Day.

While the essentials of Loyalty Day were in place by 1950, changing circumstances would occasion variations. The ongoing need to showcase loyalty prompted an unending quest for devices to attract parade-goers once the novelty had faded. At the same time, the routinized annual observance, like St. Patrick's Day or other rites tinted with a political coloration, led to occasional contretemps as leaders attempted to make political use of it.

Loyalty Day 1951 dawned not three weeks after Truman removed Douglas MacArthur from command and the general came home to a welcome full of pomp and politically charged circumstance. This unique instance of cold-war pageantry is remembered as a dramatic episode of focused public attention, the throngs angry over his ouster sharing in solemn and intense public ceremony. In fact, a study of MacArthur's visit to Chicago found the crowd curious and casual rather than formal and irate. Onlookers preferred "'being there'" to watching on television. Their supposed intensity or solemnity or "mass hysteria" were constructs of television and newspaper coverage not apparent to observing sociologists.[26]

New York's Loyalty Day planners invited MacArthur to review the April 28 parade, but complications ensued when they announced his entourage. New York's Episcopal bishop would not ride in the lead car though MacArthur was himself Episcopalian. Instead, Cardinal Spellman was to be the sole religious leader with him. "Hundreds" protested. The local branch of Protestants and Other Americans United for Separation of Church and State complained of yet "another manifestation of the dominance of the Roman Catholic hierarchy in the public affairs of New York." Plans were soon altered. MacArthur rode in the lead car and dismounted at the reviewing stand; the cardinal walked with colleagues of other faiths at the head of the procession.[27]

After 1951, Loyalty Day's custodians found it hard work to mobilize enthusiasm. Though the Korean War made the Cold War palpable, the dialogue with the May Day parade grew fainter. The decline of the American left thus posed an ironic difficulty for Loyalty Day. The chairman of the VFW Loyalty Day Committee bragged in 1955 that "the Reds are on the run." In 1956, he exulted that "most communist celebrations in the U.S.A. have disappeared from the front pages of the papers." In 1958, New York's Governor Averell Harriman boasted: "We have taken over the streets for loyalty." [28] May Day's demise and the success of past Loyalty Day parades were no boon to those that followed.

More marchers were needed. Active-duty military personnel were an obvious source, but in 1948 the Department of the Army declined to let its units take part in Loyalty Day parades lest any May 1 demonstration should be "pictured and advertised" by Soviet propagandists as "a Communist celebration." Moreover, if "trouble" arose at a parade, Army officials wanted no troops present. Organizers pled with the Pentagon and White House to reverse the policy. In 1952 they won out. The Department of Defense left the decision to individual commanders. For the first time federal troops marched, upwards of a thousand in Manhattan. Civil defense volunteers also began to do so. Though the New York County VFW anticipated the largest anti-communist demonstration in history, a steady rain dampened a crowd of 20,000 viewers—far from the one million predicted.[29]

Reducing or erasing the rival parade was another option. In issuing his 1953 Loyalty Day proclamation, New York Mayor Vincent Impellitteri regretted that the police had granted the left a parade permit; he endorsed efforts by Catholic War Veterans and a West Side business group to get approval revoked. Stating that his underlings had not, in fact, granted an official permit, the police commissioner now denied one to the May Day Committee. He refused to subject New Yorkers "to the sight of the red flag of communism while the red blood of our American boys is spilling in Korea." After litigation and posturing, the ban stood, though the police commissioner did permit a May Day rally—a small one, it turned out—in Union Square.[30]

In subsequent years, similar ploys were used. In 1954, the Fourteenth Street Association was allowed to hold a Loyalty Day fete on May 1 that gave patriots a "monopoly of Union Square" and precluded its use by "rabble-rousing elements." The Left did receive a permit to use the square that evening. In 1955, when the May Day Committee sought parade and meeting permits, they discovered that the VFW and its allies had preempted them, planning a celebration to include circus clowns and games for children. The national Loyalty Day chairman exulted that the Left had been "forced to surrender in their last feeble effort to make May 1 a communist holiday in America." In 1956 he bragged of having "driven the Reds underground." The Left's subsequent Manhattan May Days grew more invisible and marginalized.[31]

Loyalty Day also garnered official support at the national level. In 1955 GOP Congressman James Van Zandt of Pennsylvania, past national VFW commander, won passage of a bill making Loyalty Day a national observance. Despite his and the VFW's suggestion, the White House, constrained by President Eisenhower's schedule and the bill's timing, held no signing ceremony. Though applying only to 1955, the measure was deemed "the ultimate peak in public acceptance of this V.F.W. product." In 1958 Van Zandt shepherded through a bill making Loyalty Day annual. Ike's low-profile statement of approval betokened little enthusiasm. It fussed that there was conflict with a 1928 law designating May 1 as Child Health Day.[32]

It proved hard to sustain enthusiasm in Manhattan. In 1953 the VFW first predicted a half million marchers; in the event, the parade chairman lowered the figure to 250,000—then to 175,000 after reporters protested; "independent estimates put the figure at 50,000 marchers." In 1954, sponsors claimed 210,000 marchers, but police, perhaps to avoid the "recriminations" of prior years, offered no estimates. In 1955, only 20,000 paraded. (Faithful Brooklyn turned out 60,000.) Numbers were similar in 1956. In 1957, the *New York Times* merely reported that "thousands" marched. Meteorologically, the parade faced a no-win situation. While sometimes rain thinned the crowd, in 1957 *good* weather, perhaps by luring potential onlookers out of town or to the beaches, seemed to have similar effect.[33]

Drawing crowds proved a challenge unending. In 1958 Mayor Robert Wagner backed a VFW request to move the parade south into the heart of the shopping district. The city council amended the pertinent regulations. Battered by suburban competition, merchants howled. The *New York Times* ran five acerbic editorials bemoaning their inevitable losses. Said Wagner: "in these grave times when loyalty is of such vital importance to our very existence," the parade needed "the best possible showcase." Its marshal weighed up the issue as patriotism versus the "almighty dollar." Wagner, surmised the *Times*, held the theory "that loyalty is more loyal if it costs other people some money." It garnished parade coverage with a picture not of ranks coursing down Fifth Avenue but of empty aisles at Bonwit Teller's. Since the march drew a crowd only three-deep, leaving shoppers ample room to pass, its director sniffed that if stores lost money, "it's because their merchandise isn't up to standard." An average sales decline of 32 percent was reported, and crowd size did not improve.[34]

In 1959 retailers again protested that the new route cost them business. The VFW countered that marchers had all been asked to make a purchase in a Fifth Avenue store, so the parade actually boosted buying. But only 100,000 looked on. The complexities of scheduling events in Manhattan also led to confusion. President Eisenhower had proclaimed May 1 as Loyalty Day, New York Governor Nelson Rockefeller designated May 2 for the state's celebration, but the Manhattan organizers' permit required that they parade on the preceding Saturday (April 25)—while Brooklyn's march took place on May 2.[35]

In 1960 the mayor brokered an "armistice" under which the parade reverted to its former itinerary and the stores worked to promote it. Still the ranks of marchers and spectators thinned, prompting the VFW to experiment further. Their 1965 permit to march north from 44th Street triggered new merchant complaints.

In words that would have signified blasphemy in the high cold war, the *Times* carped: "We have never understood why it is necessary to prove loyalty by parading it, anyway." The outcry induced Wagner to cajole the VFW back to its usual route.[36]

In 1958, Loyalty Day faced a new rival. Law Day, celebrated on May 1, contested ceremonial ownership of the date. Conceived by Charles S. Rhyne, president of the American Bar Association, and sponsored by the ABA and local bar associations, Law Day sought to teach "that respect for law and order is the cornerstone of our American heritage." At the behest of the ABA and Justice Tom Clark, the American Heritage Foundation promoted Law Day, warning that the nation faced "an emergency of rising lawlessness among adults as well as young people." From the outset, Law Day, U.S.A. enjoyed more elite support than Loyalty Day. It won backing from governors and mayors, the NEA, National Council of Churches, FBI, PTA, and service organizations. Key figures in the Eisenhower administration endorsed it.

Law Day quivered with Cold War resonances. In proclaiming it, Ike urged Americans to "remember with pride and vigilantly guard the great heritage of liberty, justice and equality under law which our forefathers bequeathed to us" and termed America's government "an inspiration and a beacon light for oppressed peoples." The May 1 date was no coincidence. Alluding to "tanks and missiles and tens of thousands of regimented Soviet citizens [who] paraded before the Kremlin," Senator Hubert Humphrey found no better contrast between the two regimes "than their glorification of revolution and force and our dedication to law and peaceful change." An organizer of Cincinnati's 1963 Law Day declared his group's intent "to prove that if the Reds can pack Red Square, we can pack Fountain Square." [37]

With 20,000 separate observances, Law Day opened grandly.[38] Mostly lawyers orated, but in St. Louis, two great-grandchildren of Dred Scott helped reenact his famous case. The first Law Day was meant to convey not high polish but the granite solidity of Hammurabi's code and Moses's tablets. *Time* limned eighty-seven-year-old Harvard scholar Roscoe Pound drafting his speech hunched over an ancient writing desk, a judge taking inspiration from the "ax-hewn pine timbers of the oldest courthouse in California," and other jurists cracking old tomes to rediscover first principles. At Independence Hall, the chief justice and attorney general took part in televised rites; Ike spoke on TV. If mostly conservative in thrust, Law Day left space for other views. Governor Harriman lambasted his Arkansas counterpart for calling out the National Guard "not to uphold the Constitution and orders of the Supreme Court, but to defy them." [39]

Law Day and Loyalty Day were in some ways complementary: the rule of law and due process enshrined on Law Day were key elements of the system to which Loyalty Day promoted allegiance. Sponsors of Law Day declared that it aimed "to foster respect for law; to increase public understanding of the place of law in American life; to point up the contrast between freedom under law in the United States and governmental tyranny under communism."

Yet the new fete prompted confusion and competition the VFW could only regret. In 1959 a Loyalty Day supporter noted that since the president had designated May 1 Law Day *and* Loyalty Day, the date had lost its "identity." After Congress made Law Day yearly in 1961, the VFW's commander-in-chief urged the president to reject the "confusing" measure. "Anything that serves to detract from the Loyalty Day celebrations ... certainly could not be good for our country." However, Loyalty Day could not outmuscle its rival. Kennedy had already signed the bill, an aide replied, and probably would have in any case. [40]

Sustaining Loyalty Day became an ever heavier burden. Two organizers of Brooklyn's 1963 Loyalty Day complained to Kennedy how hard it was to secure an Army general to review the parade. If the public was "complacent," the armed services were "not exactly bubbling over with patriotism either." Manhattan's Loyalty Day faced new competition. In 1966, marchers 15,000 strong expressed solidarity with Americans fighting in Asia. Many wore red-white-and-blue buttons reading: "Support Our Boys in Vietnam." However, a thousand "pacifists and leftists" in Union Square rallied against the war. After years in eclipse, the Left—albeit mostly the New Left—was back. [41]

Manhattan was not the whole country, but elsewhere too, the event ebbed toward natural limits. In 1958, the National Loyalty Day Committee chairman derided Communist hopes that the VFW was tiring of Loyalty Day, yet he warned that "in some circles today patriotism is considered to be an archaic sentiment, out-of-date and nationalistic." Such a "diseased conception of modern government" made the effort all the more necessary. Robert K. Christenberry, head of the New York State Athletic Commission, the GOP's 1957 New York mayoral candidate, and chair of the 1959 Loyalty Day Executive Committee, addressed the inertia.

He noted that Loyalty Day came just weeks before "when Khrushchev has said he will throw us out of Berlin. Let's now stand together and show this Red butcher that he has underestimated the readiness of the American people." While "several hundred" posts would mark the day, given the stakes, this was "poor representation." [42]

Loyalty Day had from the outset shouted defiance at the Red menace. For the non-militant, that posture grew quaint after the Korean War ended and the "spirit of Geneva" kindled modest hopes for a less grim Cold War. Before a decade passed, only old believers upheld Loyalty Day with much fervor. Loyalty Day utterances grew shriller, full of warnings about threats of communist infiltration and diplomatic deviousness which to many Americans sounded a bit passé. Conservative Senator William F. Knowland used Loyalty Day 1955 to assail Eisenhower's willingness to negotiate the Taiwan Straits dispute with Red China. The 1956 Manhattan parade chairman warned that the perils of communism "are now taking on a new type of smooth, subtle quality." In 1965 the Westchester County VFW Council withdrew Congressman Richard L. Ottinger's invitation to speak on Loyalty Day after he voted against a HUAC appropriation. [43]

Loyalty Day faced other handicaps. It pertained to both veterans and politicians but did not insinuate itself fully enough into the concerns of either constituency to guarantee permanent national significance. Speaking little of past sacrifices, it differed from other observances by or for war veterans. Usually, the martyrs it invoked were those who bore the Communist yoke. As a chairman of the VFW's Loyalty Day Program later put it, other patriotic holidays cited "special patriotic objectives or anniversaries. But Loyalty Day is the one day that we set aside for the exclusive purpose of letting the world know that we Americans vigorously reject the evils of communism" and like menaces. [44] Time and a mellowing of the Cold War made demonstrating that rejection less urgent.

The necessary sacrifices were present and future, not past. The annual massing of school children may have implied prospective cold-war commitments. The head of the 1956 Loyalty Day campaign stressed how crucial it was to "indoctrinate the children of today" in loyalty. Adults were important, "but primarily because the wrong kind of adult thinking on the subject of Americanism exercises a dangerous influence upon the thinking processes of the youngsters who will be our adult citizens tomorrow." Manhattan's 1963 parade theme was "The Children of America." Said the parade chairman: "On their shoulders lies the great task of maintaining our future world leadership." [45]

Though the observance made reference to victims of Communist oppression, the remoteness of this constituency may have limited Loyalty Day's potency. Its eminence as public observance depended on a sense of cold-war crisis; in the absence of a mood sufficiently fearful, Loyalty Day could not sustain its salience. In the 1960s, with the breakdown of the cold war consensus, Loyalty Day fell prey to centrifugal forces operating in that decade—and saw in some of them the very demons it had been meant to exorcise. Thus, in 1967 Brooklyn's VFW commander noted "a new breed of Communist stalking the land. No longer does he march in Union Square singing 'The Internationale.'" Rather, he sought to subvert youth, as evidenced in "riots in our college campuses, the draft card burnings and the beatnik parades." [46]

Loyalty Day's limits also stemmed from its sponsors' tenuous political leverage. At parades, mayors, governors, and secondary national figures turned out, but not presidents. (Arguably, Tom Clark's 1949 elevation to the Supreme Court took a valued ally from active politics.) Loyalty Day had some clout: the ban on participation by members of the armed services was ended; a resolution mandating an annual presidential proclamation won passage. But the veterans could not defend their title to the day when lawyers—seconded by the nation's highest political leaders—impaired it with Law Day.

Loyalty Day pageantry was not the product of Establishment or *hoi polloi*. While its practitioners were hardly powerless, they generally belonged to a middle echelon. If the celebration was not invented by a mailman, it seems to have owed its modern incarnation to two active Democrats, an employee in the Brooklyn United States Attorney's Office and a deputy commissioner in the administration of Mayor Bill O'Dwyer.[47] The example of Loyalty Day, having its origins in an intermediate niche, suggests that the force field of the politics of ritual was something more complicated than bimodal.

4

Springtime for Stalin in Mosinee

"Come out with your hands on your head! I represent the Council of People's Commissars and we're taking over this town."* This order rang out not in tsarist St. Petersburg, nor in the streets of Prague, but on May Day 1950 at the home of the mayor of Mosinee, Wisconsin. These "commissars" were actually American Legionnaires seeking to dramatize the Red menace and the liberties to be lost in the event of the real thing.

Of the several varieties of pageantry devised by promoters of anti-communism and patriotism, in sheer dramaturgy none could rival this mock Communist takeover. For forty-eight hours Mosinee's coup captivated the nation's media and briefly inspired anti-communists to believe they had hit upon a new and striking form of anti-communist theatre. To the genre of anti-communist pageantry it added the novelty of uniquely dystopian fantasy.

The idea of demonstrating the feel of a day under Communism occurred first to John Decker. Lawyer, former assistant city attorney of Mil-

---

* An earlier version of this material appeared in "Springtime for Stalin: Mosinee's 'Day Under Communism' as Cold War Pageantry," *Wisconsin Magazine of History* 77 (Winter, 1993–94).

waukee, and active Legionnaire, Decker belonged to a cohort of young World War II veterans just gaining influence in Wisconsin's Legion. Though untroubled by the organization's muscular anti-communism, Decker knew it had a tendency to "bring out the band and the flags" and sensed a need to "elevate the debate to reach minds we hadn't reached." During a January 24, 1950, car trip with his friend Paul Thielen, state Legion public relations director and editor of the *Badger Legionnaire*, Decker conjectured that a mock Communist takeover would vivify the precious liberties that would be forfeit in the event of a real Communist triumph. Thielen's enthusiasm was instant.[1]

The two men laid the scheme before the state Legion's Public Relations Commission, which responded with eagerness. Mosinee was chosen as a venue. The small papermill town in Marathon County afforded several advantages. For one, Brigadier General Francis Schweinler, a prominent state Legionnaire, avidly backed the idea. As owner-editor of the *Mosinee Times*, he was well situated to sell it to the community and to mobilize the local Legion in an era when the Legion virtually "*was* the small town."

Mosinee offered ideal size and location. Its population was not quite 1,400. In a large city such political theatre would raise severe complications. In a hamlet whose "power structure" all breakfasted at the same cafe, communications were simplified. Moreover, in a metropolis Communists would surely contest such a symbolic offensive. Detroit's police commissioner opined that to hold the pageant in his city would invite both Communists and "criminal elements" to run amok. Mosinee, said Wisconsin's State Legion commander, was "far removed from the scenes where Communists normally are active." Remote, with just three access roads, bordered on one side by the Wisconsin River, Mosinee permitted control of access. Sponsors scheduled the pageant for May 1 "because it traditionally is a Communist holiday."[2]

In February, Thielen, Decker and Schweinler revealed the secret plan to Mosinee's leaders: the ex-mayor and owner of Mosinee's second biggest store, a co-owner of the department store and former chamber of commerce president, the phone company manager, two top managers at the Mosinee Paper Mill and leaders of its two AFL locals, the owner of the Mosinee Land, Log and Timber Company, the president of the Lions Club and the current head of the chamber of commerce. Four were active Legionnaires. Previously sounded out by Schweinler, these ten now approved the concept and asked the state Legion to draw up a pageant scenario, but enthusiasm was far from universal. Practical rather than philosophical reasons prompted some reticence.[3]

Officials at national Legion headquarters embraced the scheme but, in their ecstasy, altered the focus. The Wisconsinites had originally emphasized local education, but Indianapolis saw the coup more as a national public relations bonanza. A national Legion public relations functionary termed the pageant "colossal in the dramatic possibilities it has of impressing upon the American people the ultimate every-day living objectives of the red tide." When he informed a *Life Magazine* official of the idea, the latter, in language indicating shifting priorities, exclaimed, "Why didn't I think of such a stunt?" The hope that national media would embrace a "smashing pictorial story" bore fruit. *Life* quickly determined to cover it. Hearst's Milwaukee *Sentinel* planned to treat it "like a National Convention with photographers and several reporters to touch upon it from all angles—women's angles, treatment of kids, etc."

By early March, Wisconsin Legionnaires—Thielen especially—had roughed out a script. Out-of-town Legion men cast as Communists would offer "strange faces not familiar to the town's people." The sponsors also adopted some specific touches suggested by national Legion HQ, including erecting a barbed-wire stockade to house enemies of the new regime.[4]

Mosinee at large had still to be mobilized. Schweinler invited sixty-seven community representatives to attend an April 12 meeting to consider "a program that can be of tremendous importance to all of us." There Thielen, Decker and Jack Cejnar from national Legion headquarters spelled out the evolving plan. Until now the planning had been kept secret: Indianapolis headquarters entertained "some fears lest this Mosinee stunt should backfire on us."[5]

The response fell short of fevered. Thielen found it "still mixed." Mayor Ralph Kronenwetter had "qualms." To this Democrat it looked like a "Republican idea." The clamor over Wisconsin Senator Joe McCarthy's first charges of Communists in government may have given him pause. The *Daily Worker*, grinding its own axe, later quoted a "prominent townsman" to the effect that "most people here were only lukewarm to the whole idea."[6] There was other scattered opposition. Some folk feared that publicity might endanger townspeople's relatives behind the Iron Curtain. Schweinler's *Mosinee Times* reported that some citizens with "wrong impressions" of the scheme were "loud in their condemnation of it" but that most residents were "favorable."

Resistance remained slight. Kronenwetter, the weightiest potential critic, went along. Leaders at the April 12 meeting agreed to pitch in and, with Schweinler serving as general chairman, the pageant was on. To provide leeway for naysayers, sponsors stressed that participation would be entirely voluntary. Those who wished to play along would wear badges so indicating.[7]

In March national Legion headquarters lined up ex-Communist Joseph Zack Kornfeder to provide expertise. This Slovak tailor had arrived in the States in 1917 and joined the Communist Party in 1919. Trained at Moscow's Lenin School from 1927 to 1930 in "political warfare," he was then posted as "Comintern delegate to South America." He broke with the Party in 1934. A member of the emergent new calling, the ex-Communist witness, he testified before legislative committees, including HUAC; he advised and wrote on the Red menace.[8]

Later Indianapolis also brought Ben Gitlow into the pageant. Gitlow had a briefer but loftier Party career than Kornfeder. He had helped found American Communism. At a 1919 trial, his bold defense of his radical credo led to prison but also honorary membership in the Moscow soviet and a place in the Communist International. He became general secretary of the U.S. Communist Party and its vice-presidential candidate. In 1929, however, he took the wrong side in Stalin's struggle with Nicolai Bukharin. He fell victim to the Georgian's drive for sole power in Soviet and world Communism and was drummed out of the American Communist Party. Gitlow too became a redoubtable foe of communism.[9]

Though both men reportedly donated their services, their arrival prompted some misgivings: it betokened both an intrusion by professional anti-communists, possibly with careerist goals, and a national Legion effort to inject itself into a previously amateur program.[10] Kornfeder had the larger role as "chief commissar" and "technical advisor" tasked with designing such paraphernalia as entry permits and ration coupons. After April 22, he worked full-time in Mosinee. As "chief commissar," he claimed, "I was doing just what I learned in Lenin University: Use force to gain command, and then stamp out freedom."

When they unveiled their plan on April 12, sponsors found their hopes of publicity fulfilled. Thielen boasted that "the entire nation will be watching Mosinee on May 1." It was "a safe bet that 90 per cent of the daily newspapers in America" would cover it. The initial story appeared in over 1200 American newspapers, played on all radio networks "coast-to-coast" and even won Kate Smith's endorsement on her national radio show.[11]

National reaction was stirring. Praise flowed in from around the country and even abroad. "Never in the history of this nation," exclaimed Schweinler, "has a small community had the news coverage, except for a catastrophe, that Mosinee will have for their 'Day Under Communism.'" Residents were reportedly "happy, excited and more than a little proud" of the publicity.[12]

The media did pour in. Nearly sixty reporters registered, and probably others omitted that formality. Three television networks sent correspondents, as did several radio stations. Two newsreel companies, two pictorial outfits, and three wire services sent representatives. Personnel from *Life*, *Readers' Digest*, and big-city newspapers checked in. The *Philadelphia Inquirer* sent its UN correspondent. The Soviet TASS news agency sent a reporter. "The entire civilized world today knows of the capitulation of this paper-making community," boasted the Wausau newspaper. A Mosinee columnist hailed the presence of "men who have interviewed and written about presidents, congressmen, millionaires, murderers and great projects." [13]

Publicity did carry risks. Some leaders speculated that real Reds might barge in. However, Mosinee's police chief thought Communist meddling unlikely; he worried more that "some of the boys might do too much celebrating in the taverns." Even so, the Legion's national Americanism director advised against publicity too far ahead lest the Communists find a way to exploit it. Plans to display large pictures of Stalin were scrapped lest foreigners get a notion that he had admirers in Mosinee.[14]

Mosineeans at large learned of the pageant on April 12. Some had reservations. When first announced, the plan "was so startling in its implications and possibilities that a great many folks in the community were unable to grasp it," Schweinler conceded. "But since then our people have more and more grasped it and understand it, and now are for it." Still, a resident later complained that it had been "railroaded through" unapproved by citizens or their elected officials. *Life* reported that "the few who grumbled and objected that the stunt was 'foolishness' were allowed to go about their business unmolested." [15]

In the wee hours of Sunday morning, April 30, a day before the coup, six real Reds staged counterpageantry by surreptitiously leafleting Mosinee's doorsteps. One flier asked: "So This Is Supposed to be Communism. Says Who?" Its answer: "THE BOSS," "AMERICAN LEGION BIG SHOTS" and "STOOLPIGEONS." Under real Communism, "the mills are owned by the men who work in them. There are no bosses." Communism promised "equality and brotherhood." But the "money-men" who would profiteer from "a Hell-Bomb war against the Soviet Union" lied and redbaited to break unions. Who would know true Communism should attend a May Day meeting in Milwaukee, advised another handbill.[16]

So how do you know 6 people?

The details of this leafleting, including precisely when it occurred, remain a mystery. Pageant leaders expressed alarm. "This shows how well the Communists are organized in this country," Ben Gitlow warned. Detroit's police commissioner, in town to pick up tips on how to crush Red plots in the Motor City, found it sobering that "the CPUSA's underground organization" was at work in Marathon County—and everywhere else. The leaflets steeled Mosineeans' resolve, said Schweinler. "It made them really realize that they were engaged in an important job."[17]

The pageant went on as scheduled. On Sunday night reporters and residents witnessed a "dramatization" in which Communist Party "cells" plotted the morrow's takeover. At Legion Hall, Gitlow and Kornfeder offered rhetoric worthy of Lenin at the Smolny Institute. They still had their grasp of revolutionary idiom and betrayed no irony that this charade would be their nearest approach to the glorious words, deeds and results they had fantasized in younger Party days.

First Gitlow rehearsed the glorious triumphs under "our great Stalin." The "war mad, blood-thirsty, fascist minded American government" little realized how close lay its doom. "Comrades," he exulted, "the sweet wine of revenge" was imminent. "We count the hours when the poor and downtrodden workers will rise and overthrow the whole rotten regime of the United States." Next Chief Commissar Kornfeder gleefully listed insurrectionary details. Later on, he enjoined tight security, ordering that no raiding party member "even go into a bathroom without company."[18]

Soon after 6 a.m. on May Day, stealthily, trailed by sixty-odd journalists, Red plotters crept up to the home of Mayor Ralph Kronenwetter. The short, stocky Kornfeder, wearing a derby hat, approached the house along with five gun-toting, arm-banded "security police." "Come out with your hands on your head," he shouted. As the squad burst in, Kornfeder declared a takeover by the Council of People's Commissars. "What for?"

asked the mayor. "You want to live, you are going to do what we ask you," Kornfeder riposted. "We ask you to make a statement for us."

In his bathrobe and pajamas, the mayor was rousted out into the frigid dawn. Some photographers missed the shot, and others thought it needed more graphic roughness, so the insurrectionists and their captive obliged with several reenactments. Thus the pervasive media presence had an intrusive impact upon the day's events. Taking his ouster with aplomb, Kronenwetter used the occasion to announce plans to seek the Democratic nomination for Congress in this Republican district and to dismiss Senator McCarthy's charges as "just headline hunting."

A second raiding party nabbed Police Chief Carl Gewiss. "Well, you rat, you're under arrest," said Gitlow. When he refused to surrender his two-man police force, Gewiss was "shot" (and thus freed to take charge of directing traffic. Police from nearby towns helped with the vast chore of crowd control.) In short order the Communists seized the paper mill's powerhouse. They dragged class enemies to the stockade where the mayor languished. A squad stormed into Emmanuel Lutheran Church as the pastor preached to a congregation largely of journalists. Later, the Reds rounded up Reverend Will La Drew Bennett of the Methodist Church, who had publicly hidden his Bible the day before as part of the festivities.[19]

Schweinler awaited another team of Communists at his newspaper office. Kornfeder arrested him as "an enemy of the people." "So it has come to this, has it?" Schweinler postured. With the seizure of telegraph and telephone offices, Communist control of communications was absolute.

The Soviet presence grew obtrusive. Three roadblocks interdicted access to the town. Willing participants had their cars searched and persons hassled; others could come and go as they pleased. Previously pageant sponsors had issued documents—identification forms and entry, exit, ration, gasoline and camera permits—which citizens were required to produce when accosted. Propaganda banners flapped and billowed over Main Street.

Communism's culinary aspect proved especially stark. Restaurants served a uniform diet of potato soup, black bread, coffee—and nothing else. (Eventually menus expanded "under the pressure of competition.") Grocery stores enforced rigid rationing. A *Milwaukee Journal* photographer snapped a six-year-old wistfully eyeing a store sign reading: "Candy for Communist Youth Members Only." Rejecting the new regime's diet, some Mosineeans drove to Wausau for a capitalist meal. The revolution affected other modes of consumption. The dollar was devalued and prices shot up. Suits once sold for $42 now went for $252.[20]

Off the presses of the *Mosinee Times* rolled a pink-tinted tabloid, *The Red Star*, organ of the new regime. It carried a biography of Stalin whose stress on his youthful bank-robbing and purges of Party rivals undercut otherwise authentic-sounding hyperbole about this "Red Star of the Universe, beloved of all humanity!!!" A proclamation ended private property; confiscated land and other assets; annulled the Constitution and all other "bourgeois" laws; voided all debts, legal obligations and U. S. money; and proscribed all voluntary organizations, churches, and parties but the Communist. The new labor code forbade strikes, instituted piecework and required workers "to contribute to the State four extra hours of labor without compensation."

The Red Star tried to explain how so tiny a group could hope to maintain itself in power.[21] It foretold creation of an elite Military Security Police with members "trained to be cruel and heartless towards the people," a separate and superior Secret Political Police answering to Moscow, and slave labor camps. While references to "cadres," "Trotskyist and Titoist elements," and "class-collaborationist" elements added verisimilitude, a notice that "Pig" Schweinler and his newspaper had been marked for extinction betrayed a degree of local boosterism.

Mosinee's first three hours under Red rule culminated in a parade to the center of town for a mass meeting. Led by the high school band, over 500 marchers, including children, carried signs with such messages as "Stalin is the leader," "Competition is waste," and "Religion is the Opium of the People." One observer thought the paraders looked "a little bewildered." From a sound truck, Kornfeder sought to enforce allegiance. "Little boy," he barked at one diminutive onlooker, "Bow to the red flag." When they reached "Red Square," the mayor urged his constituents to "submit to the accomplished fact" to avert bloodshed. Kornfeder issued a proclamation, and Gitlow, to a mixture of boos and cheers, orated about the imminent overthrow of capitalism.[22]

Other dramatic scenes were played out. A raiding squad burst into the library, seized "objectionable" books from readers whose surprise was often rehearsed, and heaved them into the street. Minions of the new order confiscated guns belonging to a tavern-owner—a very provocative act to North Country hunters.

That afternoon, Communism engulfed the high school. Gitlow

harangued the Young Communist League as to their "special duties" in combatting religion and family ties. The paper mill was nationalized. At 1:30 p.m. the security force straddled a jeep across the railroad tracks, halted the Milwaukee Road's *Hiawatha*, held its engineer at gunpoint, and let it proceed after harassing passengers. That night at the movie house the commissars halted a film about Hungarian Cardinal Mindszenty's travails under Communist rule and substituted a paean to Stalin.[23]

After dark, Mosineeans gathered in "Red Square" to end Soviet rule with a bonfire and rally. Into the fire they threw posters, banners and other Communist paraphernalia. This most heavily symbol-laden of the day's activities provided catharsis. It rid the town of "something that was impure," said Schweinler. "We are purging our city of all evidences of the 'occupation' by clean fire." The scenario called for "loyal Americans" to attend and "'Communists' [to] cast aside their subversive roles and [to] join in raising of the American flag."

Charles Larson, state Legion commander, delivered the main address, which had some twists that pageant critics might not have expected. While Marx had called religion "the opiate of the people," Jesus, who exalted "the equality of man as a fundamental of his religion," was the truer revolutionary. This tenet had inspired the rebels of 1776. Quoting General Eisenhower on the indivisibility of American freedoms, Larson chided those who "in their anxiety to preserve democracy would pass legislation curtailing one or more of these freedoms." Vigilance against subversion was urgent, "yet we may not lose sight of the fact that we cannot produce a fine garden merely by pulling weeds."

The script called next for the crowd of between 1,500 and 3,000 to sing "God Bless America" and "start peacefully home thankful to God that they live in AMERICA." One coup perpetrator remembered what a "relief" it was "to see the flag at night and realize it had been a game and not a reality." Schweinler recalled that many left the rally in tears, deeply appreciative of their American freedoms.[24]

Two grisly realities broke the spell and gave the event an unintended symbolic backlash. As he arrived at the rally, Ralph Kronenwetter fell ill. Rushed home, he suffered a cerebral hemmorhage, lapsed into a coma, and on May 6 expired. Rev. Will Le Drew Bennett, another participant, suffered a heart attack and died on May 7. The shock of these deaths, particularly the mayor's, suffused much news coverage and cast a pall over the conclusion of the day's events.[25]

News accounts minimized the pageant's role in the mayor's demise. "No one specific incident" caused the death, said a doctor. "It was a combination of the excitement attendant to the May Day program, his high blood pressure and a slight accident he had last Saturday." (He fell into a pothole while fishing.) The Mosinee paper absolved the pageant of his death. *The Daily Worker* did not, calling Kronenwetter "the first fatality of the storm-trooper style 'revolution' here," blaming "the terrorized atmosphere" and "the wire-pullers behind these sinister 'mock invasions.'" The *Mosinee Times* riposted that the men's families confirmed its medical diagnosis and claimed that both "would despise" even being mentioned in the Communist publication.[26]

The Communists criticized more than the fatalities. They claimed Mosinee had witnessed a spurious version of Communism. The state Party vice-chairman challenged Schweinler either to debate the true nature of Communism or to let real Communists run Mosinee for a day. He accused the Legion of a "Nuremberg spectacle." Borrowing General Anthony McAuliffe's famous answer to the surrender ultimatum at Bastogne, Schweinler retorted: "NUTS." He predicted continued Communist protests, for the program "struck a hard blow to their cause" by driving "the usual Communist-inspired May Days" out of the news.

Communists kept up a drumfire of criticism. The *Daily Worker* opined that this "so-called 'Communist' police state turned out to be remarkably like the realities of the Cold War witchhunt of 1950." It said Mosinee was picked because it was a "company town" run by the paper barons. It quoted a housewife as saying that the bread and soup diet was "no different from what many of the families here have a good deal of the time." As for exemplifying democracy, the Mosinee region—very like lumbering areas in the South dominated by the same interests—was Jim Crow country where no blacks lived or were served.[27]

Critics of this political passion play included more than Communists. William T. Evjue, liberal publisher of the *Madison Capital-Times*, ridiculed the "silly hippodrome." "Dictatorship" was nothing novel in the company town. Having tried "Red dictatorship," Mosineeans should heed "the growing outlines of dictatorship that are looming over on the right ... financed by the forces of monopoly and corporate wealth." Schweinler labeled Evjue's "the nearest thing to the Daily Worker" among the country's newspapers.

Other liberal critics included the *New York Post*, its columnist Max Lerner, and Eleanor Roosevelt. Schweinler disparaged Mrs. Roosevelt's credentials in light of "her own attitude" on the Alger Hiss case and other evidence of Communist infiltration. The liberal Catholic journal *Commonweal* held that "to create deliberately an unreal, gruesomely playful atmosphere of fear in which to consider the primary political, spiritual and religious problem of the age is a very dangerous business." [28]

Nearer the political center, the *Minneapolis Tribune* termed Mosinee's hucksterism "just a little frivolous and superficial." It lamented "the carnival atmosphere" of New York's Loyalty Day and Mosinee's pageant and suggested that their sponsors "would do much better to concentrate on broadening the base of democracy." After an Iowa town imitated Mosinee, the *Des Moines Register* hoped Americans "do not go in for a 'rash' of this sort of thing. There is enough of hysteria and precious little of thoughtfulness about Communism . . . as it is." [29]

But critics were a minority. The flood of media attention showed that Mosinee captured the national imagination. A Stevens Point paper said the event earned "more national attention than any past news development in the history of central Wisconsin." Mosineeans exulted over the "nationally famous names" in town. Coverage blanketed the nation and even made the foreign press. Indianapolis headquarters crowed that the Legion and Mosinee "were on the air almost continuously" for two days. Letters poured into Mosinee, the vast bulk favorable, the only cavils being that the project had not portrayed Communism more horrifically. A St. Louis man was moved to poetic transports beyond even the planners' fertile imaginations. One of his verses depicted "teen age girls . . . led away and ravished by the men. Others who remained behind were fearful of their end." [30]

The media coverage was impressive, but not every journalist treated the drama as its sponsors might have preferred. The pageant was subject to a gamut of competing perceptions, thus mirroring differences among those who put it on. There were unresolved tensions on the part of sponsors, participants and observers as to the level of performance—desired as well as accomplished. The distinction between play and reality, between fun and seriousness, often became murky.

Some sponsors wanted the "Day Under Communism" to be a sober undertaking. The Legion's national public relations director advised "that this be done in a serious fashion and that there be no horseplay . . . whatsoever." Schweinler agreed: "There is NOT to be any 'horse-play' of any type whatsoever." People were ready to take part "in a most serious and thoughtful manner." Indeed, Schweinler hoped they would be "seriously serious."[31]

On the other hand, John Decker, whose idea it was, saw the pageant as at least in part an outlet for some fun or a "lark" (not a unique notion for a Legion event). Generally Legion national headquarters, while not disparaging the project's seriousness, tended to view it more light-heartedly. The operative word was "stunt," reflective perhaps of the penchant for publicity which prevailed in Indianapolis.[32]

Viewers' perceptions of the pageant also varied from gravity to whimsicality. Detroit residents took a particularly literal view. Detroit's police superintendent claimed to have learned "how easily a coup . . . could be put over on any community" and how to resist one in his city. (He did not reveal his findings lest he forewarn the enemy.) Though Carl Cederburg's radio broadcast to Detroit conveyed the hijinx that occurred, he shared the *gravitas* of his city's top cop. The *American Legion Magazine* also struck a somber note. "It can't happen here? It did happen" and showed how easily a coup could be carried off.[33]

The intensity of performance impressed some reporters. One recalled: "One had to be on hand to realize how many persons accepted the coup as a possibility. They believed . . . that the Communists were about to take over everything." "Swept away by the idea," *faux* Communists were "meaner than Hell." A local newsman argued that the Red victory parade might well "have ended up an hilarious riot but everybody realized the seriousness of the thought that it 'could happen here'"; occasional "bantering" aside, "marchers were of serious mien."[34]

Most outside media took a more tongue-in-cheek approach. Even the nearby *Wausau Daily Record-Herald* was not above joshing. It lamented that the state Legion leaders on hand (who of course enacted the coup) failed to save Mosinee from the Reds. The *Milwaukee Journal* reported Kornfeder spent four years in Russia "learning how to behave in the meanest possible way and all his instruction is paying off beautifully." The *New York Times* made light of the drama, and the *Washington Post* termed the uproar over the Communists' leafleting a "miniature 'cold war.'"[35]

Some coverage was equivocal—perhaps reflecting the ambivalence of participants unsure how sternly to comport themselves. But such treatments tended to give the balance of the doubt to gravity over levity. A Wausau newsman found that while some Mosineeans acted as if on a "holiday," there prevailed "a general overtone of serious consideration of what the day was intended to convey." A Milwaukee reporter monitored reactions to the Red victory parade: "some smiled and some didn't, but, clearly the demonstration was being taken seriously by the townsfolk." *Life* conveyed a mixed message. It termed the pageant a "stunt" and the leafleting by real Reds an effort "to spoil the fun." Still, it concluded, Mosinee demonstrated "a firm belief in Americanism." [36]

Yet some scribes rejoiced in the Kilroy-Was-Here irreverence and the bumbling they saw—saving traits that precluded Mosinee's ever succumbing to Communism's dour sway. A *Milwaukee Sentinel* editor gloried in the snafus and burlesque. Kornfeder resembled "a character in any musical comedy," while the mayor needed two retakes to master a serious face during his arrest. It was comforting that "true Americans . . . couldn't transpose their roles" or become what they were not. To another writer, the "reassuring air of fantasy" proved "you can't go to bed as an average American citizen and rise up in the morning as a dyed-in-the-wool Communist." Mosinee's Communists could not take away "the grain of salt and sense of humor with which most average Americans are equipped." [37]

Pageant participants perceived the layers of seriousness and play in differing ways. Some mixed up appearance and reality. The coup preliminaries confounded one soldier passing through. "Say! What's all this about Communists taking over here? Don't you have a veterans' organization to stop something like that?" When paper mill workers learned that the new Soviet labor code imposed an ill-paid twelve-hour day, confusing fiction with fact, they grumbled authentically until set straight. Said one account: "although the Mosinee dramatics were a kind of game, many townsmen frankly admitted they were scared." One of them hoisted defiant countersymbols, the Stars and Stripes and a sign reading: "Any communist molesting this American flag is a dead duck." He also strung up an effigy bearing a placard: "This commie tried to pull down the Red, White and Blue." [38]

Thus, there was some confusion between reality and pretense. Yet while Mosinee's offered more counterfactual play and fantasy than did other cold-war pageantry, it fell short of the reversal of worlds and social bouleversement occasioned by "carnival" in other societies. [39] Perhaps the insistence that participation was voluntary, the media's obtrusiveness, which anchored a temporary "play" world to ongoing reality, and the in-

tentional catharsis of the closing ceremonies helped mitigate the poten-
tially unsettling, deracinating quality of the experience.

Some citizens refused to enter the pretend world of communism. A few
locals made a game of running the "roadblocks," daring the police to respond. (The meaning of these actions might, of course, be ambiguous:
did the checkpoint-runners reject this form of coercion playfully or defi-
antly, from within the premises of the pageant or from outside?) Others
evaded the grim Soviet diet by stealing away to Wausau for a square meal.
Mayor Kronenwetter maintained a mildly subversive playfulness.[40]

The media transfigured the pageant. Their omnipresence altered the
target audience from local to national, and thus performance too. Newsmen received an exact schedule of events, but "to avoid crowds" the public
did not. The mayor's arrest was rerun until cameramen were satisfied. At
Red Square, newsreel men stirred the crowd into "raising its fists." One
story noted journalistic "horseplay." A local woman complained that
"sensationalism and violence," the "appeal to publicity" and the "rehearsed photography" replaced "genuineness and dignity."[41]

Yet the crush of newsfolk so impressed other locals as to reconfigure
the event. A millworker confessed he was "lukewarm" until he saw "how
seriously all the newspaper people regarded this threat; I realize now we
must wake up."[42] To most sponsors, the vast media coverage defined success. Yet by its own dialetic this massive attention made Mosinee a one-
shot affair.

Some hoped a universal model had been found. A Green Bay paper saw
a precedent in how a traveling play version of *Uncle Tom's Cabin* had once
proven better than a book in educating Americans about slavery. Detroit's
police commissioner endorsed imitations, for Mosinee rebutted the
claim, "It can't happen here." "In another year," predicted a *Detroit News*
writer, "500 or more communities in the United States will adopt the
Mosinee Plan for teaching Americanism." Schweinler expected the exercise to "prove invaluable to those communities who follow us." On May
14, Schweinler and Ben Gitlow touted the program to the newly founded
All American Conference to Combat Communism. Multiple Mosinees
would "wipe the Communist May Day off the map." Schweinler cherished
the loud applause and the comment that Mosinee "can provide the spark
that will enlighten our people and drive all 'isms, except Americanism,
from among us."[43]

However, reruns were few. The first and nearest parallel occurred in

Hartley, a hamlet in northwest Iowa whose chamber of commerce and Legion post, seconded by Legionnaires from Nebraska, scheduled a Communist takeover for Flag Day. It was to include Communist proclamations, flags and shock troops, arrests of capitalists and clergy, a parade to "Red Square," indoctrination of students, rationing and a soup kitchen. A "Flag Day, American style" and the destruction of the day's Communist trappings would close the dramatization. A dance would follow.

The Mosinee precedent loomed large. The local paper and its editor played a key role in the pageant. To stem "rumors" and soothe those disturbed, perhaps, by Mosinee's fatalities, the *Hartley Sentinel* declared that "all demonstrations and arrests will . . . be made in a peaceful manner and no rough tactics will be tolerated." Hartley also braced for intrusion by real Reds, as at Mosinee. None came, but "pro-Communist letters" did trickle in. The CP's district chairman termed the event a "Nuremburg spectacle," the same charge leveled at Mosinee.

Hartley added new wrinkles. People of neighboring communities were invited to witness the event, which, it was hoped, might promote local business. "Influential capitalists" would be tried, and homes inspected. A plane was to drop "surrender leaflets." Unlike Mosinee, Hartley imported no ex-Communist experts: James Green of Omaha, national Americanism Chairman of the Legion and candidate for national commander of the organization, played the role of commissar.

Hartley faced an unforeseen challenge: a sudden rainstorm disrupted outdoor simulations and reduced the crowd. Some forty "guerrillas" described as "soaked-to-the-skin" snatched control of government and public utilities. Officials were arrested, some "executed." Reds seized the *Sentinel* and passed out copies of "The Hammer and Sickle." Townsfolk queued up for ration cards and submitted to a pass and roadblock regimen. Books were burned. The downpour wiped out the parade to Red Square and drove the mass meeting inside.

The ambience differed from Mosinee's. Hartley had no media invasion, and its enthusiasm was lower. Some merchants would not take part; a grocer locked up and went fishing. A few homemakers demurred at having their houses searched; one would sic her dog on any "Communist" who tried. Some townsfolk rejected "playing around," citing the cautionary deaths in Mosinee. "They know Communism is bad," said a town official. "They feel that when you play with something that is bad, somebody's going to get hurt." Ersatz Reds were warned not to "push people around" for some of them were "all steamed up about this." Some youngsters groused about interrupting vacation to report to school to be harangued by Commissar Green.

It proved hard to convey the level at which the putsch was to operate. It was a "demonstration," not a "celebration," the *Sentinel* emphasized. Legionnaires were lauded for "serious and orderly," unrowdy demeanor and residents for obeying rules. On the other hand, townsfolk at the mass meeting "demonstrated vocally against" proclamations of Communist takeover. A few Hartleyites—the foreign-born especially—found it hard to fathom that the coup was only in play. Some women planned to sing hymns on a streetcorner, but the rain aborted their protest. The new regime arrested many youths for tearing down Communist flags "and otherwise staging demonstrations."

Yet outside reaction was negligible. Voluntary surrender to "communism" no longer lured reporters. The *Des Moines Register* ran a story—and a critical editorial. "Vastly more subtle" real Reds did not "stoop to clumsy rough-houses, public mass arrests, or ostentatious book-burnings." Feigning Communism "with displays of physical violence is really misleading." Far better to worry about "the *invisible* violences done to men's reason and gentility by suspicion, disunity, intolerance, and dogmatism." In rebuttal, Hartley's editor declared the pageant successful in stirring people into "more zealously guarding their freedoms." [44]

In December 1951, Rushville, Indiana, fell to Communism, but with a much different script and level of participation. The *Indianapolis Star* sent a photographer and reporter to confect a photostory. The reporter termed his article a "fictionalized account of what could happen anywhere in the United States" and "a composite of the fate of thousands of persons behind the 'Iron Curtain.'" Photos depicted uniformed Reds jailing a man, invading a church, seizing nuns and clerics and regimenting youth. There was no community participation aside from those who posed for pictures. Indeed, the distinction between events staged and those simply made up was unclear. Unequipped to print pictures, the Rushville paper did not even cover the episode. [45]

The underlying premises in Rushville were even gloomier than in Mosinee: the major cities having been bombed, Red "occupation parties" now mopped up the hamlets. Religious overtones were also heavier. "On this First Sunday in Advent," coverage began, "Christianity faces its greatest peril at the hands of the blood-hungry Communist masses of the

Anti-Christ"; the only recourse was "a great moral resurgence and prayer." Communists swept into a Catholic children's mass and carried off the priest and nuns while restraining parishioners at gunpoint. The newly mandated prayer began, "Our father who art in Moscow."

The script also included book burning, nationalizing the hotel, indoctrinating school children, seizing "stately mansions" and collectivizing farms. Communists "looted" stores already scantily stocked. They took over the newspaper. A mass grave containing bodies of 476 martyrs was later discovered.

Opposition was also scripted and punished. A man who wrote "freedom" on a tavern men's room wall was "beaten to death" at a "labor camp." As undercover worship services spread, religion inspired resistance. The outcome of the coup was left in this limbo of frail optimism.[46] Given its artificial quality, it is no surprise that national media ignored Rushville's non-event.

The efforts of some New York state American Legionnaires in conjunction with the Crusade for Freedom gave further evidence of the decline of this sort of pageantry. In 1953, with the Mosinee model in mind, they proposed that a "Red underground" seize city halls in eleven upstate cities. To redeem these towns, "Freedom Forces" would have to obtain signatures for "Freedomgrams" to be sent to citizens behind the Iron Curtain and contributions to the Crusade for Freedom. Proponents announced reassuringly that the project was "so filled with safeguards it amounts to nothing more than a pageant." However, resistance to the idea mounted swiftly. Local officials objected to "scare psychology," and two police chiefs termed the plan "absurd and ridiculous." After various local officials vetoed it, the scheme quickly collapsed.[47]

The Army offered the most elaborate dramatization of the communist yoke after Mosinee. Exercise Long Horn, an elaborate maneuver involving nearly 100,000 troups in Texas in 1952, was part of a notional war beginning with an Aggressor army invasion and pursued with nuclear attacks. The Aggressors were led by the Centralist party. (Even in that era's raveled U.S.–Soviet relations, one did not label enemy forces Communist or Russian.)[48]

Centralists were to control the town of Lampasas for three days, pretend to suppress civil liberties and otherwise behave ruthlessly. Having won city government approval, the Army asked citizens to "enter into the military government play in order to make it as realistic as possible" without disrupting "normal life." A liberation was also scripted so as to give military government units practice in restoring "law and order."

On April 2, Aggressors entered Lampasas. They erected roadblocks; seized the newspapers and radio station; raised a Centralist flag (a Texas Lone Star on a triangular green field); and shut churches, businesses and schools. Martial law, curfews and nationalization were declared but not enforced. The next day Lions Club members and kin were interned at a concentration camp. During a flag-raising, a U.S. plane dropped leaflets promising liberation. Summary trials and sentences of hard labor or death were meted out. A band played the Aggressor national anthem.

The Centralists decamped on April 5, hypothetically leaving a third of the town destroyed, food lacking, typhus spreading. Local officials had collaborated; teachers had been converted to and students steeped in Centralism. When a U.S. military government team arrived on April 8, it dissolved the Centralist Party, hunted down enemy agents and collaborators, ended looting, weeded out Centralist currency and rationed food. That Lampasas was "well imbued with democratic principles and ideals" eased restoration. Liberation was curtailed when Long Horn was ended ahead of schedule.

The Army lauded the town's "enthusiastic cooperation," but not everyone played along. Some resented interruption of routine. Others would not submit even to a charade of Communism. Aggressor goons dragged the balky sheriff away from work kicking and screaming, authentically angry. At the high school, drama escalated when three students and the football coach refused to stand at attention. Soldiers moved in to compel obedience, one brandishing a rifle butt. An officer broke up the melee. With a level of earnestness that was unclear, some students pondered guerrilla activity to "pay back" the 82nd Airborne.[49]

The media were intrusive. Over forty reporters showed up on April 3, when, for their benefit, most antics were scheduled. While the coup "distracted from the actual reality of events to some extent," it earned "much publicity" for military government efforts, said one Army report. Another concluded more snappishly that the simulation "approached being staged more for the benefit of the news media than as a training aid." The Army itself subverted realism. A gag newspaper declaring Texas a sovereign nation promised "better government, lower taxes and more rain." Despite these efforts, media coverage was sparse.[50]

There were other snafus. The complexities of provisioning 97,000 troops were unrealistically solved by having supply trains under a single command cross the battlefield under neutral flags. Such hardships as twenty-three fatalities (including a murdered officer), mix-ups in paratroop drops, and tank operations hampered by gumbo mud from a chill rainstorm brought the maneuver to a close eighteen hours prematurely.[51]

War games by nature pose circumstances contrary to current but suggestive of future fact. Long Horn had many precedents. The run-up to World War II, encompassing frightening new military and paramilitary tactics, occasioned imaginative exercises. Air war's adolescence led to a profusion of mock bombing attacks. In 1938, Army planes foiled a pretended bombing of Tampa, Florida. In 1939 a Red Army invading Wisconsin covered its crossing of the Mississippi with a theoretical bombing of La Crosse.[52]

Other changes in warfare shaped training. In a 1941 exercise, troops landed by notional submarines raided a fort in New Jersey. Anderson, South Carolina, fell to an attack abetted by "fifth columnists" who filtered in as tourists. To imitate "tactics employed in Europe," town officials were hauled off to concentration camps. Unprepared U.S. forces added further, ironic unreality to such illusionism. The Third Army used mock wooden anti-tank guns in 1941 maneuvers; to indicate that they had "fired," troops waved a flag.[53]

After 1945 the armed services occasionally held simulations for the benefit of civilians. These may have been ploys in the interservice competition for defense funding. On May 17, 1947, 101 Strategic Air Command B-29s from distant bases filled the skies over New York and other eastern cities. SAC's commander told a New York audience that "everybody should be tickled that we . . . carried no bombs" but also warned that the display revealed the Air Force's decline in strength since the war.[54]

Some Cold War-era simulations addressed vulnerabilities. In June 1950, Army "saboteurs" damaged a control room at the Soo Locks and a telephone exchange before being driven off. In July 1956, fifty-two Marine reservists seized utilities and the Air National Guard headquarters in Des Moines and briefly silenced radio and TV stations. The company, led by a sergeant, plotted the coup on its own during national Civil Defense Week to show America's unreadiness. These exercises had minor impact.[55]

Mosinee proved a disappointing precedent in anti-communist pageantry. Reprises were few—this was no folk movement. Some civic activists kept the model in mind. The idea of a "This is Communism Day" as part of a "Wake Up America Week" or of Jaycee-led "mock Communist seizure[s]" cropped up in memoranda at the American Heritage Foundation, but without apparent result.[56]

Several factors explain Mosinee's irrepeatability. Its success as a media "stunt" proved self-limiting. It won vast publicity which repeat performances, almost by definition, could not equal. Since the sponsors' view that such pageants would not work in larger cities was probably well-grounded, imitations were confined to small towns and local audiences—and not many of either. The scheme's value for local civic education was never fully tested since that aim and the quest for media coverage competed with each other.

The timing and brevity of the age of mock communist coups merit consideration. Mosinee and Hartley, the only such exercises in a civilian context, occurred in mid-1950, Anti-communist anxiety ran high; the Korean War's June 25 onset elevated them further. However, the resultant mood of crisis probably made it hard to stoke interest in such projects. Why play at a communist threat when a real one was at hand?[57]

Moreover, by June 1950, other more overtly political anti-communist dramatics had matured. Legislators had learned to supply the market for theatrical anti-communism. The Mosinee project gestated just before Joe McCarthy burst on the scene; it took place in his first hundred days. His own and imitators' antics may have crowded out such home-grown pageantry.[58]

The coming of more professionalized diversions may also have worked against reruns. Save the two "commissars," Mosinee's were amateur performers. TV had not yet invaded small-town America, but soon it would. Civic workers would find it ever harder to mobilize participants and audiences for any civic pageantry. The box that beamed attractions from Hollywood and New York and an endless panoply of goods may have helped empty the streets.

Patriot activists stressed that our freedoms brought prosperity and choice beyond the imaginings of Iron Curtain drones. But paradoxically, these blessings devalued the older media and generated competition that interfered with their message.[59] So there would be not 500 Mosinees, but only one or two.

5

"The Cold War Belongs to Us All"

Patriotizing the American Calendar

While willing to employ dramatic scenarios to advance their aims, patriotic and civic activists spent most of their energies inventing traditions that were more than one-shot episodes. Like religious devotion, loyalty was to be inculcated through repeated observance—in some cases daily (as in Pledging Allegiance in schools), in others occasionally (playing the National Anthem at athletic events), in still others annually. The "high" Cold War encouraged efforts to patriotize the American calendar and occasions at which such usages had previously been exceptional. Many patriotic practices which may seem to have grown up with the country are of surprisingly recent vintage.

Although Americans, it is argued, have long reverenced the state in what sociologist Robert N. Bellah labeled a "civil religion," they entered the Cold War lightly equipped with occasions for so doing. July 4, Memorial Day, and Thanksgiving were old enough to be time-honored, but the patina of age brought with it a degree of secularization. National days became occasions for leisure more than patriotic reflection.

Other patriotic observances had a tentative quality. Flag Day won national status in 1914 but languished after World War I until interest revived in the late 1930s. Not until 1949 did Congress act to raise its status.

Discussion was brief. The bill's sponsor noted that it "simply calls on the president to issue a proclamation requiring the display of the flag on all government buildings." The Republican House leader had to ask: "Does he not do that now?" "No, sir," was the reply. The House assented; armed with a terse committee report that "enactment will serve a valuable and patriotic purpose," the Senate concurred without debate.[1] And none too soon: the American Legion saw "as great a need" to support the flag and what it stood for in this "new and strange conflict," the Cold War, "as there ever was in any time of violent conflict."[2]

Flag Day came just weeks after I Am An American Day. The latter had a following that included the Legion and National Education Association and suggested a promising cold-war future. As one patriotic activist informed President Truman, despite its "Junior" status, it "has attracted greater attendance than any annual patriotic public rally in our nation's history."[3] The day now lent itself to Cold War, anti-communist rhetoric, but it no longer commanded the attention it received during World War II. Patriotic leaders devised other celebrations—some of which would have the ironic effect of killing I Am An American Day.

Armed Forces Day was one such event (and Loyalty Day another). Both holidays emerged in the first half-decade after World War II with rather specific cold-war functions. By 1950, the rise of what Daniel Yergin has labeled the "national security state" and the merger of the armed services into a single cabinet department prompted the establishment of Armed Forces Day.[4]

In 1947, for economy and efficiency Congress melded the Army and Navy plus the newly fledged Air Force into what became the Department of Defense. As World War Two's near-limitless defense spending faded into history, interservice strife over money and weapons erupted into battles royal. Each service tried to torpedo its rivals' pet projects: the Navy belittled the Air Force's giant B-36; the Air Force ridiculed the Navy's supercarrier. These rivalries made a minefield of the Pentagon.

Armed Forces Day extended unification into the ceremonial realm. It was a means of "dramatizing" the new unity of national defense. Previously, Army Day had been marked on April 6, when the U.S. had entered World War I; Navy Day, on October 27, the birthday of Teddy Roosevelt, the Navy's great booster. Air Force Day was a three-year-old tradition. One congressman even plumped for a day for the Marines. Replacing these separate days and the parochial interests they served, Armed

Forces Day was meant, in part, to sublimate interservice rivalry.[5]

Scheduling it was not easy. The first date suggested, March 23, ran afoul of bad weather, Lent, and such fund-raising efforts as that of the Red Cross. The Joint Chiefs of Staff fixed on the third Saturday in May, but new complications loomed. The Justice Department harumphed that they had ignored the fact that May's third Sunday was I Am an American Day, an event dear to it and statutorily fixed. Even so, in 1950 President Truman proclaimed the third Saturday in May as Armed Forces Day.[6]

The Defense Department attached great importance to its new day. Adopting the event as one of its projects, the Advertising Council helped publicize it. Truman agreed to offer brief remarks at a banquet in Washington on the eve of Armed Forces Day. At a similar dinner in New York the next day, Secretary of Defense Louis Johnson spoke over a nationwide radio hookup.[7]

The day called naturally for parades. The 35,000 marchers on Manhattan's Fifth Avenue included fifteen bands, units from each service arm, the West Point cadets, veterans, women's groups and contingents from such children's organizations as the American Nautical Cadets, American Girl Reservers, American Sailorettes and Blue Jacket Guards. President Truman, General Eisenhower and Admiral William D. Leahy reviewed Washington's procession. In Europe, 85,000 troops also paraded. The Berlin march symbolized American "determination to remain in this city." Many American communities held parades.

But not just parades. Eight B-36s from Carswell Air Base overflew the capital of each state in the Union. The Navy's Blue Angels looped and wheeled over Brooklyn. Military bases held open houses. A quarter-million thronged Bolling Air Force Base to see a show aimed at the "little guy who pays the bills." It starred a blimp, artillery, tanks, a parachute drop and a ninety-plane flyover. Showman Arthur Godfrey rode in the rear seat of an F-80 Shooting Star to describe the experience for the crowd. Stationary exhibits made up a sort of military petting zoo. Ten thousand people visited the Naval Ordinance Lab at White Oak, Maryland, to view a jeep and its passenger suspended by a plastic thread, a helicopter air-sea rescue, a huge airshow, infantry maneuvers, and divers in a water tank. The Navy brought 340 vessels into port and invited the public aboard. A remote-controlled four-and-a-half-foot-long model airplane trundled the streets of Washington to herald Armed Forces Day attractions.[8]

Successful devices reappeared in future years. Parades multiplied. Massive air armadas were frequent, though conditions sometimes imposed limits. Bad weather caused a 175-plane flyover of Manhattan to be scrubbed in 1951. New York's 1952 parade was "streamlined" and aerial maneuvers cancelled to save fuel during an oil strike. Open houses at land bases and on naval vessels attracted multitudes. In 1951, thousands clambered aboard the battleship *Missouri* and other ships. Hundreds of thousands attended air shows presented at Coney Island.[9]

Military hardware appeared annually in parks and squares in New York City. In 1956 there were displays at nine Manhattan sites alone. An F-84 Thunderjet was on view in City Hall Plaza. Exhibits ranged from aircraft (sometimes cut-away or wingless) and their engines to tanks to an experimental Army cold-weather suit. The Navy brought a fifty-foot-long model aircraft carrier to Gotham in 1954. At Coney Island, Air Force helicopters performed a "barn dance" maneuver. Navy salvage divers welded inside a 10,000-gallon water tank. In 1951 Bolling Air Base regaled visitors with a million square feet of exhibits. Band concerts were a heavy draw.[10]

Some promotions strained a bit. From Governor's Island in 1951, the Signal Corps sent a greeting that circled the globe in one-eighth of a second; on its return, it activated a "miniature atomic pile," whose fissioning detonated a magnesium bomb which cut a ribbon, thus releasing pigeons from a coop. In 1959 a fireworks firm aided a mock Marine beach landing on Long Island by destroying a pillbox with an "atomic" explosion. For 1955 Armed Forces Week, 116 antique cars rallied at Fort Dix. A 1958 display at New Jersey's Raritan Arsenal ranged from missiles to Girl Scout cookies. More practical was the 1955 Armed Forces Day project of some Seabees who built lean-tos at a Long Island Boy Scout camp. The De Land, Florida, Chamber of Commerce expressed the hope that Private Elvis Presley, then in training in Texas, might be detailed to sing at their 1958 Armed Forces Day gala. The Army vetoed the request for Presley's services.[11]

Some Armed Forces Day activities linked present with past challenges to American freedoms. In 1952 Columbia University students dug earthworks on Governor's Island like those their predecessors built in 1794 when a French invasion threatened. In 1954 the Army put on a costumed pageant depicting Governor's Island's three-century history. Repeated in following years, the pageant included such vignettes as the purchase of the island from the Manhattan Indians and the soldiery of past wars. Speeches by the Dutch and British consul generals in 1955 emblematized Free World solidarity.[12]

A major theme of early Armed Forces Days was interservice unity. In 1950, newsmen at Bolling Air Base reportedly "gaped in amazement" as Air Force flacks touted the Navy's carrier plane demonstration and Navy public-relations men hyped Army and Air Force events. In proclaiming Armed Forces Day in 1952, President Truman declared the several services "welded into a unified team." In 1951, the U.S. Military Academy band, giving its first outdoor public concert in history (telecast from Radio City by NBC) played the anthems of the four services.[13]

After 1950, formal exorcism of interservice rivalry receded in importance.[14] The next three Armed Forces Days, during the Korean fighting, put more emphasis on mobilizing morale in a Cold War grown hot. Interservice cooperation remained a leitmotif, but a wider mutuality between soldiers in Korea and civilians at home took precedence. The *New York Times* warned in 1951 that the event was no "festival." "It may be dress parade and the bands playing here in the United States. It is fox holes and mortar fire and flak in Korea." New Yorkers viewed "exhibits illustrating the teamwork between industry and the military." A 1951 Armed Forces Day speech avowed that "today there is practically no delineation between those of us in uniform and those in civilian life." The secretary of labor declared in 1953 that the "soldier in the field and the worker at the machine are inseparable in plan and action." In 1958 the secretary of the navy stated: "The cold war belongs to us all." [15]

A recurrent theme of Armed Forces Day oratory was the need to gird for protracted conflict against the communist world. In 1951 Admiral Forrest P. Sherman, chief of naval operations, warned that the nation might face more "relatively small wars" for which it must maintain military strength, deploy forces around the globe, aid allies, and make sacrifices at home. Pentagon officials often used the occasion to emphasize the ongoing need for heavy defense expenditures.[16]

After the Korean War ended, talk of the urgency of a mobilization that yoked civilian and military spheres declined, but building consciousness of the military establishment remained a major goal. The armed services' role in preserving national freedom persisted as the central theme. Starting in 1953 and continuing through the 1960s, the motto of Armed Forces Day was "Power for Peace." Military correspondent Hanson

Baldwin tartly summarized the day's message in 1952 as "justification for past arms expenditures—and . . . pleas for even greater strength."

But commitment went beyond dollars. Whereas our defenders had once been professionals scarcely linked to civilian life, now, said the *New York Times*, "that is all changed. They are 'our' armed forces because they are a part of the total fabric of our lives, civilian and military." Members of many families had borne or would bear arms. As "the highest degree of loyalty and devotion" was expected of those who served, "it is right, therefore, that we give a corresponding degree of loyalty to them." Three years later, the *Times* reminded readers who took national defense for granted that it rested on "the solid foundation of personal service and often sacrifice by individual men and women." A 1961 *Times* editorial stressed that "our armed forces are still civilians under arms." [17]

Armed Forces Day frequently evoked calls for civilian gratitude. In 1954 Mayor Robert Wagner urged New Yorkers to recognize "the sacrifice and devotion to duty" of members of the armed forces. New York Governor Averell Harriman proclaimed Armed Forces Day in 1955 as a "public expression of respect" for U.S. servicemen and women. "Their calling," said the *Times* of the marchers of 1960, "is a proud one—the defense of our homes and liberties—a task which all of us . . . gladly share." [18]

The observance also permitted comment on immediate issues. In 1950, Truman speculated that had Congress passed his universal military training program, there "would have been no cold war." In an Armed Forces Day dinner speech just after he fired MacArthur, Truman urged an end to "bickering" and "playing petty politics." General Omar N. Bradley and Secretary Marshall also warned against seeking a quick military fix. At a 1954 Armed Forces Day banquet Eisenhower deplored the "unworthy scenes" of the Army-McCarthy hearings. Ike seized on festivities in North Carolina that combined Armed Forces Week and the anniversary of the signing of the Mecklenburg Declaration of Independence to support Army Secretary Robert T. Stevens, then embroiled in those hearings. In 1959, just before retiring as Army Chief of Staff, General Maxwell D. Taylor restated his opposition to the administration's reliance on a defense based on "massive retaliation" at an Armed Forces Day event. [19]

Armed Forces Day allowed for some multivocality on defense issues. In 1951 General A.C. Wedemeyer urged schools to shore up the home front and dismiss "fuzzy thinkers or those identified with alien movements." History must teach patriotism. "Legends in song and story are a valuable

part of that history. I deplore the tendency to scoff at the fine old stories"—like young Washington and the cherry tree. In 1953, General
Bradley, retiring as chairman of the Joint Chiefs of Staff, leery of the Administration's "New Look" defense policy, warned the nation not to put
"economy ahead of security." Defense Secretary Charles E. Wilson retorted that "We believe Uncle Sam's big old pocketbook has been open
just too wide." Armed Forces Day 1955 gave Senator Stuart Symington a
chance to air his warnings, soon to become a staple of Democratic criticisms of Eisenhower defense policies, that the United States lagged behind
the USSR in developing an intercontinental ballistic missile.[20]

Armed Forces Day also served to reinforce aspects of nuclear deterrence doctrine. A vast 1951 atomic energy exhibit at a Manhattan armory
aimed to acclimate Americans to life in the atomic age. One display, entitled "Cheer Up!" belittled the notion that "super-bombs" could cause an
earth-destroying chain reaction. Civil defense workers joined the New
York parade for the first time in 1952. In 1953 the secretary of the Air
Force reminded visitors that the Strategic Air Command's "destructive
potential" had "deterred the outbreak of another world war."[21]

The event became a sort of Free World answer to the annual Soviet May
Day display of military might. The parallel was never explicitly avowed.
Indeed, an account of 1950 Armed Forces Day parades stressed that in
none "was the strength of American equipment and material emphasized
as the Russians stress theirs in Moscow demonstrations."[22] Still, a spo-
radic dialogue arose. From 1951 on, Soviet military attaches sat on the reviewing stand in Washington in reciprocity for similar courtesies to
American attaches at Moscow's May Day parade. A weapon glimpsed on
May Day might bring a glossing response on Armed Forces Day. In 1954
the Air Force chief of staff alarmedly cited the new medium and heavy
bombers unveiled on May Day. In 1955 he fretted about the swarms of
long-range bombers and a new supersonic fighter observed over Moscow,
and the Atlantic Fleet's commander warned that Russia was "feverishly
building" a Navy which had moved in fifteen years from seventh to second
largest in the world.[23]

Yet flashes of detente also sparked between the two rallies of armed
might. In 1956, after "one of the briefest and least warlike" May Day parades "ever seen in Red Square," the White House responded by pruning a
District of Columbia flyover from 216 B-47s back to forty-five. In 1956 a
Soviet official was first welcome at the New York Armed Forces Day

parade. Soviet officers watched the Berlin parade in 1959. In 1960 a party led by the Soviet Air Force Commander was to fly an Ilyushin-18 to Washington's Armed Forces Day ceremonies, but the downing of an American U-2 "spy" plane deep in Soviet territory prompted them to postpone the invited visit to a "more suitable time." [24]

Armed Forces Day never rivaled May Day's symbolic pitch, nor perhaps its level of military readiness, but it was used to show off new weapons. The Navy Skyray interceptor was featured in 1951. Guided missiles festooned later parades. The Nike debuted in 1954, the Snark and Redstone in 1956. Though New York's 1959 parade exhibited smaller guided missiles, one reporter saw little other "military 'hardware' not familiar in the Korean War." Infantry carried the old M-1 rifle—or even 1903 Springfields. [25]

Through the 1950s, Armed Forces Day maintained a high but gradually declining profile. The 1953 presidential transition had some impact. Truman took the event seriously, reviewing all three Washington parades while president. Eisenhower held the day in less awe—not his only avoidance of the embrace of the armed services whose appropriations he struggled to restrain. On the third weekend of May 1953, Ike was heavily scheduled. He visited Williamsburg on the 177th anniversary of passage of the Virginia Burgesses' resolution favoring American independence, garnered an honorary degree at William and Mary, played golf (albeit at an officers' club in Norfolk), yachted up Chesapeake Bay, and attended church at the Naval Academy. However, his defense secretary, not he, reviewed the Armed Forces Day parade in the nation's capital. He also missed that procession in 1954. He did attend an Armed Forces Week function in North Carolina, but there the lure was the anniversary of the Mecklenburg "Declaration of Independence." His alacrity in finding alternative pageants in lieu of the main Armed Forces Day observances is noteworthy. [26]

Even with Ike's deemphasis, Armed Forces Day became a solid fixture of the American patriotic calendar. Through 1958 the Manhattan parade numbered upwards of 25,000 marchers. Crowd estimates ranged as high as 1,250,000. The last two Eisenhower years saw declines on both sides of the police barricades: 13,000 and 14,000 marchers in 1959 and 1960 and some 100,000 onlookers in each year. [27]

The services strove to provide entertainment. The displays at Bolling Field resembled "a gigantic fairgrounds" to one reporter. Army Engineers "lent a carnival touch" to the 1954 show, erecting a "midway 'front' with gaudy sideshow signs" with messages such as "Earth Eating Dragon" captioning a bulldozer. Aerial acrobatics and ship visits always drew crowds. Weapons and simulated combat enthralled children. Kids at Bolling in 1953 used mine detectors to find dummy mines in a sandbox. In 1954 at a Bronx armory, a thousand youngsters aimed bazookas at their moms and spun about on anti-aircraft guns. In 1955, as a mock assault at Fort Jay reached a flamethrower-led climax, a throng of kids, some clad in Cub Scout or Davy Crockett gear and "brandishing side arms and pop guns," were so "carried away by the excitement" they rallied to join the attack. MPs could barely restrain these peewee reinforcements.[28]

The 1960s brought change—first apathy, then opposition. In the Kennedy years, only 10,000 marchers entertained about 50,000 spectators. Under Lyndon B. Johnson, rising opposition to the Vietnam war brought drastic alterations. Parades gave supporters of the Vietnam war a chance to show the flag—but anti-war forces mobilized too. They dogged Armed Forces Day parades and critiqued "hands-on" demonstrations and play at base open houses.

Armed Forces Day itself undermined a neighboring event. Locating it on May's third Saturday clotted a Spring patriotic calendar already crowded with Loyalty, Mother's, Memorial and Flag Day. But the heaviest damage befell I Am An American Day. It and Armed Forces Day usually shared a weekend, doubling demands on bands and marchers and producing patriotic overload. Despite its legal seniority, the patrons of I Am An American Day rescheduled their event. Their good intentions proved fatal.

By 1951, I Am An American Day sponsors like the American Bar Association, American Legion, NEA, B'nai B'rith, National Conference on Citizenship and Justice Department lobbied to move it to September 17, when the Constitution was signed, and to rename it Citizenship Day.[29] Urging the change, a Justice Department official cited both spring's patriotic gridlock and iffy weather. While Washington's 1951 Armed Forces Day lured over 200,000 people, I Am An American Day drew a mere 3,000. The fall, he said, better suited schools, which could adopt "'carry on' programs." Congress approved the shift in February 1952.[30]

Outraged I Am An American Day partisans implored Truman to reverse the deformation. One linked it to a "vicious trend" away from Americanism toward "'One World'—'World Federalism.'" The Hearst press assailed "the little man in the White House." What next—would Citizenship Day become "World Citizenship Day"?[31] Sons of the American Revolution expressed a similar fear. Constitution Day's patrons also protested sharing September 17.[32]

Purists sought a reversal. One blamed the new date for halving attendance. It found entertainers busy with new shows, civic groups unfocused after the summer break and citizens who had welcomed a spring day in the park now contemplating winter hibernation. One founder of I Am An American Day took heart that many state governors kept on proclaiming it in spring. Also confusing, for a time some jurisdictions still used the old name "I Am An American Day" in September, and some organizations employed the old date.[33] I Am An American Day, which could once draw a million people to Central Park, was throttled, and its new incarnation also clouded the status of Constitution Day.

Patriots clamored for more events. Some latter-day isolationists would declare October 23 United States Day to counter the erosion of American liberties under "world government and law by treaty with the alien controlled United Nations." To a call for a United States Week, Frederic Fox, the presidential aide who handled observance of patriotic and devotional events, gently replied that, with Columbus Day, Citizenship Day, United Nations Day, a National Day of Prayer and Civil Defense Week, the season was too crowded already.[34]

A clergyman who wrote speeches for Eisenhower, Fox knew the limits of public observancy. His duties included energizing the annual National Day of Prayer that Congress mandated in 1952. Truman scheduled the first one on July Fourth. Subsequent dates varied; none worked well. The day lacked "focus." In 1957 Fox selected the first Wednesday in October, a nice fit on church calendars. Still no pulse. In 1958 Ike read a "longer-than-usual" Proclamation at a news conference. A special Psalm was chosen. Still, attendance at Ike's church remained flat. Only twenty-three people, bodyguards included, worshiped at the 1960 presidential service. Yet the National Day of Prayer, with "heavy holy momentum," lived on.[35]

The day coincided with a rising national religiosity. A toy firm offered a doll whose flexible knees enabled it to kneel in prayer. Congress added the phrase "under God" to the Pledge of Allegiance in 1954. Signing the law on Flag Day, Ike praised it for "reaffirming the transcendence of religious faith in America's heritage and future." The motto "In God We Trust" became official on coins and in 1954 went on a stamp. Since this stamp would often be sent overseas, a sponsor exulted at the now-global message "that we, as Americans, believe in spiritual values." Ike, most of his cabinet and leaders of the three major faiths introduced the stamp on national television. Himself unchurched until his election, Ike understood that the nation and its leader needed to be religiously anchored.[36]

In keeping with that aim, the Fraternal Order of Eagles promoted the new stamp. The American Legion sponsored an annual "Back to God" program. On February 1, 1953, Ike filmed a message to a religious service televised from New York; on hand in person, his vice president declared Americans uniquely privileged to hear the president pray at his inauguration. On July 4, 1953, Ike, Nixon and the cabinet launched "The March of Freedom," a movement to defend the seven freedoms listed in the Twenty-third Psalm and so affirm America's "spiritual heritage" and the divine basis of its freedoms.[37]

Civic, veterans, and fraternal organizations also worked to broaden patriotic observance. Sertoma International gave copies of the Declaration of Independence to schoolkids and in 1952 began a drive to have the National Anthem sung at sports events, providing singers and handing out the lyrics. In 1955, at the American Legion's behest the National Football League changed a prescribed referee's signal. The previous sign had frustrated Legionnaires seeking to instruct grade-schoolers: they snapped off a flag salute only to find that the kids thought it denoted unnecessary roughness. In 1958 the American Heritage Foundation determined to supply every school in the nation with a high-fidelity recording of the National Anthem.[38]

Civic activists labored to make holidays more patriotic. Conscious of his role as leader of national rites, John F. Kennedy supported such efforts. In 1961 one of his aides researched how often Eisenhower had taken part in Memorial Day ceremonies at Arlington Cemetery. (He went to four and sent deputies four other times.) Though Kennedy considered the day "almost a religious holiday," he sent a substitute.[39]

On July 4, 1962, Kennedy spoke at Independence Hall in Philadelphia. In 1963 he endorsed a campaign to "Ring the Bells for Freedom." Over his signature and with his picture on the cover, *This Week Magazine* ran a story heralding the revival of bell-ringing on July Fourth, as first espoused by John Adams. "All over America, at the time the Liberty Bell in Philadelphia is given a ceremonial tap, bells in churches, schools and public buildings will ring out a message of liberty and independence."[40]

Sponsors continued to lament public inattentiveness to the numerous occasions for patriotic expression. Patriotic days shared a natural history. Early on, they had vibrancy, but then routine set in. A civic holiday was easily preempted by a beach outing. Guardians of these days protested and strove to reinfuse them with their original meanings, but often to no avail.

Los Angeles Mayor Fletcher Bowron encountered the problem in 1946. He would not make June 14, the centenary of the raising of the Bear Flag at Sonoma, a holiday. He preferred to mark the centennial of the raising of the American flag over Los Angeles, on August 13, but he also fretted that "hardly a corporal's guard" attended the city's Memorial Day rites two weeks before, "but instead the big majority spent the day in search of pleasure" and in "recreation other than for purposes patriotic."[41]

In the 1950s, distempers could strike swiftly at America's celebratory nerve. Competition offered one threat. Loyalty Day lasted longer than I Am An American Day, but its patent on May Day stood for only eleven years; then the upstart Law Day materialized. The lifespan of patriotic observances could be cruelly short.[42]

Sometimes competing purposes undercut patriotic content. In 1952, after just the third Armed Forces Day, *New York Times* military affairs correspondent Hanson W. Baldwin lamented how the observance had strayed from its original purpose. Energies were squandered on "justification for past arms expenditures" and "pleas for even greater strength." Deeper meaning had vanished. "The advertising urge in the United States, with strong backing from the Pentagon," threatened to make Armed Forces Day "like many of the other national anniversaries that have been so commercially and shamelessly exploited into an observation without a meaning, a monument of tinsel, a day without symbol."[43] Baldwin was not alone in ruing the nation's inability to celebrate seriously. Those who complained that fellow-citizens failed to approach occasions for patriotism or reverence with sufficient solemnity faced an ongoing existential struggle, one which offered occasional successes, but no final victory.

6

The Cornwallises Send Regrets

Historical Commemoration in the 1950s

History, long prescribed as cod-liver oil for civic irregularity, remained as a sovereign remedy during the Cold War. While policymakers often rummaged for ancient precedents and lessons, some leaders wanted more of history than that. Seeking to root Americans in their past, they stressed less history's pragmatic lessons than the inspiration to be derived from early heroes, less tested solutions than ancient values. On frequent occasions little analyzed by historians, cold-war America paid homage to a variety of hallowed places and olden times.[1]

Patriotic activists turned to history especially in times of turmoil. The aftermaths of the two world wars produced similar anxieties—and responses. Beside Red Scares, both eras displayed a softer side in efforts to instill patriotism by applying the balm of tradition to current social eruptions. On September 17, 1919, Constitution Day was marked under the aegis of the National Security League, a bulwark of "one-hundred-percent Americanism" during the war and the Red Scare. In 1920, with due pomp, Secretary of State Robert Lansing placed original copies of the Declaration of Independence and Constitution on display.

Similar preservationist ceremonies followed World War II. In 1951, these two charters were enclosed in helium-filled cases to halt their deterioration. President Truman quoted Justice Oliver Wendell Holmes: "We live by symbols." As the two documents were ceremoniously enshrined, Truman contrasted the American and Soviet revolutions, "the rule of law and the concepts of justice" rooted in these sources as against the Soviet constitution's empty promises.

The decade after each world war witnessed rising interest in historic preservation. After World War I Henry Ford assembled the pastiche of Americana that became Greenfield Village, and a 1926 tour of Williamsburg inspired John D. Rockefeller, Jr., to underwrite restoration of the mouldering former capital.[2]

Rockefeller had aesthetic motives but also felt the site could teach "the patriotism, high purpose, and unselfish devotion of our forefathers to the common good." The "critical days" before World War II reinforced his commitment.[3] One GI's wartime visit provided confirmation. Chancing on a portrait of Washington, he braced, saluted and said, "you got it for us, General. And, by God, we are going to keep it." Told the story, Rockefeller tearfully declared, "then it was all worthwhile."[4]

Historic preservation and restoration matured in the 1930s. Williamsburg and Greenfield Village opened their doors, and the federal government assumed a growing role in managing historic sites and professionalizing historic preservation during Herbert Hoover's presidency. The National Park Service (NPS) acquired control of Monticello, Mount Vernon, Jamestown and Yorktown. It later took over a number of Army military parks. Several public works agencies carried on restoration projects, and the Historic Sites Act of 1935 formalized a government role in preservation.[5]

The political culture of World War II and the Cold War encouraged preservation. Perilous times drew Americans, said an NPS historian, "to the national historical parks and shrines for a renewal of their faith in their country's traditions and . . . destiny." They sought "direct emotional experience" on hallowed sites. Donald Culross Peattie, who often wrote on patriotic themes, found Americans flocking to sites which "we call, not too accurately, our shrines." During World War II, he stood before the Liberty Bell in a throng of diverse ethnicities, races, and creeds: on every face glowed patriotic pride.[6]

Colonial Williamsburg tried to address Cold War issues, for as John D. Rockefeller, Jr., declared, the site beamed "a beacon light of freedom to the world." Williamsburg's staff searched for a function associated with

America's free-world leadership. Its most ambitious effort began in February 1950, when "the world situation" offered a "compelling incentive" to take "a more important role in the drama of our times." A Special Survey Committee was established to define that role, to enable Williamsburg to serve as "not just a reminder of the past, but a living force in our country today." [7]

The committee consulted with leaders of government, the military, education, the media, and institutionalized patriotism about how Williamsburg might delineate principles that set the Free World apart from the Communist Bloc. They traveled, with State Department cooperation, to global trouble spots. Nothing dramatic resulted. The Special Survey managed to distill the philosophical issues "between free world and slave state" down to a short list: "the dignity and integrity of the individual," "individual liberty," "responsibility of the individual," "opportunity," "right of self-government" and "faith." [8]

In other ways Colonial Williamsburg labored to carve a place for itself in emerging cold-war pageantry and educational activities, becoming a shrine of American democracy. When the Freedom Train was conceived, Kenneth Chorley sought without success to bring it to Williamsburg. [9]

In 1949 Williamsburg hosted the Voice of Democracy program, an annual contest launched in 1947 by the U.S. Office of Education and several business associations. High-school students recorded brief essays entitled "I Speak for Democracy." From state victors four national winners were chosen. In 1949 the four visited Williamsburg for ceremonies carried on radio; General George C. Marshall spoke. In 1951, under an altered format, in-state winners took part in a "Democracy Workshop." [10]

Youth was a continuing target. From 1957 on, the annual Williamsburg International Assembly brought in foreign graduate students about to return to their homelands. They took part in programs that taught "some of the concepts that have helped fashion America's tradition of liberty, and have fostered . . . democratic institutions throughout the free world." In 1958, a student burgesses program began. High school students came to Williamsburg to discuss the issues raised by a set of study materials on the theme of "Democratic Leadership in the World Today: A Challenge to Youth." Subsequent years saw a focus on issues of "national purpose" which informed the period. [11]

Williamsburg achieved its highest visibility through commemorative events. On July 4, 1949, its powder magazine and guardhouse were dedicated, with General Walter Bedell Smith the chief celebrant. As the former ambassador to the USSR approached the guardhouse, six men in Continental Army garb presented arms. Warning, over two networks, that America could enjoy peace "only by remaining stronger than potential aggressors, Smith lauded the restoration of "this original arsenal of democracy." As the magazine was formally opened, amid cannonades and Air Force band music, a squadron of F-86's zoomed over in tight formation.[12]

Williamsburg also began marking "Prelude to Independence," the May 15, 1776, Virginia Burgesses' resolution for American independence. In 1953, President Eisenhower graced the occasion with brief remarks in the restored House of Burgesses. Secretary of State John Foster Dulles spoke in 1954, UN Secretary General Dag Hammarskjold, in 1956.

Williamsburg hosted many illustrious guests, including royalty from Britain, Japan, Belgium, Greece, Morocco, Jordan and Cambodia. Grateful State Department protocol officers helped plan such trips, which, said a travel writer, were "fast becoming de rigueur for foreign dignitaries." Tours often began at the restored church at Jamestown to evoke America's spiritual roots, glimpsed the surrounding wilderness and the primitive reconstructed village to show the "rude and humble beginnings" of a nation now "glittery and glamorous and prosperous," then moved on to Williamsburg's elegance and pageantry.[13]

Williamsburg offered a backdrop for rites confirming America's Free World leadership and, notably, its ties with Great Britain. Any rift between Hanoverians and colonials was long forgotten. In 1954 the Queen Mother paid a call. Visiting Bruton Parish Church on Armistice Day, she was asked if she would like to join in the prayer, using the pew once reserved for royal governors. Asking whether George Washington had owned a pew, she endeared herself by declaring, "I would prefer to kneel there."[14] In 1955, the former rebels reciprocated by giving the first Williamsburg Award to Winston Churchill, an honor that trustees hoped would confirm Williamsburg's status as "a symbol in the endless struggle for freedom and self-government." Churchill responded that the two nations "shall not go far wrong if we keep together."[15] A Williamsburg visit by London's lord mayor inspired further reference to the two nations' "mutual conviction that man's right to freedom is sacred and inalienable." Colonial Williamsburg's Kenneth Chorley repaid the compliment in 1958, telling a London audience that the American Revolution had raised what "were issues between brothers," that "our republic . . . rests upon a foundation of British thought."[16]

The 350th anniversary of Jamestown's founding occasioned the grandest expressions of Anglo-American unity and marked a high point of an important ceremonial genre of the 1950s, the observing of historic anniversaries. Such remembrancing of things past and their linkage to the current crisis constituted an important facet of cold-war patriotism. Some anniversaries of the 1950s were important, but not so much their intrinsic significance as their sheer number suggested how central they were to the political culture.

The nation commemorated events from two epochs which Robert N. Bellah has aptly termed America's Old and New Testament eras. Several anniversaries of colonial and revolutionary events, of Genesis and Exodus, fell in the 1950s. Americans celebrated the 175th anniversary of the Declaration of Independence, the 200th of the Albany Congress and the births of John Marshall and Alexander Hamilton, the 250th of Ben Franklin's, the 350th of the founding of Jamestown and of the Hudson and Champlain discovery voyages. The Lincoln sesquicentennial and Civil War centennial addressed New Testament themes of Christian "death, sacrifice and rebirth."[17]

Why this flurry of historic occasions? Part was calendrical luck: many memorable events dated back in multiples of twenty-five or a hundred years from the 1950s. Also, as historian Dumas Malone noted, several remembered heroes had links with universities then marking their own anniversaries—and sometimes publishing the complete works of the selfsame founding fathers.[18]

Some events had but local carry. Several New York entities marked the 1954 sesquicentennial of the Alexander Hamilton–Aaron Burr duel, chiefly with exhibits such as the coroner's jury's report on the duel and the pistols used on the fatal day in Weehawken. There was no reenactment. Some states and cities also had 100th birthdays: Iowa in 1946, Wisconsin in 1948, and Minnesota in 1959. California observed centennials of statehood, various episodes in its revolt against Mexico, and the gold rush. Kansas City marked its centennial in 1950.[19]

At times, commemorations so encumbered the calendar that memorializers tripped over each other. On July 2, 1959, the Statue of Liberty hosted ceremonies for the 75th anniversary of its own presentation by France, the 150th of Lincoln's birth and the 350th of Henry Hudson's discovery of the river bearing his name. In early 1957, Hamilton admirers who booked passage on a cruise ship bound for Nevis to celebrate the bicentennial of his birth might well bump into Virginia Historical Society members retracing Captain John Smith's voyage of 350 years before.[20]

Commemorators drew on each other for advice and precedent. The Battle of New Orleans Sesquicentennial Commission counseled with Battle of Lake Erie celebrants. The Hamilton Bicentennial Commission contacted its Marshall and Jamestown counterparts. The Civil War Centennial Commission cooperated with the Lincoln Sesquicentennialists and sought information from the American Heritage Foundation.[21]

The National Park Service, especially its Historical Division, provided staff and direction for most commemorations. It had a natural eagerness to link them with its national parks: budgetary stakes were high. There evolved a variant of the "iron triangle" that characterized the linkage between a specific interest group, relevant committees and members of Congress, and the appropriate executive agency. Just as a defense firm, concerned federal lawmakers, and a Pentagon agency might coalesce around a weapons program, so there developed ties between local backers of a restoration project or commemoration, congressmen with either a local or ideological affection for the program, and the NPS. A quasi-profession of commemoration seemed to be emerging.

The first celebration, the sesquicentennial of Washington's founding, merged the aims of District of Columbia boosters and those with broader patriotic goals. Backers of the 1950 National Capital Sesquicentennial envisioned a "Temple of Patriotism" with dioramas of "the fifty greatest scenes in American history," a "Cavalcade of American Freedom" that would outdo the Freedom Train, a pageant of "American Government on Parade" with a float for every federal agency, a costumed reenactment of the first session of Congress held in Washington—and more. The capstone was to be a Freedom Fair, a trade show for industries "interested in helping along our international picture to combat communism." The National Capital Sesquicentennial Commission (NCSC) declared the festival's "overall theme" to be "FREEDOM." Truman wanted the fair to "bring home to every American, and to the world, the full significance of our great heritage of freedom." [22]

The grander of these schemes—especially the Freedom Fair—hit a wall of skepticism. Some congressmen hesitated to fund a showcase for Truman's Fair Deal. One Republican found "something anomalous about an administration that sponsors bills to collectivize and socialize America, while paying lip-service in a projected fair to freedom." He waggishly proposed a "welfare state exhibit." An Indiana solon balked at the fair's three-million-dollar appropriation—six times what he sought for flood control "to keep Vincennes from being washed downriver." [23]

With late and paltry appropriations, the Freedom Fair languished. In 1949 charges surfaced that a leasing agent had sought a kickback. Senator Joe McCarthy demanded an inquiry. The NCSC denied complicity, but the scandal helped postpone the Fair's opening from July 4, 1950, to 1951. The illness of one leader and the fact that other NCSC members were from "non-promotional enterprises" or "past the age of ready enthusiasm" slowed progress. Ultimately constraints of funding, time, site selection, and other problems doomed the fair. In May 1950 the commission pulled the plug on a project slated to attract fifteen million tourists. Local businessmen bemoaned losing a chance to reply to the "false ideologies" assailing Americans. A citizens committee termed it "a moral defeat of this effort to 'sell' our youth on the virtues of the American heritage." [24]

The sesquicentennial opened on April 15, 1950, with a reenactment of the laying of the district's first stone. President Truman welcomed all. A Metropolitan Opera diva sang arrayed in a gown modeled after that of the statue of Freedom atop the Capitol, the symbol of the sesquicentennial. Fireworks streamed skyward and jets overflew what the NCSC bragged was the "most spectacular patriotic pageant" since Washington's inauguration. In the main talk, Vice President Alben Barkley, taking his text from Tom Paine, contrasted America's liberating revolution with communism's "counterrevolution of tyranny." [25]

The sesquicentennial progressed, sometimes improvising. The Sesqui Commission promised "an interesting and memorable event" every day from April 15 to November 22. There were concerts, an art exhibit, new stamps, and a contest to write a centennial theme song. Each state and territory had its own special day. On Indiana's, a chorus of 3,000 women performed "Hoosier Heritage." I Am An American Day and Flag Day occasioned special programs.[26]

The cultural centerpiece was a symphonic drama by celebrated author Paul Green which opened at a new amphitheatre in Rock Creek Park. A dramatization of George Washington's life, "Faith of Our Fathers" was steeped in spirituality. "Tonight," stated its prologue, "we send our

thoughts along the deep earth where our forefathers sleep. . . . In our re-
membrance they live again and are not dead." Under the famous picture
of Washington praying in the snow, the souvenir program printed lines
from the old hymn: "Faith of our fathers! we still survive/To win all nations unto thee." The drama evoked the early years of the new nation,
though rather skimpily, according to critic Brooks Atkinson, who praised
Green but thought his script "not quite adequate to so memorable an
occasion." [27]

"Faith of Our Fathers" returned in 1951 despite first-season losses.
Green revised it to exalt yet also humanize Washington and to link him
more firmly to the capital city. It opened as slaves and neighbors sang
hymns outside Washington's sickroom and ended with his "Apotheosis."
The pageant closed when it failed to get another subsidy. "Some of our
Congressional friends," Truman grumbled, had missed the program's
"immense contribution to the real awakening of patriotism in this
country." [28]

The sesquicentennial fell a bit short. Beyond its limited funding, observers also cited disabling levels of apathy among blasé Washingtonians.
Having government as a permanent industry, local business interests had
little motive to hustle for the added revenues a Freedom Fair might bring;
some even feared it might stimulate competition. The bare-bones sesquicentennial fell well short of initial expectations. [29]

The 175th anniversary of the Declaration of Independence in 1951
proved more gratifying to sponsors. Taking the lead after local efforts
flagged, the American Heritage Foundation strove to foster a "serious"
celebration of the Fourth. The main observances took place in Philadelphia, but the AHF worked to promote a national "year of Dedication"
aimed at such ailments as "individual cynicism and neglect [and] the
creeping deadly erosion of national integrity and idealism." [30]

After the Freedom Train, the AHF had operated sporadically, seeking
projects in which to apply methods perfected in 1947–48. The 1951 anniversary proved timely. The country's "psychological state," wrote an AHF
official, "was undoubtedly ripe" for it: with peace expected in Korea there
was a "tendency to relax our efforts." In February, the AHF convinced
Philadelphia's Independence Home-Coming Committee to launch a rededication program. It hired C. M. Vandeburg to work with that group
and to map a national program. President Truman also named a federal
commission to mark the 175th. The local committee and the AHF did

most of the work; the final plan was approved by those two groups, the Ad Council, and a representative of the federal commission.[31]

Philadelphia's four-day celebration began Sunday, July 1, with "Rededication services" in 1,600 churches. Youth Freedom Day, July 2, featured the Battle of Germantown reenacted in Franklin Field. On July 3 veterans, armed forces units, civil defense workers and historic floats paraded. The Fourth began with speeches at Independence Hall, one warning that the battle "between oppression and freedom" raged just as in 1776. A pageant depicting a day in old Philadelphia ended with a hundred lawyers reenacting the signing of the Declaration and a ringing of the Liberty Bell. Oak seedlings planted in "hallowed earth" from Independence Square and historic places in the other twelve colonies were presented to representatives of all the states for ceremonial planting. Unable to attend, Truman spoke from the Washington Monument. The American Revolution had aimed not "to wipe out the British Empire" but to gain freedom, and so in Korea, he said, we fought not "to conquer China, or to destroy the Soviet Empire" but to secure "the right of nations to be free and to live in peace."

As it had for the Freedom Train, the Advertising Council unleashed a promotional blitz: radio, TV and newspaper kits, national advertisers' guides, posters and car cards. The AHF and its allies sought to stimulate activities in the nation's major cities. The campaign produced "thousands of proclamations" by mayors and governors and a special July Fourth issue of *Life*. The campaign slogan was "Now Freedom Needs *You!*"[32]

The AHF counted the event a triumph. It toted up 90,000 sermons on July 1;[33] "hundreds" of radio and TV programs; 7,500 outdoor ads; speeches by national leaders (Chief Justice Vinson, Justice Clark, General Marshall). Perhaps forty million saw television spots or coverage. Ten thousand cities and towns held observances. Legion posts arranged public readings of the Declaration. Fans witnessed "a visual event" and recited a rededication pledge at ballgames. The House of Representatives convened in extraordinary session to hear the Declaration read. This once, July 4 was rescued from "aimless" celebration.[34] There would be subsequent efforts to invigorate July 4th, but only the 1976 bicentennial would equal the 175th.[35]

The AHF saw the Fourth as a "test case" for its methods and goals. It was "but one of the many national holidays" whose meaning had been "lost in the tempo of modern living and neglect." Vandeburg noted the happy fact that "the aging nation is approaching a series of city, state and regional anniversaries." After 1951, however, others would take the lead as the AHF focused its energies elsewhere.[36]

The initial remembrances of the Eisenhower years were less imposing. The Albany Congress bicentennial was a case in point. As for other observances, a new postage stamp was issued (though it did not mention the Albany Congress), and the Mint struck a medal of Franklin's "Join or Die" cartoon. Congress voted to affirm Albany's title as "Cradle of the Union." But initiative remained largely local. There was a reenactment of the Congress, a historic pageant, a parade with forty-seven floats, church services, an outboard regatta, a state dinner and a colonial ball featuring "top-ranking television and recording acts."

And speeches. However local the observance, the rhetoric reached for universals and yoked 1754 to the here and now. "Just as the theme of the Albany Congress of 1754 was unity," said one orator, so was the bicentennial's. That Britain and Canada sent representatives to Albany accented the theme. Governor Dewey urged "rededication" to the premises of 1754—that "spiritual and physical strength and unity" were attainable without demanding "conformity." To win a cold war "which may last decades or centuries," he cautioned, "we must understand the right of other nations to differ from us as we differ from them."

Some Albanians called for annual "Cradle of Union" fetes. The mayor deemed it valuable "to reemphasize the continuing need for the spirit of unity." Local Congressman Leo O'Brien noted enviously that Massachusetts was "always celebrating some historical event, like Bunker Hill Day and Paul Revere Day." [37]

Usually, and almost by definition, commemoration of the past entails a conservative outlook. Most who labored to build public reverence for the Founders would acknowledge the conservative nature of their efforts even as they strove to keep them nonpartisan. But not every bygone deed or hero evoked such values, for not every token of memory was conservative, and so not every commemoration of the 1950s merely cherished an *ancien regime*. The bicentennial of John Marshall's birth offered space to invoke liberal attitudes, even in a conservative age.

September 1954 was John Marshall Bicentennial Month, but William and Mary College paid its son a full year's homage. Honoring the man who first spaciously defined the Supreme Court's power proved nettlesome in the year of the *Brown* ruling. Ironies abounded when Chief Justice Earl Warren, who had delivered that opinion the past May, led the celebration commission.[38]

Warren's keynoting of William and Mary's celebration caused a stir. The governor and other state leaders boycotted it. Lieutenant Governor A.E.S. Stephens pled a prior engagement, the Richmond Tobacco Festival, but the governor's office announced that Stephens would attend the ceremony—then go to crown the Tobacco Queen. Warren's address warned of "waves of passion, prejudice and even hatreds [that] have on occasion swept over us and almost engulfed us." The quest for equal justice often required that "we . . . wipe some things from the slate and start again." He invoked Marshall in defense of federal supremacy.[39]

As was the usual practice, the commission stimulated initiatives by other groups. The ABA helped distribute the commission's handbook, drummed up speakers, and encouraged local bar groups to lead celebrations. The NEA and American Library Association also pitched in. State bar associations distributed a film dramatization of *Marbury v. Madison* supplied by the du Pont Company. The commission hired two PR men to press home a publicity campaign in the final weeks. They boasted that "hundreds of ceremonies were stimulated throughout the Nation."[40] As in most other commemorations, the National Park Service, especially its Historical Division, played a big role.[41]

Some of the commission's grander ideas were snaffled by lack of funds. The $82,500 Congress voted looked puny next to the $259,500 requested and precluded publishing Marshall's papers. One commission member hoped to reenact Burr's treason trial as "a lesson to this generation when we hear so much about guilt by association, and when characters at times are being destroyed without proof." Legal scholar Edward S. Corwin was asked to write a short life of Marshall, but he did not finish before the Marshall year ended. Moreover, Warren declared it "not written in an inspirational manner" suitable to young readers and "critical" of Marshall's achievements and of the Supreme Court of both Marshall's and later eras. It was not printed.[42]

The ceremonial climax of the bicentennial came on August 24, 1955, when Chief Justice Warren and President Eisenhower addressed the American Bar Association's annual meeting at Philadelphia's Independence Park. Ike found Marshall had much to teach a world riven between those committed to "a government of laws" and those endorsing "a government of men who rule by decree." Lauding Ike's presence and message,

Warren shifted emphasis to Marshall's "insistence upon the independence of the judiciary." Could the world see "that the provisions of our constitution guaranteeing human rights are living things, enjoyed by all Americans, and enforceable in our courts everywhere," he said, "it will do much to turn the tide in our favor and therefore toward peace." [43]

In other ways the Marshall anniversary showed that the past could be reverenced with a variety of messages. A New York State Supreme Court justice noted that at the Burr trial Marshall had first "authoritatively" elaborated the Fifth Amendment freedom from self-incrimination. One author claimed Marshall would have upheld *Brown* against the "recalcitrance and contumacy" of "certain state and local authorities." The Marshall year also gave voice to polite anti-McCarthyite rhetoric. [44]

Ben Franklin's 250th birth anniversary was exceptional. His multiple virtuosities, scattering his appeal, perhaps explain the absence of a federal commission to mark the event. Congress did authorize seventy-one Franklin medals; of these and other medals there was no end of giving. America's first postmaster general also was honored with stamps at home and abroad.

Though the festivities had no official geographic center, Philadelphia naturally took the lead. In 1952, twenty-one organizations "with a Franklin tradition" met there at the Franklin Institute to map a global celebration by "voluntary, individual action all over the free world." There were over 500 sponsors in forty nations, including universities, academies of science, engineering societies, orchestras and other institutions reflecting Franklin's catholicity. On his birthday in 1956, 205 separate celebrations took place in the United States. [45]

Given Franklin's many talents and callings, he was multiply invoked— printers, journalists, scientists, admen, savers and entrepreneurs hailed him. Politicians too. To Richard Nixon he was "a superb political operator." A celebrant termed Franklin's Poor Richard one of the earliest "apostles of free, individual enterprise . . . the only ideology in the world today that can still inspire millions of people and defeat various isms." Defense chief Charles E. Wilson claimed that Franklin, in a sense the nation's first secretary of defense, would not blanch at the huge current defense needs. In Franklin's name, a White House aide rallied admen behind the crusade for world freedom. Richard Nixon also mobilized Franklin in support of the Cold War.

Other shades of Franklin were summoned too. Eleanor Roosevelt claimed him as a humanitarian. A publisher cited him to warn against "such patriot-appealing phrases as 'national security,' and 'national prestige' and 'national interests' as excuses for muzzling or intimidating the press." Philadelphia sent three Franklynia trees honoring his "long labors for world peace" to Hiroshima University "dedicated to the hope and belief that never again will a nuclear explosion disturb the friendship between peoples." Like Marshall, Franklin admitted of a degree of political polyvalence.[46]

In some ways the Alexander Hamilton bicentennial was also atypical. The Treasury Department, not NPS, served as the lead federal agency. Although Hamilton advocated activist government, conservative themes marked the fete. Grayson Kirk, president of Hamilton's alma mater, Columbia University, praised the Federalist's approval of bold national action but warned: "Leviathan is still Leviathan even when it is benevolent." At the bicentennial commission's first meeting, Democratic Senator Harry Byrd, dean of southern conservatives, nominated GOP conservative Karl Mundt as chair. Commission member Edward R. Burke, once a right-wing senator from Nebraska, offered the aid of the conservative American Good Government Society, over which he presided.

Mundt, the celebration's prime mover, brooked no nonsense about his hero. When Senator Paul Douglas playfully proposed honoring Andy Jackson too, Mundt replied that Hamilton merited single homage to balance that given Thomas Jefferson. What about Aaron Burr, asked Douglas? "We are on the Hamilton side of the feud at this time," replied the barely amused South Dakotan.[47]

Mundt placed his hero on the right. Contrary to "some self-styled liberals," he said, the American and French Revolutions differed vastly. France's left its heirs unable "to erect stable political institutions," while Hamilton's offered a model to emerging nations. Ideally, the bicentennial might revive "interest in the whole constitutional concept." Professor Louis Hacker of Columbia University also developed a theme of decorous upheaval: "Revolutionary fervor is one thing; public responsibility is another. The leaders of new countries must understand that the processes of building are slow and painful; they require the honorable discharge of obligations."

The bicentennial commission showcased an essay contest with fifty-five high-school winners—a totemic number (one per state and commonwealth). They toured Washington, Philadelphia, Valley Forge and

Mt. Vernon; met the president and other leaders; and held a mock constitutional convention. This focus on adolescents may have encouraged the
celebration's accent on Hamilton's youth and dash, which blurred slightly
its conservative emphasis. The *New York Times* noted his "invincible
youth," and even Mundt lauded his "breathing the spirit of youth into the
Government and Constitution" along with his fiscal sobriety.[48]

Eisenhower proclaimed January 11, 1957, as Bicentennial Day, two
hundred years after *one* of the birthdates ascribed to Hamilton.[49] Ceremonies occurred in Washington, New York, Chicago, several Army posts,
and Nevis, Hamilton's birthplace. Mundt spoke near the Hamilton statue
at Manhattan's Federal Hall. Wreaths were laid on his tomb by representatives of Hamilton's church, artillery unit, college and other institutions to
which he had had ties. New York City named a bridge for Hamilton.[50]

Jamestown's 350th anniversary (more exactly, the Jamestown–
Yorktown–Williamsburg celebration) outdid prior festivities in tourism
and glamor. Virginia's planning for 1957 began in 1952, Washington's in
1953. Expecting 2.5 million visitors, Colonial Williamsburg, the state and
nation budgeted $25 million for new or refurbished facilities. The armed
forces supplied costumed halberdiers. Full-size replicas of the *Susan Constant* and two 1607 companion ships were built; the commander of NA-
TO's Atlantic forces presided at the keel-laying. Paul Green wrote a new
pageant-drama for outdoor performance. Getting a jump on lesson-
drawing, he suggested that the reasons Jamestown's "communistic system" failed 350 years before "may still be valid." [51]

The anniversary occasioned endless avowals of Anglo-American unity.
Where Captain John Smith's tiny fleet had weighed anchor, U.S. Ambassador Winthrop Aldrich praised the two people's "intimate and unique relationship." That same day, replicas of Smith's ships were christened in
Virginia by the wives of the governor, a former U.S. ambassador to Great
Britain, and Britain's ambassador to the United States. When a *Mayflower*
replica sailed from England to Plymouth, Massachusetts, Ike sent a telegram that termed the ship's name an emblem of "our heritage of freedom
and our historic ties to lands across the sea."

The festival's opening on April 1 bore out John Donne's dictum that
Jamestown was "but the suburb of the Old World." Jeremiah Clarke's
Elizabethan trumpet voluntary was the musical theme of the festival. Britain's ambassador and London's former lord mayor took part and the
queen's spokesman claimed that the Declaration of Independence had

benefited Britain, too: had the colonies lost, ideals of liberty "would have died in Britain as surely as they would have died in America." Virginia's governor asserted that British and American festival exhibits "accurately portrayed the role of the English-speaking peoples in developing and safeguarding democratic principles." [52]

Hitches did arise. Its seaworthiness in question, the *Susan Constant II* wisely accepted a Coast Guard tow on its voyage to Washington. A banquet to honor "distinguished Virginians" ran afoul of southern racial protocol. *Who's Who* produced the name of Dr. Clilan B. Powell, physician, entrepreneur and publisher of Harlem's *Amsterdam News*. Belatedly learning Powell was black, the Virginia Chamber of Commerce righted its "mistake" by lifting the invitation. Powell declared that since the governor had issued it, he alone could rescind it, and termed the fiasco "fodder for the communist propaganda machine"; at length he and six other African Americans declined bids. If they had shown up, the hosts had a table ready—up in the balcony.[53]

Virginia put on an engaging show. On May 13, a Captain Smith impersonator stepped ashore from a longboat as the three replica ships stood off in the river. Richard Nixon greeted him. Three Air Force jets roared overhead bringing from England copies of the original colonial charter and the seal of James I; the trip lasted less than eight hours, as against Smith's 128 days. Nixon urged the nation "to show the hardpressed peoples of Europe, Asia and Africa that they, too, may realize the benefits which Americans today enjoy if they will share the faith which motivated the settlers of Jamestown." (The Red Army newspaper *Krasnaya Zvezda* took a different tack. It labeled the first settlers indentured servants and criminals who owned slaves and treated Indians with "crafty, mercenary, bestial brutality.") [54]

At the festival's naval review, the 114 ships, from nations with NATO ties or links to settling the New World (thus excluding Iron Curtain regimes),[55] stretched fourteen miles in double line. when the governors conference met in Williamsburg, Ike hailed the American tradition of decentralized power. "Today, against the dark background of Eastern Europe, we see spotlighted once again the results of extreme and dictatorial concentration of power." In October, the battle of Yorktown was reenacted. Descendants of Lafayette and other French heroes of the American Revolution attended. However, Lord Cornwallis's heirs sent regrets.[56]

Queen Elizabeth and Prince Philip's royal progress climaxed the festivities and provided "the biggest stimulus yet to public interest in these historic shrines." On October 16 they deplaned at Patrick Henry Airport, greeted by ten thousand. They went to services at Jamestown's rebuilt church, toured festival exhibits, attended Paul Green's pageant, and visited Williamsburg. In Washington, a million onlookers cheered, but their trip to New York City proved an even bigger sensation. Arriving by water, the queen saw the *Mayflower* replica. "She has very good eyesight," burbled New York's Governor Averell Harriman, his awe typifying the response to the royal visit.

The queen shared fully the gala's hands-across-the-sea sentiments. She stressed the two nations' common experience. The festival "illustrates these two stories, yours and ours," she asserted, ". . . both stories of experiments and adventure in freedom." Ike's toast to her declared that "the English-speaking people march forward together, to stand steadfast behind the principles that made the two nations great." [57]

Jamestown raised the standard for the 350th anniversary of Henry Hudson and Samuel de Champlain's explorations. In planning the 1959 commemoration, New York State officials eyed covetously the tourism Jamestown enjoyed. The New York-Vermont Interstate Commission on the Lake Champlain Basin had begun preparations in 1955. Governor Harriman proclaimed 1959 a "Year of History," urging the entire state to mark its past. Congress established a Hudson-Champlain Celebration Commission and appropriated $50,000. Leaders tapped local, state and national energies. The Dutch Hudson River counties were eager to celebrate. Perhaps recalling the glittery Hudson tercentennial of 1909, New York City geared up for a "massive demonstration" of its "unique position as the industrial, commercial and cultural center of the world." Early proposals included battle reenactments; art, historical and industrial exhibits to be borne down the state's waterways by barge; and a full-scale copy of the *Half Moon*. Entreated to donate a replica of Hudson's ship as they had in 1909, the Dutch asked after the latter's fate. After performing ingloriously in the 1909 aquatic spectacle, when under full sail it rammed a replica of Robert Fulton's *Clermont*, it had suffered neglect, rot, fire and, ultimately, destruction. There would be no barge displays and, alas, no *Half Moon*. [58]

Opinions varied over what to celebrate. Italian-Americans lobbied to add Verrazano to the explorers' pantheon. Others put forward Irish fishermen or Phoenicians as discoverers of the great river. Erie Canal fans vied for notice, as did the State of New Jersey. At New York's opening program, controversy was avoided by honoring Verrazano on the first float, Hudson on the second. (As for the Irish, New York legislators presented commemorative medals to the mayor of Dublin.)[59]

With celebrations stretching from Manhattan to Canada, local option thrived. Ethan Allen Day, with a mock capture of Fort Ticonderoga, was superimposed on the Hudson River theme, as were Armed Forces Day, Loyalty Day, Memorial Day, Navy Day and the 170th anniversary of Washington's first inauguration. The centennial of John Brown's Harper's Ferry raid was marked at his farmhouse. In July a "Canoecade" retraced Champlain's voyage and reenacted his battle with the Iroquois (played by "a motley over-painted crew of summer campers and local artisans"). Many towns mounted historical pageants.[60]

Observances bristled with international themes. Britain's military attaché presented eighteenth-century muskets from the Tower of London to the Fort William Henry Museum. France's role in the region's history was showcased with a re-creation of Champlain's expedition. At opening ceremonies, both Governor Nelson Rockefeller and Vice President Nixon noted that as an Englishman, Hudson had captained a Dutch ship, and the Italian Verrazano had earlier entered New York harbor on a French vessel.

New York's Dutch heritage won due notice. Forty legislators junketed to Amsterdam, and a magnum of Hudson River water was poured into a canal. Rhetoric did not quite match Jamestown's apostrophes to Anglo-American unity at Jamestown. Governor Rockefeller lauded Holland for its "divine spirit of religious tolerance," its "unequenchable aspiration to liberty"—and some of "our favorite foods, such as waffles." The Hudson-Champlain Celebration Commission intoned: "From these early settlements came an influence on our history, culture, law, commerce, and traditions of liberty . . . which is constantly reflected in the position of the United States as the leader of the nations of the free world." [61]

Not graced like Virginia with a queen, New York did host young Princess Beatrix of the Netherlands. A crowd of 200,000 saw her disembark from the *Rotterdam*. She cruised the harbor, reviewed troops, and avowed Holland's kinship with New York City and America. They shared a belief "in human dignity, in the freedom of man and in the right of the individual to life, liberty and the pursuit of happiness." After a detour to

Washington and lunch with the president, she journeyed up the Hudson, stopping to see Eleanor Roosevelt and various sites and visiting Albany for a parade, a ball and other ceremonies.[62]

A martial tone resounded. "No single aspect of [its] work," said the celebration commission, "received as much approval" as the participation of armed services units. In Manhattan's night-time parade, "the city's historic past vied with its vigorous present and its military insurance for the future"; historical floats and marchers in the garb of sixteenth-century Italian maritime republics were interspersed among Terrier, Nike-Hercules and Bomarc missiles. Sixteen Navy ships visited New York Harbor on June 11. The U.S. Military Academy Band played at Fort Ticonderoga before the Green Mountain Boys reenacted its capture. At Lake George, Military Display Day featured a parade, an Air Force chopper's air-sea rescue, a jet flyover and Marine amphibious landing. Rockland County's pageant, "Muskets to Missiles," closed with "a simulated launching of Nike Ajax and Hercules missiles." [63] Defense officials' interest in this pageantry exceeded the recreational. Several used the Hudson-Champlain celebration as a sounding board for claims for an expanded mission or budget.[64]

In all these commemorations the message was one of growth and change. From tiny European seeds had sprung a vast American oak, sheltering power and abundance, spirituality and dedication to liberty. The contrasts earned frequent note. The *New York Times* remarked that Hudson's 160-ton "vlie boat" made six knots; the USS *Northampton*, its 17,200 tons tied up in the North River for the celebration, could do thirty. Nixon compared Hudson's five-month voyage to his own itinerary that day—breakfast with the president in Washington, Manhattan at noon and a date in San Francisco that night (for which his flight would be an hour late). In accepting the first published volume of Jefferson's papers in 1950, President Truman compared the nine days his recent 7,000-mile trip to the Pacific Northwest had taken with the twenty-eight-month-long Lewis and Clark expedition.[65]

That time brings improvement is an American axiom, but some ancient truths endured. The chief of the international Franklin celebration recalled what a French savant told him: had America faithfully followed Franklin's teachings, "there never would have been any communism or even socialism in the world." Historian Dumas Malone saw the revival of interest in American history as a rebuttal to the "dominant impression created on foreign visitors . . . that we are present-minded and future-minded."

The past anchored a stormy present, and remembrances nerved Americans for a stressful new global role. Malone surmised that "a bewildered and beleaguered society like ours, feeling insecure in the present and unsure of the future, is seeking to tap the wisdom and experience of the Fathers." By Jamestown's pageantry and pomp, the *New York Times* suggested, "we may be again reminded that though we are a young country we do have our history and our traditions." These could be burnished with reenactments, costumed pageantry and the westward flow of Old World royalty and diplomats honoring the young nation's past.[66]

The commemorations of the 1950s naturally laid stress on the sufferings and sacrifices of the nation's founders. However, this theme would reach its fullest elaboration in the Lincoln Sesquicentennial and the Civil War Centennial.

7

Patriotic Gore

The Lincoln Sesquicentennial and Civil War Centennial brought both closure to the commemorations of the 1950s and a shift in thematic content. Again, Robert N. Bellah's distinction is apt. Earlier observances mostly paid homage to discoverers or liberators of the promised land, to America's Old Testament or Mosaic age, while Lincoln and the Civil War evoked New Testament trials—"death, sacrifice, and rebirth." Like the earlier celebrations, these two anniversaries expressed the nation's sense of its Cold War mission and its appointment with destiny.

At the Civil War Centennial's close, however, certainty was ebbing. A country nostalgic for moments of historic consequence would soon be battered by them. The civil rights movement had begun to veer from the style that once admitted it to the national consensus. On college campuses, blotches of disorder were erupting. The war in Vietnam stirred dissent. By 1967, two years after the second "stillness at Appomatox," Bellah would term the troubled present the nation's "third time of trial." [1]

Although the Lincoln Sesquicentennial took place in the seemingly still tranquil 1950s, even so, there were signs of disquiet. The political debate filled up with expressions of doubt as to the "national purpose" and intimations of America's decline. Sometimes the discourses of the different groups—commemorators and alarm-criers—converged.[2]

Though observing the Lincoln Sesquicentennial might seem predestined, some lobbying proved necessary. The Lincoln Group of the District of Columbia took the main initiative. This assemblage of Lincoln enthusiasts included Congressmen Fred Schwengel of Iowa and Leo Allen of Illinois and others who would subsequently play active roles in the sesquicentennial.[3]

That Lincoln deserved commemoration none disputed, but to details of personnel and politics, there were objections aplenty. Occasions for partisan preferment complicated the memorializers' task. While it was a central Sesquicentennial theme that Lincoln transcended party—indeed, transcended nationality—a Republican he had been. A Republican, his heirs insisted, he would remain.

In 1957 Eisenhower appointed the Lincoln Sesquicentennial Commission. Republican Senator John Sherman Cooper of Kentucky became chairman and Indiana Republican Congressman F. Jay Nimtz, an active sponsor of the celebration, vice chair. Bertha Adkins, women's director of the Republican National Committee, headed the executive committee. This GOP trifecta disturbed Peter Mack, an Illinois Democrat and commission member. Naming an executive director proved contentious. Nimtz proposed John Allen, a Republican activist and leader in Lincoln Group centennial initiatives. Others held out for a figure less political and more scholarly. At length, historian William E. Baringer was named executive director and Allen, assistant executive director, an arrangement about which several commissioners were dubious.[4]

Congressman Mack remained a critic. He assailed Allen's high salary and how Republicans "sneaked him in the back door." He derided plans to spend $740,000. He assailed the lavish outfitting of offices for an agency set to expire inside two years. Glumly, Chairman Cooper conceded the need for greater economy. Embarrassments multiplied. In June 1958, word leaked that minutes of a meeting had been stamped "Confidential." [5]

Limited funding precluded the sesquicentennial committee's grander schemes. There would be no movie nor, as some hoped, any Lincoln "trailer-museums." Mostly, the commission advised and encouraged other groups, public and private, to celebrate the Lincoln Year. Baringer compiled a chronology, Lincoln Day-By-Day. A Lincoln Handbook was published.[6]

Despite the squabbling, the Lincoln legend brought comfort in an uncertain cold-war age. A delegation visited Japan, and Lincoln scholar Roy Basler of the Library of Congress lectured across Europe. Ike expressed delight that a New Delhi group was creating a museum to honor Lincoln and Tokyo high-school students listed him as "the most respected of all world figures." Further, Tolstoy had ranked Lincoln "the only giant" among world statesmen, Sun Yat-sen bottomed his governing principles on the Gettysburg Address, and India's Prime Minister Nehru drew strength from the mold of Lincoln's hand he kept on his desk.[7]

Lincoln became a Cold War asset. Visiting heads of state added Springfield to their itineraries. There, Willy Brandt, mayor of embattled West Berlin, declared the "House Divided" speech "perhaps even more applicable" to present-day Germany. Placing a life-size log cabin in front of Berlin's Amerikahaus, Americans extended the parallel. The Voice of America marked the anniversary of the Gettysburg Address with tributes by Ike, leaders of Britain, West Germany and India, and a Malayan schoolboy, Brazilian librarian and Ghanaian preacher.[8]

Even the Soviets paid homage. In 1959 Nikita Khrushchev visited the Lincoln Memorial. After a homily by Ambassador Henry Cabot Lodge, Jr., he bowed from the waist and continued: "This is why we honor him and bow to him." Lincoln "was a truly great man, a human man, because he dedicated his life to the struggle for freedom." Russians at a U.S. exhibition in Moscow named Lincoln America's greatest figure.[9]

The arts also took note. Norman Corwin's play "The Rivalry" treated the Lincoln-Douglas debates. Richard Boone, who played Lincoln, excerpted his role on the Ed Sullivan show. NBC-TV broadcast the program "Meet Mr. Lincoln." Radio ran Lincoln dramas. A special joint session of Congress on Lincoln's birthday witnessed the premier blending of poetry and statecraft. Ike and other notables heard actor Frederic March render the Gettysburg Address. Then poet and Lincoln biographer Carl Sandburg's oration hushed and enraptured them from his opening line: "Not often in the story of mankind does a man arrive on earth who is both steel and velvet, who is as hard as rock and soft as drifting fog, who holds in his heart and mind the paradox of terrible storm and peace unspeakable and perfect." It was mildly embarrassing that, with scores of GOP lawmakers out on the hustings for that yearly party rite, so many of the attentive faces were Democratic.[10]

Still, the Lincoln Year had limited impact. Despite the many local observances, the anniversary probably had less *eclat* than Jamestown's, favored as it was by the queen. But if brevity curtailed its effect, it also shortened the time critics had to carp. That was an advantage denied the Civil War centennial.

The Civil War Centennial unfolded as a culmination, if not last gasp, of "high" cold-war-era celebration, soon to yield to the less ordered public ceremony of the 1960s. No earlier observance triggered so many resonances with the nation's global role or became so embroiled in politics, media and popular culture. All public rites are subject to competing uses and readings, but no mobilization of the past in support of the present prompted as much friction as the Civil War anniversary.[11]

It was not at first obvious that the centennial should be celebrated. As Virginia Senator Harry F. Byrd asked a would-be commemorator, "Why do you and I want to call attention to the Civil War? The South got the hell beat out of it." A speaker at the first national centennial convocation hoped "to avoid any sort of activity or exercises that would tend to revive the bitterness and the hatred engendered by that great conflict." Karl Betts, who chaired the Washington, D.C. Round Table's centennial committee, assured that centennial sponsors had no desire to "stir up hatred and passions out of the past. We don't fight those battles any more, we study them."[12]

The civil rights issue injected a further irritant. As whites sought fraternally to mark the 1861–65 fratricide, African Americans grew restive at a century's scant progress and the gap between cold-war rhetoric and practice. Centennial preparations coincided with critiques of the creeping pace of change; observances took place as freedom rides, sit-ins and marches proliferated. The *Brown* decision and other provocations grated on southern sensibilities. When some in Dixie protested the 1954 ruling, said a southern trade journal, "the outside press landed on the region." To the South the Confederate flag took on renewed totemic importance. In 1958 the State of Mississippi warned "Yankee business concerns" selling beach towels imprinted with the Stars and Bars that they risked fines and jail time.

The approach of final roll call for the handful of surviving Civil War veterans elicited a diminuendo foreshadowing of sectional acerbities. In 1955, Congress had voted to pay the medical expenses of the last living Union veteran. When bills for similar aid to the last three Confederates came up the next year, South Carolina Senator J. Strom Thurmond warned that the subsidy would subvert states' rights, and the United Daughters of the Confederacy termed it a Yankee "insult." [13]

The centennial run-up coincided with the deaths of the last Civil War soldiers. Curiosity, but something more, stimulated national interest in the corporal's guard of Civil War veterans left in the 1950s. The Sons of Union Veterans of the Civil War held their 1954 encampment in Duluth to honor there the only surviving Union veteran. In 1959, the sole living Civil War veteran, 116-year-old ex-Confederate Walter Williams, joined Houston's Armed Forces Day parade in an ambulance. [14]

It was an eventful year for Williams. Research cast doubt on whether he had been old enough to serve with General John B. Hood as he asserted, but Texas officials upheld his claim. On his death in December 1959, Eisenhower, as Congress had mandated, decreed a period of national mourning, stating that "the wounds of the deep and bitter dispute which once divided our nation have long since healed," leaving "a united America" with lessons to teach "a divided world." The governor of Texas and representatives of the other Confederate states attended as Williams was buried with full military honors. [15]

Misgivings about the centennial yielded before a hope that it might serve as a touchstone for patriotism and Cold War civics. Three senators who led in promoting it stated, borrowing from a decade-old speech by Eisenhower, that the observance "must be a new study of American patriotism." It must bring "deeper understanding of the immense reserves of bravery, of sacrifice, and of idealism which lie in the American character." [16]

The centennial's constituency included the Civil War round tables which flourished in numerous cities. By 1955, claimed one Civil War buff, almost thirty round tables existed, several with the word "Centennial" in their names. This figure may have been conservative: in 1958 a historian put the number at over a hundred. In 1956 the Washington, D.C., Civil War Round Table began campaigning for a national centennial. Members drew up legislation to create a centennial commission. [17]

As allies the round table warriors could count the travel industry. The American Automobile Association, foreseeing "the greatest domestic travel in history," began coaching its travel counsellors in the fine points of Civil War tourism and lent its moral support to the centennial. By 1960, an AAA spokesman boasted that Civil War sites were "competing with famous tourist attractions of Europe." [18]

More importantly, the National Park Service hoped the centennial might serve Mission 66, its long-term project to acquire and refurbish Civil War battlefields. The NPS sought leverage over any observance "lest it take a political turn, and the service be faced with a major task of fighting off unsound, one-shot commemorative proposals, instead of turning the event to aiding in proper, permanent development of [Civil War battle] areas." The CWCC supported the NPS and its Mission 66.[19]

The centennial also engaged historic preservationists, who blanched at incursions into hallowed ground by such phalanxes of progress as housing tracts, shopping centers, and tourist gimcrackery. A Pennsylvania congressman noted that a famous hill on the Union right at Gettysburg "is now a junkyard and a garage dump"; an NPS official decried the presence of a motel athwart Daniel Sickles' defense line on the Emmitsburg Road. He termed "commercial and industrial encroachment" the "biggest single threat to the historical and memorial character" of Civil War sites. In many skirmishes over Civil War preservation, a powerful strain of antimodernism emerged.[20]

Congressmen and senators also took interest in the centennial. Several solons who guided Civil War measures through Congress belonged to the District Civil War Round Table. Fred Schwengel, GOP congressman from Iowa, had a passion for the Civil War and history in general. Representative William M. Tuck of Virginia shared a fascination with the War Between the States.

Though a rival group based in New York and Chicago offered a more academic-sounding plan, a variant of the D.C. Round Table's proposal won bipartisan support. Congressman Tuck's bill called for a Civil War Centennial Commission of twenty-five members, four each from House and Senate, twelve selected by the president (two from the Defense Department), plus the director of the NPS and librarian of Congress or their designees; the president, vice president and Speaker of the House were members ex officio. The Senate approved a similar bill; Ike signed it in September. Funds were briefly a problem when a Senate panel halved a House-approved 1958 appropriation of $100,000 as adjournment neared. Tuck, normally tightfisted but also the CWCC's vice chairman, moved swiftly to convince Senate leaders to reverse the cuts. No less than Harry F. Byrd of Virginia, inveterate foe of government extravagance, convinced colleagues to restore the full amount.[21]

In December, Eisenhower named twelve public members. Mostly

Yankees, they were Pulitzer Prize-winning historian Bruce Catton; Professors Avery O. Craven of the University of Chicago, John A. Krout of Columbia and Irvin Bell Wiley of Emory; W. Norman Fitzgerald, a Milwaukee manufacturer and Civil War Round Table president; William S. Paley, chairman of CBS; Aksel Neilson, a friend of Eisenhower's; Consuelo N. Bailey, former lieutenant governor of Vermont, and Alvin L. Aubinoe, a Maryland builder; Assistant Secretary of the Army (and former Congressman) Dewey Short; Vice Admiral Stuart H. Ingersoll; and retired Major General U.S. Grant 3rd. Senators John W. Bricker, Edward Martin, Joseph C. O'Mahoney and Clinton P. Anderson and Congressmen Tuck, Schwengel, Wint Smith and Frank M. Coffin, the director of the National Park Service, the librarian of Congress, and the *ex-officio* members filled out the panel.[22]

Elected to lead the commission, the 76-year-old General U.S. Grant 3rd, grandson of the eighteenth president, had impeccable credentials as a patriot and commemorator. He had served briefly as associate director of the George Washington Bicentennial Commission. He was active in the National Council on Historic Sites and Buildings, the American Planning and Civic Association and the Washington Civil War Round Table. His resume termed him "one of the most ardent patriotic and civic workers in America."[23]

As executive director Grant named Karl Betts of Catonsville, Maryland. A boyhood pal of Eisenhower's, Betts brought to his task a passion for the Civil War and a public-relations approach acquired in a career in advertising. He had led efforts to lobby for creation of the CWCC. His enthusiasm for battle reenactments sometimes subverted the commission's official position of disdain or neutrality toward that popular feature of the centennial. He often dilated on the "vast romance" of that "'storybook' war," which was "a common ordeal from which no one lost but everyone gained." At times Grant had to check his zeal. He once cautioned Betts not to boast that a Bull Run reenactment would draw "the greatest audience ever to witness an outdoor spectacle in America," citing welcomes like Lindbergh's in 1927. The two made a congenial but ill-starred partnership.[24]

For their planning, Betts and Grant found the Freedom Train an especially fetching model and collected data about it. Reflecting the altered state of American transportation, their "Mobile Museum" in its most ambitious version would carry Civil War exhibits throughout the country by train, ship, truck and/or plane. However, funding and logistics proved problematic, and the Mobile Museum never got past the wishing stage.[25]

Like other federal commemorative bodies, the CWCC functioned according to a decentralized model: it could cajole, coordinate, inform, suggest and advise, but most initiatives had to come from states and localities. His office could not, Betts insisted, supervise the "hundreds" of projects in the works. Indeed, the CWCC devoted much of its initial energy to convincing states to create centennial commissions, as eventually forty-four did.[26]

Yet the CWCC's challenge was less powers or funds than to avoid aggravating sectional and racial tensions. Endlessly the centennialists reassured those loathe to rake up ancient carnage and division that it was not to be a "celebration" or vaunting by victors, but a "commemoration" of spirituality and sacrifice on both sides and a "re-dedication" to these shared virtues. Betts warned a speaker that "there is nothing in this heroic episode of our past that we want to *celebrate* during the centennial years. We desire, rather to *commemorate*" deeds and sacrifices "which feed the springs of our national greatness today." Grant spiked the idea of any "period of jubilation." The mood was to be not "merriment or jollification" but sober "reappraisal." [27]

Fears of division paled before awareness of the centennial's utility for teaching cold-war patriotism and unity. Congressman Tuck stressed how in the unity forged by the war "the sons of both North and South have subsequently fought side by side for human freedom, justice, and the dignity of the individual." He captured the observance's civil-religious purpose in a call to improve battlefields like Sayler's Creek so all Americans, not just Virginians, "may come to worship at these shrines." Eisenhower stated a recurrent centennial motif: "Our free country was purchased at great price. . . ." [28]

These themes pervaded the first National Assembly of local, state and national commemorators in January 1958. Ike's decade-old call for "a great ground swell of patriotism" was especially urgent, said one CWCC member, "in these dangerous and desperate times." The assembly voted that "the Centennial observance must be a new study of American patriotism" yielding "deeper understanding of the immense reserves of bravery, of sacrifice and of idealism which lie in the American character." [29]

Yet CWCC leaders thought the nation's hard-won unity still so fragile that they blocked a proposal to study the Civil War's origins lest it revive sectional feelings. Such sensitivity persisted through the centennial. In like spirit, state centennial commissions also evaded pointed assessments of the war's origins, thus diffusing sectional guilt. Mississippi's listed the causes as "those which bring about all wars—greed, fear, ignorance, apathy, and emotionalism," flaws to which no section was immune. The head of New Hampshire's commission gave parallel counsel—borrowed from a South Carolina commission publication—against allocating blame "or fighting the issues over again. Americans from every section produced the divisions that led to war. These divisions grew out of hate, greed, fear, ignorance, apathy, selfishness and emotionalism—evils from which this generation is not free." [30]

The CWCC strove to make the celebration national. Betts found it "something of a problem" to enlist "the active interest of our Southern friends." One ploy was to hold the CWCC's second National Assembly in the South. In Richmond in 1959, the executive director waxed enthusiastic about centennial activities all over the country by "people of opposite political faiths." These energies betokened "a *tremendous idealism*" at work.[31]

The affirmation of enduring unity became the centennial's rhetorical cement. In what soon became a litany, the first National Assembly concluded that "what was lost in [the Civil War] was lost by all of us; what was finally gained . . . the preservation of the American Union as the instrumentality of freedom for all the peoples of the world—was gained by all of us." Betts termed the war "a common ordeal from which *no one lost* but *everyone gained*." It had "trapped those appalling passions which might not be cooled, however paradoxically, except by the heat of war. And out of the cooling came *reason*, the national settling of all minds upon the principle of unity which gives us our strength and everlasting hope." [32]

No orator unlimbered heavier metaphoric artillery than Dewey Short, ex-congressman and now assistant secretary of the Army, at the Second National Assembly. The Civil War's murky origins were "the product of the time," a result perhaps of "growing pains" in a time America was "bursting, as it were, its seams in boundless expansion." Yet from the hellish conflict came lasting good, for "out of the holocaust, heartbreak, misery, terror and tragedy of civil war came unity." Given that achievement, "that this Nation was to become a world power was part of its destiny."

Short laid out a comparison. In 1959, as in 1859, freedom was at issue. "Today, we are locked in a struggle with an ideology that is attempting to destroy the concept of freedom." A century had passed, details varied, but "the mosaic of events is strikingly similar." For Bleeding Kansas or John Brown's raids, substitute Berlin or Korea. Was Short equating Southern slaveocracy and Soviet communism? Not at all, for Yanks and Rebs had battled for the same thing: freedom—of men and of states respectively. Miraculously, the war had left only pure memories and a unity that "had no room for villains." Short concluded with his sense "that the Civil War was America's Gethsemane and Calvary." "After the Crucifixion came the Resurrection of a new purified, unified and glorified power." [33]

The theme of unity proved timely to many orators. Grant boasted that centennial efforts by "Republicans and Democrats, Jews and Gentiles, Northerners and Southerners, Easterners and Westerners" showed the world "the finest possible demonstration of unity and goodwill." Betts termed the Civil War's outcome "notice to enemies wherever they be that in any sly or overt attempts to undermine us they're barking up the wrong tree." Similarly, Robert E. Lee, IV, told a conclave that, war's "wrath" and Reconstruction's "beastliness" notwithstanding, "the people came back together. . . . [W]hen the chips are down there is one country here, and let no outside force be ever deceived." [34]

Coinciding with the spirited debate over national purpose during Eisenhower's second term and the 1960 election campaign, the Civil War Centennial looked back on an age when commitment to transcendent goals shone clearly. Kentucky's centennial commission cited the Civil War's "noble examples" of courage and sacrifice which "can benefit an 'easy-living' generation that may at any moment be called upon to make sacrifices equally as great." Programs for the 1961 reenactment of First Manassas told spectators that the spectacle aimed at "reminding you of our common heritage—and indeed of reminding the world—that our people have always been willing to fight and to die if need be for their beliefs—and their principles." [35]

While much of Grant's rhetoric fit in companionably with the national purpose discourse, on less public occasions he veered further right. Grant often fretted much about "our heterogeneous population." Once, seeking corporate aid for an educational program, he cited two right-wing tracts to prove that schools and colleges were honeycombed with "un-American teachings" which crowded out "lessons of American history and patriotism." "The poison of socialism and internationalism" was at work. The schools, he stressed, must be helped to stimulate "unity," "a revival of patriotism," and "a better understanding of our constitutional government and of the subversive efforts that are aimed to destroy its basic principles." While no Henry Adams in decrying the nation's decline (and surely more positive about his grandfather's presidency), Grant endorsed a public statement identifying the Civil War as "America's days of greatness." [36]

Grant's unease with America's heterogeneity twice plunged the CWCC into controversy. In 1959, Grant, who was commander in chief of the Military Order of the Loyal Legion of the United States, printed in that group's newsletter an article asserting that international financiers ("the Rothschilds") had helped foment the Civil War. Widely perceived as anti-Semitic, the essay had first appeared in Father Charles Coughlin's journal and more recently in a notorious segregationist publication.[37] Grant termed the document an "illuminating account of the scheming [Lincoln] had to meet from abroad" which had never "been contradicted to our knowledge."

Jewish groups rose in protest. The Anti-Defamation League urged Grant to disavow this "vile anti-Semitic canard." Grant regretted not checking its origins or authenticity, but he had addressed it "only to a supposedly friendly group" of Civil War buffs, not a broader public, and was astounded that anyone took seriously its more outrageous claims. Its "distortion into an attack on the Jews in general" he deemed "too far fetched to be likely." He suggested that the ADL's director himself had "given to this article the anti-Jewish twist." Betts told a concerned White House that no anti-Semitism colored the story; mention of the Rothschilds and Benjamin Disraeli had no significance. The ADL had made "a large mountain out of a molehill." Later Grant expressed regret at missing some of the article's inaccuracies; when he had stated "that the article had never 'been contradicted to our knowledge' . . . apparently 'our knowledge' was at fault. . . ." In two months the disturbance had subsided.[38]

These distractions forgotten, dignity characterized the centennial's formal opening. Ike's proclamation called the war "a demonstration of heroism and sacrifice by men and women . . . who valued principle above life itself. . . ." They came from both sections "of our now magnificently reunited country." Church bells, sermons, and reverent gratitude for century-old sacrifice and restored union marked the official beginning of the observance on Sunday, January 8, 1961. Simultaneous rites at their respective tombs honored both Grant and Lee.[39]

Betts and U.S. Grant 3d, with limited staff and funding, intended that the national CWCC be a clearinghouse for state and local agencies, which would sponsor and carry out most of the commemorative activities. It provided advice and information, arranged for speakers, published a monthly newsletter, and acted as a cheerleader. Its pamphlet "Facts About the Civil War" was in constant demand. (The pamphlet's critics noted that it managed to evade a single mention of the term "slavery.")[40]

Not long after the centennial opened, Grant and Betts found themselves under siege. The rising salience of civil-rights issues brought them up short. Betts assumed the centennial was immune to political stresses raised by such controversies and, indeed, gloried in its seeming ability to transcend them. He cavalierly predicted that "any possible complications resulting from the integration problem will soon disappear." He deemed it praiseworthy when Arkansas under segregationist Governor Orval Faubus proceeded with centennial plans "despite its troubles with integration and the Little Rock crises." [41]

The CWCC's 1961 National Assembly was set for Charleston, South Carolina, for the centennial of the attack on Fort Sumter. At such assemblies, members of the national CWCC and its state counterparts foregathered with Civil War buffs, book and gun sellers, and others. The chairman of New Jersey's centennial commission learned that segregation ordinances would forbid one of his members, who was black, to eat or live at the host hotel, though she could attend meetings. New Jersey and three other states vowed to boycott the assembly. Some suggested moving it from Charleston. The CWCC parried complaints by reiterating that delegates had charge of their own arrangements. These and any hotel's policy, said Grant and Betts, were local matters. Having no jurisdiction, they could do nothing.

Wrong, rejoined the president. Facing pressure to take action for civil rights, JFK called on the CWCC to assure equal access to all its activities. Its executive committee was at first resistant, declaring its powerlessness over hotelkeepers. Kennedy insisted, however, until Grant agreed to hold official proceedings at the U.S. Naval Station. There the races would not be segregated. Following Navy rules, however, the sexes would! Husbands and wives would have to bunk separately.[42]

The proceedings themselves produced more rancor. At an unofficial, segregated luncheon, a speaker disparaged Lincoln's parentage and derided New Jersey's protest. Before the same orator addressed an official session, an alarmed Betts got him to delete a page of his incendiary text. Still, he offended Northerners with claims that the Civil War was no anti-slavery, egalitarian "crusade," that secession had had ample precedent, and that the Fourteenth and Fifteenth Amendments, "railroaded into our Constitution," underlay "our present racial unrest." After Grant denied New Jersey's request to respond, one of her delegates held an angry press conference.[43]

Charleston climaxed but did not end the trouble. Grant's and Betts's approach engendered misgivings. In 1958 one CWCC member, Avery O. Craven, lamented that "serious issues" which had led to the war were being ignored; "one would think from the emphasis on battles and battle-fields that the men were fighting just for the fun of it." Betts assured him that clearer focus was "bound to emerge." Eventually the centennial's theme "may be concentrated in a phrase or a paragraph which will have real meaning." Unpersuaded, Craven warned that "blundering along with no clear notion of what we are doing or want to do, may get us into as much trouble as it did the men of 1850–1860."[44]

Other critics feared that commercialism and sensationalism would prevail. Proliferating reenactments stirred unease. Drama critic Brooks Atkinson, foreseeing a "whole series of battles in a carnival spirit," wondered if the centennial must end "with the shooting of Raymond Massey [who often portrayed Lincoln] in a theatre box by a disgruntled actor?" Another complainant found the centennial little more than "military dumb shows." The CWCC declared its neutrality on reenactments. It disturbed Grant that some saw the observance as "only a giant refighting of the war." States might hold reenactments (which the CWCC could hardly forbid and would in fact assist), but he envisioned a centennial replete with more varied and "dignified observances."[45]

While echoing the CWCC's official noninvolvement, Betts rarely restrained his enthusiasm for reenactments. He helped plan the first large-scale mock battle (First Manassas). He was elated that the centennial's early months would witness this and two other dramatic recreations and took pride in aiding such projects. To critics, he responded: "the American people will have pageants. They will stage [them] whenever the urge becomes strong enough...." He lauded Southerners for "commemorating their defeats as well as their victories."[46]

The commission faced other objections. Some feared that the celebration would create division. Advocates of civil rights thought it conveyed too pro-Southern a point of view; Southerners believed otherwise. Some objected to the CWCC's preponderantly Northern membership. There were murmurings of opposition in Congress. Critics of a more extremist bent assailed the centennial as a scheme which could only benefit the likes of the Soviets, international Jewry, and race mongrelizers.[47]

The many tawdry Civil War commercial tie-ins especially outraged critics. Elated that "the Civil War has come to the appliance industry!" GE's Hotpoint Division suggested that savvy merchants find "an old Civil War cannon" and offer it as a contest prize or "run a 'Bivouac Sale' or 'Battlefield Sale' and sell Hotpoint appliances from a big tent." There were candied minie balls and Grant-and-Lee cocktail trays. The Wisconsin centennial commission chairman reported the view that Japan would win the Civil War rerun "because of the junk they have unloaded." An acerbic cartoon predicted "Centennial-burgers" and "Blue and Gray popcorn." The *New York Times* lamented a centennial "desecrated with fiestas and souvenir hats and ashtrays." [48]

Conceding the problem, Grant suggested that Congress had created the CWCC lest the observance "run wild and be unsuitably commercialized." The commission appointed one panel to guide advertisers in using centennial themes decorously and another to draft a code for war-related advertising. The latter stressed that the centennial was a "commemoration," not a "celebration," urged that flags and other icons not be debased and that ads not "needlessly fan long-forgotten animosities." "Appropriateness" mattered: don't run ads about Lee on Lincoln's birthday or vice versa. To those offended by the garishness, the CWCC could only plead that it had no control over the outpouring of products. Conversely, since its objectives also put a premium on publicity, the CWCC had a soft spot for showbiz. Thus, it praised the "attention-getting gimmicks" in Hagerstown's celebration.[49]

These concerns and the wounds left by Charleston festered through the spring and summer of 1961. One congressman sought to deny funds for any segregated centennial activities. Only deft defense by allies staved off a raid on CWCC's appropriation by other solons. Some CWCC members wanted to meet, but Grant, busy tending his ailing wife at home in New York, begged off. He proposed an executive committee session for mid-September, but impatient commissioners, particularly members of Congress, petitioned for a meeting to air their discontents and act on "the commission's person[ne]l problem." They had "full confidence" in Grant's leadership but called for Betts's "early withdrawal."

On August 30, the commission met, Grant grudgingly present. A motion to remove Betts triggered rancorous debate. Grant and a few others defended him; the rest said he must go. One member found Betts lacking in "vision, wisdom and statesmanship"; he had to be removed to salvage the CWCC's battered reputation. As soon as Betts was ousted, Grant said he, too, must leave, given his burdens at home and his colleagues' "arbitrary and inconsiderate demands." Admiral Ingersoll also quit in indignation. Betts objected that no formal charges had been lodged, but his public protest suggested that he had been undone by press criticisms of "too much Hollywood" and complaints that the commission did not employ "scholars to brood and muse on our premises." [50]

The CWCC limped through the fall rallied by its Vice Chair, Fred Schwengel. Reinforcements were amarch. In December, Allan Nevins was named chairman of the commission and James I. Robertson, Jr., executive director. The two historians were auspicious selections. A Pulitzer Prize winner and distinguished Civil War scholar, Nevins identified whom the centennial was to commemorate and to address with eloquence and inclusiveness. He vowed to "discourage observances that are cheap and tawdry, or . . . divisive" and to labor to help Americans "understand the mingled tragedy and exaltation of the war, and to draw from it lessons both practical and moral commensurate with its importance." Whites North and South had died for high principle as had "a host of Negroes. . . . We must honor them all." [51]

Centennial motifs now sounded more harmoniously, yet most notes were the same. "Above all," said Nevins, "our central theme will be unity, not division, for out of the brothers' war slowly emerged the basis of a firm union of hearts." At the centennial of Appomatox, "we shall treat it not as victory or defeat, but as . . . the beginning of a century of increasing concord, mutual understanding, and fraternal affection. . . ." The war would be interpreted so as to "deepen the patriotism of all Americans, North and South," Nevins declared. The aim was to "commemorate," said Robertson, not "celebrate." Nevins, like Grant, knew that "the embers of sectional emotionalism can easily burst into flame" but even so commissioned a series of books which would state forthright opinions. The centennial was to be used to expand understanding of the war's roots and results. [52]

The CWCC abandoned ambiguity regarding reenactments. Local agencies were still free to conduct them—and did—but the commission opposed them because "they do not accurately or adequately portray" the

war's "horror, tragedy and heartache." A 1962 reprise of the battle of
Antietam was the last the Interior Department permitted on National
Park Service property.[53]

Still, the genre persisted. Countless battles and lesser events were
re-created. Actor Robert Ryan played Lincoln at a reenacted second inaugural narrated by Adlai E. Stevenson. Such performances were popular
with civic leaders, the tourist industry, and the attending public. Some localities were sadly disadvantaged. Florida's Civil War Centennial Commission could sponsor no reenactments because that state's Civil War
experience had largely consisted of a naval blockade. "The destruction of
Jacksonville . . . and the capture of Pensacola and its forts are events not
easily re-enacted, to say the least." [54]

Not even Nevins and Robertson's sensitive leadership could insulate
the CWCC from all strife. The centennial of the Emancipation Proclamation brought Nevins's nearest approach to a crisis. Some Southerners
objected to marking the event at all. Of Lincoln's praiseworthy deeds, an
edict envisioning race war on Dixie's women and children was not one,
insisted a critic. Southern centennial leaders urged a return to previous
policy which left such programs to state commissions. If the CWCC handled this one, what next? They also disliked seeing current thinking about
race read back into the past and then linked with present controversies.
Nevins stood firm.[55]

Pushed and hauled by the tricky currents of civil rights, the Kennedy
White House determined that the CWCC would conduct a September 22,
1962, observance of the centenary of issuance of the Proclamation, while
the U.S. Civil Rights Commission would mark its actual implementation
on January 1, 1963. The first would stress the event's "historical" nature;
the second, its "progressive aspects." [56] From the start Nevins and Robertson pushed to have Kennedy speak at the September rites. He was formally invited in January; in February he gave Nevins personal
"assurances" he would speak and in April "seemed to look forward to participating." Staffers pressing for Executive leadership in civil rights seconded CWCC efforts from the inside.

However, vagueness settled over the White House like a summer heat
wave. One assistant reported the date "firmly on the President's calendar,"
yet another deemed the prospects "a little shakey." Doubt reigned until
August 22, when JFK's aide Theodore C. Sorensen confessed to a "mixup
. . . somewhere along the line": the President would not show up. Some

New Frontiersmen evidently feared to jar the delicate political balance that obtained in the South and the Democratic Party; Kenneth O'Donnell apparently vetoed the appearance. When Nevins and Robertson saw him in August, the key Kennedy aide "amazed" them by professing ignorance of the long-planned event and conceding that he had committed his chief to be out of town on September 22.[57]

Kennedy's withdrawal necessitated rapid footwork. Ambassador Adlai E. Stevenson agreed to speak; his and UN Secretary General U Thant's involvement gave the ceremony a suitably international aura. Further plans called for Mahalia Jackson to sing and for the Marine Band to play a piece by the black composer Ulysses Kay, and Archibald MacLeish wrote a poem. New York's Governor Nelson Rockefeller was to present his state's copy of the Emancipation Proclamation for temporary exhibit.

Trouble still beckoned. That no black leader was scheduled to speak angered local civil-rights leaders. Returning to the capital on September 16, Robertson stepped off a train into an "explosion." The district branch of the Southern Christian Leadership Council even threatened a boycott. Robertson and several commission members "labored far into the night" to contain the detonation. After hasty telephoning and diplomacy, Federal Judge Thurgood Marshall was added to the program.[58]

The September 22 ceremony played out smoothly. Marshall, Kay, MacLeish and Stevenson's contributions won plaudits, but Mahalia Jackson stole the show. Spelled by his brother Bobby, President Kennedy, who spent the day in Newport, sent a recorded message. An estimated twelve million watched the proceedings on television. The commission had managed to sound a grace note, albeit while holding its breath.[59]

The CWCC continued to step gingerly. Memories of Charleston prompted a hesitancy to hold its 1963 assembly in Boston, lest equity require locating the next in the South, thus risking "a racial problem." Boston won out. Atlanta's subsequent pitch for the 1964 meeting raised fears of another bout over segregation. However, the city promised desegregated facilities. The CWCC avoided further "playing with fire" by not holding a session on the Emancipation Proclamation at the Boston assembly.[60]

However, the centennial could not stand clear of current political discourse. For the centennial of the battle of Gettysburg, former President Eisenhower defined the duties of citizenship in conservative terms, fretting that some Americans lacked "sturdy self-reliance" and that the dedication to self-government invoked in the Gettysburg Address was atrophying. Yet the same occasion prompted liberal voices. One declared racial equality the Civil War's "unfinished business," and another termed that failure a national "shame." President Lyndon B. Johnson used Lincoln's birthday in 1965 to tout advances in civil rights, calling for still more—and, in the context of widening war in Vietnam, to assert American eagerness to take "principal responsibility for the protection of freedom on earth." [61]

It exaggerates to argue that the Civil War Centennial ended as a Babel of such discordant messages, but there was, in the increasingly heated politics of the mid-1960s, a blurring of focus. Activities such as reenactments continued, but after 1962 news stories were fewer. An orator at the 1964 National Assembly raised the question: "Will the Centennial Kill the Civil War?" [62] In some respects this might have been viewed as a positive achievement by the CWCC's leaders, yet the rhetoric of unity which had so consistently characterized the centennial rang with greater irony as the fault lines of the 1960s opened up.

Some of the centennial's late exercises illustrate the increasingly mixed messages. Naturally, the surrender at Appomatox afforded the main closure. Lee's submission itself was not reprised. The National Park Service stood by its 1961 policy: no reenactments in its domain. At the ceremony, onlookers and participants carried a profusion of Confederate flags. The Lost Cause appeared alive, and the unity consistently invoked during the centennial, somewhat shaky. While Robert E. Lee IV and U.S. Grant 3rd took part and the mood was generally lighthearted, some local residents were heard to utter resentment against efforts to impose civil rights upon the South.[63]

The ultimate in garbled messages issued from Durham Station, North Carolina, on the anniversary of General Joseph Johnson's surrender to William Tecumseh Sherman. Vice President Hubert H. Humphrey assailed "radicalism." He left unclear what form of it he feared but termed that of the Reconstruction era "a vivid example of the mindless, vengeful kind of extremism that even today, if left unchecked, could bring our great democracy to its knees." He called for a national unity in which the South would help "bring an end to obstruction and paralysis and liberate the energies of a mighty people." He foretold a day when "senseless struggle of class against class, region against region, and race against race will be ended." But which extremists did this sturdy champion of civil rights mean? Die-hard segregationists? Or, given his echoing of the "Black Legend" of Reconstruction, was it civil-rights firebrands?[64]

These confusions aside, it would be wrong to dismiss the centennial as a defeat for official commemoration. Fiascoes there were, but successes outnumbered them. Most of the Civil War Centennial occurred in the "good" Sixties, when social conflict rose but a sense of progress and cohesion persisted. Luck of the calendar saved the nation from celebrating important anniversaries during the cacaphonous "bad" Sixties.[65] Still, already by mid-decade commemorative efforts faced growing competition from forms of pageantry of different origins. While growing numbers of the American public might be termed alienated, they constituted only a minority; much of the rest of the audience, while not disaffected, were distracted but still amenable to messages issued by the forces of order and propriety.

8

"Shame on Them"

The Decline of Cold War Pageantry

By the late 1950s the public support for American cold-war pageantry was subsiding. In the 1960s the consensus from which that support sprang also ebbed. American enthusiasm for thick pageantry, for suffering pretended perils, had always had narrow boundaries. Mosinee became dim memory, not common practice. Those who craved counterfactual play might throw themselves into civil-defense activities. Interest in recurrent observances like Loyalty Day and Armed Forces Day declined too. The Freedom Train was history, though some of the documents it carried lived on in occasional newspaper supplements or on airport walls.

Patriotic activism was hardly dead. Its usage had become less obtrusive yet also more customary—school flag-raisings, the National Anthem played regularly at sports events. While patriotic practice thrived on these levels, larger projects, the more elaborate civic pageantry initiated by the center and right-of-center of the political spectrum, declined. Farther right, however, and farther left, public ceremonial display enjoyed renewed vitality. We deed the 1960s to the Left. The machinery of our memory keeps rewinding footage of civil-rights marches, Pentagon levitations, and varied leftist street theatre, but these images are a construct shaped and later consented to by the media. The Left may have owned the 60s, but not exclusively. While usually edited out, the Right was present and active.

As respectable centrist pageantry lost momentum, the Left and Right experimented with protest techniques. Some seeds of sixties dissent struggled to emerge from the scree that fell from the summit of fifties consensus. Civil defense drills, those Cold War fixtures, occasioned counterpageantry by pacifists and critics of a nuclear and thermonuclear world who challenged the culture of consent that such drills aimed to reinforce.

Nuclear attack drills of the 1950s proved vulnerable to mild subversion. Happily, leaders found, most civilians took shelter obediently. However, in a 1954 drill in Massachusetts, while the public complied "almost without exception," jeering Harvard lads disobeyed orders to take cover. The first Operation Alert, a nationwide simulation in which fifty-four cities were bombed (causing twelve million hypothetical deaths), debuted successfully in 1954. But in 1955's Operation Alert, twenty-nine pacifists were arrested in New York City for a sit-down outside City Hall. There were protests in 1956 and 1957 as well.[1]

The civil rights movement thrived on public display. Visual images remain indelibly etched in our memory: lunch-counter sit-ins (whose participants' beatification owed much to the rednecks who poured mustard or stubbed out cigarettes on their heads), the 1963 March on Washington, and the violence demonstrators met in Birmingham in 1963 and Selma in 1965.

The last instances showed how change-seekers often gained by their foes' heavyhandedness. Likewise, students protesting HUAC's 1960 San Francisco hearings became actors willynilly in a televised ceremony when police dragged them bumpingly down stairs at city hall.[2] Women Strike for Peace also devised effective counterpageantry. When HUAC summoned its leaders in 1962, instead of the usual sullenness the committee evoked, supporters showered witnesses with bouquets and nursed babies.[3] Berkeley's Free Speech Movement earned favorable publicity at first, but the revolution devoured its young when the Filthy Speech Movement lost the moral ground more decorous pioneers had gained.

When left wing dissent emerged in the sixties, observances that once held near-monopolies of the streets found their claims contested. In New York City in 1965 and 1966, for example, protesters upstaged Armed Forces Day marchers and crowds by sitting down in the street, disrupting the parade briefly until police hustled them away. In 1967 the organization which had organized the two previous protests held a separate "Flower Power Day" meeting, so the Armed Forces Day parade occurred undisrupted, but with only 6,000 marchers.[4]

Armed Forces Day became a zone of symbolic combat between endorsers and critics of the Vietnam War. Those who turned out to cheer the passing ranks had more pointed political aims than had pre-1965 crowds. They backed the troops in Vietnam and bore witness against anti-war demonstrators. Said New York's 1968 parade marshal, Marine General Lewis Walt: "It's the best gift we can make to the boys in Vietnam." Mayor John V. Lindsay, a foe of the war, left the reviewing stand after only ten minutes.

Manhattan's 1970 Armed Forces Day, also a support-the-war outing, transpired amid growing tension. Now construction workers, who had recently disrupted an anti-war march to city hall and beaten up "long-hair" demonstrators, led pro-war, anti-protest marches. Peter J. Brennan, head of the Building and Construction Trades Council of Greater New York and a leader of the "hardhats" who supported President Nixon's Vietnam policy, organized a pro-war rally in front of city hall four days after the parade. Over 100,000 workers rallied on May 20 with signs such as "Stop Leftwing TV" and "Impeach the Red Mayor." In the explosion of dissent after Nixon ordered troops into Cambodia, no politician turned out for the 1970 parade.[5]

Armed Forces Day was now beleaguered. In 1968 the Fort Dix Army base agreed to end its practice of using clown and Vietcong soldier silhouettes as firing-range targets for youngsters to shoot at. Two churches had complained that such entertainment taught "aggression, violence and the joys of war to children." In 1970 a number of Armed Forces Day open houses were cancelled, some at the request of nearby civil jurisdictions. In 1971, Mayor Lindsay "appeared briefly" on the reviewing stand but left as soon as the first unit trooped by.[6]

Loyalty Day met competition too. On that date in 1968, a Vietnam peace parade processed in two columns into Central Park's Sheep Meadow for an anti-war rally. Mayor Lindsay arrived late for Loyalty Day. His very coming angered some marchers. One spectator's placard read, "Lindsay for Dogcatcher"; another, "Hypocrite Lindsay Go to Your Pink and Yellow Friend [*sic*] at Central Park." So he did, quitting Loyalty Day after just ten minutes. In 1970 his remarks supportive of draft resisters so outraged veterans that Loyalty Day leaders thought of barring him from the event. A mayoral spokesman said "the parade is not on his schedule, not even as a drop-in." The brief march, viewed in places by more police than spectators, did without him or many other politicians. Numbers kept falling, and the last (at least visible) Manhattan Loyalty Day parade took place in 1975. "Shame on them," said a VFW official of the absent politicians. Loyalty Day was no longer a command performance.[7]

Events of the 1960s propelled preservatist forces into the streets, but these had never been alien turf to them. Loyalty Day had initially aimed to preempt such public spaces from the Left; nor were its sponsors alone. When the Left demonstrated at the 1949 Smith Act trials of the Communist Party's leaders and later on behalf of Julius and Ethel Rosenberg, anti-communists counterdemonstrated. As advocates of clemency for the Rosenbergs picketed the White House, a group across the street had carried signs with such messages as "No Mercy for the Traitors."[8]

The Right mobilized against other felt menaces in the 1950s. These included the censure of Senator Joe McCarthy, which triggered a very public petition drive and rallies in late 1954; the 1955 Geneva Conference; Soviet suppression of the 1957 Hungarian Revolution. Later, liberal opposition to the loyalty oath required of recipients of federal student loans triggered pro-oath demonstrations by college conservatives.[9]

Such activists found jolting the news that Soviet leader Nikita S. Khrushchev had accepted President Eisenhower's invitation to come to the United States. Though most Americans approved of the 1959 visit, many conservatives saw in it a bitter betrayal to a diabolical enemy. J. B. Matthews, an anti-communist of long standing, headlined his column "Eisenhower Invites the Undertaker." Most skeptics agreed that, since the junket was a *fait accompli*, Americans should greet Khrushchev with "civil and polite silence," with a "handshake but no embrace," or with courtesy but no applause.[10]

The visit opened the prospect of political damage to the administration. As he geared up for his 1960 presidential run, Vice President Nixon took on the chore of selling the *demarche* to hardcore anti-communists. He had some success at the American Legion convention, which even gave tepid approval. The VFW, however, vowed to boycott Khrushchev, though less stridently than some delegates desired. Some strict anti-communists excoriated Nixon for his stand; those who remained allies fretted for him. Conservative journalist Ralph de Toledano suggested that he might safely argue that American anti-communism was not so weak that a passing wave by Khrushchev would cause it to fall apart.[11]

Beyond the political danger lay a further, if lesser, threat that the visit might leap the boundaries of politics into show business and illusion. Senator J. William Fulbright, while favoring the exchange, warned of the risks in seeking to "arouse great hopes by splendid pageants." A reporter suggested that Khrushchev, on a trip slated to include both Hollywood and Disneyland, would be himself subjected to a bit of "Potemkin"-style "fantasy." The ultimate effort to locate the event in illusion was an ad agency's proposal that Khrushchev be prevailed upon to crown the winner of the Miss America Pageant.[12]

Foes of the visit struggled to find means of protest. Five congressmen and senators, liberal and conservative, joined to urge Americans to attend special worship services to express "spiritual unity with the victims of tyranny" and to wear black armbands and observe mourning. Various religious, ethnic, anti-communist and Iron Curtain nationality groups planned to picket. Several Catholic prelates proposed to bombard Khrushchev with prayer. Protestant groups also announced prayer vigils.[13]

Protestors agreed that unseemly or violent demonstrations should be avoided. Freedom House, an entity opposing all forms of totalitarianism, recommended a stance of "civil silence." Others proposed ostentatious absence (though thus sacrificing a certain visibility). The AFL-CIO Executive Council voted not to "give recognition" to Khruschev, stressing that he was not welcome at their convention. Some union chiefs who did meet with him pressed him hard enough to anger him.[14]

A gathering of leaders of patriotic associations suggested Americans would be "shocked" to see Washington parade routes "decorated with the 'Red flag, the hammer and sickle,' bought and paid for by American taxpayers and placed side by side with the 'Stars and Stripes.'" Yet they hit on no single agreed response. Some counseled a day of prayer; some, silence, or better, absence; newspapers might black-border their front page when Khrushchev arrived; citizens might wear black bands. Some groups did carry out such protests.[15]

Others objected more dramatically and militantly. Police arrested a self-described Hungarian freedom fighter for posting an anti-Khrushchev sticker on the Soviet UN delegation's door. The *National Review* peddled great numbers of "Khrushchev Not Welcome Here" stickers.

A Polish refugee began a hunger strike outside the White House. Two Bostonians draped a plaque of the Declaration of Independence in black. Hours before Khrushchev arrived in Pittsburgh, a fourteen-car motorcade traveled the downtown streets carrying such signs as "Butcher of Budapest." Police had to break up a shouting crowd of demonstrators, both pro- and anti-Khrushchev, outside UN headquarters.[16]

However, the visit itself and the many who rushed to be part of it upstaged the protests. San Franciscans angled for tickets to a banquet for Khrushchev, and the rush for invitations to a similar feast in Hollywood nearly became a donnybrook. Sponsors of a Philadelphia protest rally hoped to draw 15,000 but fewer than 1,000 came. On the other hand, over 2,500 attended a prayer service in St. Patrick's Cathedral on the eve of Khrushchev's arrival, and a like crowd attended an anti-communist rally in Carnegie Hall on the day itself. There, William F. Buckley, Jr., publisher of the *National Review*, termed it emblematic of "the social history of the White House" that it now welcomed Khrushchev whereas it had ostracized the late Joe McCarthy. Three nights later, the Conference of Americans of Central and Eastern European Descent and American Friends of the Captive Nations sponsored a "Let's Answer Khrushchev" rally.[17]

Opponents of the visit could take heart from the crowd reaction to Khrushchev's progress through the nation's capital. One reporter described it as "big but undemonstrative," more curious than adulatory. A few black armbands appeared; police persuaded some individuals with skull-and-crossbones flags to furl them. One onlooker termed the motorcade "more like a funeral procession than a parade." Another reported that the reaction to Khrushchev was "dead-pan . . . a wonderful commentary on the marvelous instinct of the American People." Newsman James Reston declared that "probably never on a ceremonial occasion of this sort have so many people turned out and made so little noise." The premier met similar passivity in New York.[18]

Though Khrushchev met with and encouraged both, generally his visit contributed more to detente than confrontation. Most of the noisier critics seem not to have crossed his path. He was heckled at a luncheon of New York business leaders and found Los Angeles Mayor Norris Poulson so irritating that he threatened to go home, but the tonic of a cheering welcome in San Francisco prompted him, to his guards' horror, to plunge into a crowd to banter and shake hands. Next it was on to Iowa and his first hot dog, then a friendly reception by large crowds in Pittsburgh. On balance, the trip seemed to undercut the viewpoint of the brittler anti-communists. One of them expressed chagrin that "many Americans *did* applaud this butcher of the Ukraine." [19]

Patriots also gagged at the 1959 visit of Fidel Castro. Although as a threat Cuba was no USSR, Castro's presence seemed nearly as dangerous and subverting. It scandalized the president of Freedoms Foundation that Princeton professors, some of them leftists, invited him there, "and in the whole spirit of a spring panty raid, he's welcomed." [20]

Intrusions into American space during 1960 proved yet more distressing. The fall opening of the UN General Assembly attracted Khrushchev, Castro and other world leaders. The year past had heightened Big Two asperities and American suspicion of Castro, who was becoming, before one could fairly use the term, something of an inspiration for the American counterculture. As he deplaned bearded and in his customary fatigues, Castro was greeted by 2,000. En route to Manhattan stood clusters of critics, but well-wishers surrounded his hotel shouting "Viva Fidel," and Castro greeted them from his balcony. He abandoned that hotel in a well-orchestrated huff and showily took up residence in Harlem. Arriving a day later, Khrushchev paid an ostentatious visit to him there.

Khrushchev was more combative in 1960, but so was America's greeting. The day before he debarked, demonstrators marched with placards calling him "murderer," "hangman," "monster" and "Red Hitler." Members of the International Longshoremen's Association picketed his arriving ship from tugboats. A typical sign said: "Dear K! Drop Dead You Bum." Outside the UN and the Soviet legation, anti-Soviet Ukrainians, anti-Albanian Greeks, anti-Greek Albanians, pro- and anti-Castro Cubans, and other angry pickets clashed. Some threw eggs at policemen and firecrackers at their horses; the police answered with billyclubs.[21] If these episodes fell short of the turmoil of the 1960s, neither did they conform to the remembered placidity of the 1950s.

In the 1960s, the Right continued to make its presence known. Conservatives at the University of California protested the Free Speech Movement. As foes of the Vietnam War generated protest demonstrations, others held rallies in support of it. Members of Young Americans for Freedom organized protests against radical takeovers on college campuses. Amid those roiling forces of radical change, these contrary efforts were difficult to see.

Patriotism and evangelical civicism did not vanish but were increasingly embattled. A sense of beleaguerment prompted the right to hunker down with the American flag. This identification was evident in the early 1960s, a response to misgivings about appeals for "peaceful coexistence" and a sense of cold war crisis reawakened by Khrushchev's statements under the "we will bury you" rubric, Kennedyesque rhetoric about the need to outcompete the Soviets, and flaring troublespots around the globe.

Patriotic practice took on renewed importance in this era of tensions. The Alabama VFW urged holding flag-raising ceremonies at every high-school football game. The Civitan Club of St. Louis offered flag decals for sale. A citizen of Miami, Florida, responded to Khrushchev's boast that Americans' grandchildren would live under Communism by orchestrating a "Rededication to God and Country Period" on October 14–15, 1961, with parades, a contest and a rally. A Florida legislator wrote Kennedy shortly after the Cuban missile crisis suggesting that having radio stations play patriotic music would help with the crucial task of building "the patriotic spirit of the American people." The VFW asked Kennedy to appoint a "President's Americanism Corps" to encourage patriotic observance.[22]

New Left dissidence would reinforce the bond to the flag; the negative symbolism of flagburning would redouble it. "We don't care if they hold up peace symbols," said a Jersey City ironworker. "But if they desecrate the American flag or hold up the Viet Cong flag, we're going to fight." Vice President Spiro Agnew unadmiringly termed 1969 anti-war demonstrations a "carnival in the streets." Many Americans came to feel a need to "show the flag," which came to stand for law and order. It broke out on police officers' uniforms, on trucks and over gas stations. Giving eighteen million decals to subscribers, *Reader's Digest* began a "boom" that led to some fifty million flag stickers festooning store windows, homes and cars. The Fraternal Order of Eagles, with more prescriptive intentions, gave out decals captioned: "The Flag—Love It or Leave."

There was much organized patriotism. In 1968 Freedoms Foundation and some eighty other organizations launched Operation Close Ranks, an annual effort to promote continuous flag-flying from Memorial Day through July Fourth "to rekindle fires of positive patriotism." In Paoli, Pennsylvania, "The Committee to Get Your Kids to Wave a Flag Before Some Misguided Protest Group Nabs Them" mounted a Memorial Day parade for children. The VFW spearheaded "Operation Speak Out," a program of patriotic rallies and other manifestations giving voice to the

"Silent Majority" as a "rebuttal" to the anti-war Moratorium demonstrations of October and November of 1969. During the same period "Honor America Week" called on Americans to fly their flags, leave a light on at home throughout the week and drive with their lights on.[23]

Many on the Left, including some liberals, conceded the Stars and Stripes to the Far Right. The author of the Broadway musical "1776" lacked zest to fly the flag given its current "identification with right-wing causes." However, other liberals sought to retain title to it. Congressman Jonathan Bingham assailed "the right-wing attempt to take over the flag as its personal property—it belongs to all of us." Even evangelist Billy Graham, hardly anathema to conservatives, lamented that "we have allowed the word 'patriotism' to get into the hands of some right-wingers." By wearing a flag, one could avoid being bashed with one. Running for the U.S. Senate, Adlai E. Stevenson III affixed a flag button in his lapel.[24]

The flag decals suggest that conservatives were less besieged than they feared. Their eventual, albeit conditional, triumph came with the American Revolutionary Bicentennial. Carping and dissent shadowed the preliminaries, which began in the 1960s. The inert American Revolutionary Bicentennial Commission appointed by Lyndon B. Johnson drew gibes; Nixon's replacement appointments inspired suspicions that he was politicizing the ARBC to turn the Bicentennial into a personal triumph. Broad criticism of ARBC bungling led to the agreement to begin anew in 1973 with an American Revolution Bicentennial Administration. Secretary of the Navy John W. Warner was named administrator, and ARBA performed better than its predecessor.

Criticism persisted. The Left assailed official plans as those of the Establishment, as they were. ARBA's membership and approach were too white, too male, too non-ethnic, too pre-sixties, and, as Watergate mysteries unfolded, too Nixonian. Others assailed the observance as a "Buy-Centennial" awash in tawdry products (such as red-white-and-blue toilet seats and Bicentennial coffins).[25] An effort to hold a World's Fair in Philadelphia foundered on a dearth of funds and a surplus of opposition from neighborhoods not wanting it in their backyards.

A New Left-inspired People's Bicentennial Commission asked veterans of the 60s to invent a bicentennial reflecting the truly revolutionary demands of ordinary people, not the "Tory" interests of Nixon's corporate allies. The PBC triggered a congressional inquiry; a pamphlet warned that "the Communists plan to subvert the Bicentennial Celebration!" At a reenactment of the Boston Tea Party, PBC adherents rowed a Nixon effigy about the harbor and heaved oil drums into the water to protest oil prices. When official reenactors cried, "Down with King George," radicals in the audience responded: "Down with King Richard." [26]

ARBA rolled with the punches. Like prior commemorations, it made a virtue of the absence of a single site. This one "would be everywhere." ARBA did not coopt the Left—it didn't have to—but it did absorb some 1960s themes, or at least language. In valediction Warner recalled that "untold millions were inspired to do 'their own thing' for their community, for their country" in the observance. A bicentennial poster enjoined: "Get Into America." ARBA gave its imprimatur to virtually any project, however tangential to the Revolution: thus, a reenactment of the 1777 Dominguez-Escalante expedition through the Southwest won ARBA recognition. In this sense authorities ratified the 60s' multiculturalist imperative. ARBA praised Americans' awareness that "they were a pluralistic society built on diverse racial and ethnic contributions, cultures and heritages. The celebration of this diversity" was central to the observance. [27]

The ARBA claimed victory. Americans had fond memories of the Tall Ships which sailed into New York, of the gigantic fireworks display in Washington, or of other celebrations or projects. Bicentennial officials had the tumult of the 1960s much in mind. Their *Final Report* declared: "We entered the Bicentennial year having survived some of the bitterest times of our brief history. We cried out for something to draw us together again." They thought they achieved that goal, enabling Americans to come together and to share fun and a good feeling about their country which qualified as patriotism. It was deemed a victory that the large crowds at the major Bicentennial events avoided violence. The climactic July 4th weekend came off with "hardly a murmur of dissent and no reported terrorism."

The bicentennial weekend did make many people feel better, although one headline calling July 4 a "day of picnics, pomp, pageantry and protest" hinted at the new equivocality about patriotic pageantry. There were, for instance, two counter-rallies in Philadelphia. The City of Brotherly Love had scheduled a parade, but its Mayor, Frank Rizzo, fearing violence, had requested 15,000 troops to keep the peace. The troops were neither dispatched nor, as it turned out, needed. [28]

What seemed, then, to work was a variety of products and productions: Tall Ships, an international naval review, the corporate-sponsored, twenty-car American Freedom Train, brilliant fireworks, and the local celebrations—whether the 1,776 frisbies tossed from atop a Wisconsin hill, the bicentennial parks created in numerous towns, the thousands of fire hydrants painted up with tricorned patriot faces, or the garish ash-trays and shot glasses. Americans survived the bicentennial—and even enjoyed it. But it would never be as easy again as it had been in the early Cold War to anneal the people into a patriotic mass. And even then, it had never been easy, nor had hard work guaranteed success.

Conclusion

When the Left reemerged in the 1960s, moderate-to-conservative programs to instill patriotism and citizenship faced a rising cynicism about the beneficence of American institutions and values. A mood of obstreperous dissent prompted by discontent with limited progress toward racial equality, by the increasingly unpopular war in Vietnam, and by other fracture lines in American society crowded out the civic lessons which once so weighted public discourse.

Yet the decline of cold-war patriotic and civic pageantry resulted from more than simply the advent of the oppositional politics of the 1960s. The political culture of the 1950s carried several elements of its own self-destruction. Their defenders hoped that the virtues of the American way of life might help subvert the Soviet system. In the end, so they did, but they also had an ironic subverting effect upon the American system too. Many of the blessings of American life tolled off by their celebrants gradually, cumulatively, made celebration harder to achieve. Even in the amenable 1950s, patriotic and civic activists encountered and complained about obstacles to their work. Their labors came to seem Sisyphian. Barely did they conclude a project—even a successful one—before they discovered a pressing need to renew their efforts.

Guardians of citizenship had an endless task. Even the indefatigable Mayor Fletcher Bowron had sensed the limits of his constituents' devotion to civic duty, citing the sparse turnout at 1946 Memorial Day ceremonies, when most Angelenos found other amusements. Likewise, a flack for Los Angeles County's 1948 centennial festivities bemoaned the "wide apathy" toward them.[1] Some in public life even learned to treat patriotism's ceremonial and iconic demands offhandedly. An aide to Vice President Nixon recalled a request which, "in a rapture of patriotism," sought soil from Mount Vernon, the Washington Monument, the Lincoln Memorial, the U.S. Capitol, and the White House in which to plant a tree on Washington's Birthday. He won "everlasting gratitude" by sending "varicolored dirt collected from a parking lot behind the New House Office Building."[2]

Yet committed patriots lived to wage a high-stakes, long-term struggle. In a 1960 advisory about Loyalty Day, an Alabama VFW leader took a long and Spenglerian view. Patriotism distinguished rising nations, but "when a nation reaches the zenieth [sic] of its power, the first sign of stagnation and decay is apathy." At that point "pledging alligence [sic] to the flag is consider [*sic*] rather a corny and useless ritual by the sophisticated and apothetic [*sic*] citizen." The commentator (silent on the role of spelling's decline in the collapse of nations) saw more evidence of decay in the exalting of "personal individual welfare above that of the citizens in general."[3]

Such elegies for lost civic virtue grew common in the late 1950s. In 1959 Navy League officials devised Project Alert, a program to instruct the citizens of Lubbock, Texas, in the nature of the Communist threat. The manual for Project Alert, which, it was hoped, would provide a model for other communities, opened with a quote that also set out the danger of decline. "Great nations Rise and Fall—the people go from Bondage to Spiritual Faith . . . to Great Courage . . . to Liberty . . . to Abundance . . . to Selfishness . . . to Complacency . . . to Apathy . . . to Dependency . . . back again into Bondage." The need for such a program arose from "a gradual dilution of national character and integrity and a lack of moral leadership on the part of both parents and youth."[4] Though more ornate, such jeremiads resembled those of Tom Clark and others on behalf of the Freedom Train.

The strivings of patriotic veterans and civic organizations to augment patriotic observance were not invariably appreciated. The Eisenhower White House received mail about the growing practice of playing the National Anthem at athletic and other public events; attitudes ranged from merely inquisitive to critical. Some targets of patriotic endeavor felt oppressed. A lad "representing the 7th and 8th grades" of his school protested that his teacher, who was "getting worse and worse every day," had warned students who had not mastered the National Anthem, "we won't pass. Please tell me what to do." [5]

The Kennedy administration, in its "ask not" mode, made broad demands of Americans. These often ran parallel to the American Heritage Foundation's calls for more engaged citizenship. The AHF, Ad Council and State Department cooperated to publish the pamphlet *Challenge to Americans*, which once again connected active citizenship with the Cold War context. During planning a White House aide suggested to the AHF that the booklet put "primary emphasis" on "patriotism"; "the threat of Communism on both the domestic and international scenes could then be given secondary attention as the negative aspect of this." The pamphlet told Americans "What You Can Do to Help." It urged the active citizenship the AHF had always preached and made a Kennedyesque call to "strive for excellence." Further, Americans should "observe patriotic holidays, display the flag, and stimulate conscious appreciation of the principles and ideals for which our Nation, our Flag and our Heritage stand." [6]

Many Americans responded positively to the Kennedy summons, but not necessarily in patriotic observance. JFK conceded and excused this circumstance in his 1963 Loyalty Day proclamation. "Understandably, our people avoid ostentatious displays of patriotic fervor." Even so, "in these trying times . . . it is entirely fitting and proper and in the national interest to set aside a special day each year on which to express our unceasing devotion and loyalty to this Nation." Though alarmed at the right-wing extremism then on the rise, the Kennedy administration endorsed efforts to build patriotic consciousness. [7]

Despite all the civic striving, to some observers Americans seemed no more attuned to citizenly duty than they had been ten or fifteen years earlier. Thus, a suburban New York elementary school principal discovered in horror that just three of his hundreds of pupils knew the National Anthem's words. A VFW activist warned that, despite a decade of effort, "only a very small percentage of Americans are aware of the existence of Loyalty Day." Was this slack patriotism "a sign of the decadence of which the Communists so often speak?" [8]

Patriots had so striven to fill up the American book of days that the struggle for time on the sacred calendar could be quite Darwinian. Crowding squeezed I Am An American Day out of spring into September where, combined with Constitution Day, it vanished. Loyalty Day, a patriotic newcomer itself once, became a victim of the upstart Law Day. Patriotism sometimes suffered from the American appetite for the new.

The American Heritage Foundation exemplified some of the challenges confronting civic and patriotic activism. It faced a recurrent difficulty: on one hand, it pressed its claim on contributors and allies that the need for its services was urgent and ongoing; on the other, it had to document that past efforts had succeeded. The AHF never quite squared this circle. Its leaders concluded that "indifference will always be with us. This is the price we pay for freedom." One staffer offered a philosophical gloss, in terms historians of the American Revolution might call "republican," that "Freedom is a fragile flower that requires our constant care." [9]

The AHF's efforts to stoke political participation showed that the good fight was unending. It launched its first get-out-the-vote drive in 1950. Expanding its efforts in the next election, it boasted that while 51.5 per cent of the eligibles had voted in 1948, 62.7 per cent did so in 1952. Yet in 1956 the figure fell to 60.4 per cent. To the AHF such statistics might suggest the movements of a roller-coaster, but more dispassionate observers perceived a snail. An official of the Rockefeller charitable interests responded skeptically to a fund solicitation by noting that while the total vote had risen 1 per cent from 1952 to 1956, population had grown 8 per cent. [10]

Starting in 1949 the AHF also campaigned to imbue American holidays with more meaning. Evidence of success (aside from the 175th anniversary of the Declaration, a special case) is sparse. The problem persisted. In 1961 the AHF was still seeking to use holidays as "springboards for rededication programs" to inculcate Americans with the need to understand their roles in the long-term global struggle with communism. [11]

The Kennedy years opened auspiciously for the AHF. JFK had been elected after and partly thanks to an extended debate over national purpose. His inaugural address implored Americans to ask what they could do for their country, not vice versa. Both Kennedy and Khrushchev spoke of an across-the-board competition between the two powers, thus stimulating renewed talk that Americans needed to "rededicate" themselves to winning what had come to be called the Cold War's "protracted conflict." The Ad Council, AHF and White House cooperated to this end. Their product, *Challenge to Americans*, called for "a greater spirit of rededication and sacrifice," and summoned "every individual . . . to make this hour of challenge our hour of greatness." Kennedy supplied a suitable foreword.[12]

The AHF also faced the challenge of improving upon triumph. After the Freedom Train, said an AHF officer, "we found ourselves the victims of success."[13] What was left to do? The AHF canvassed the notion of mounting another Freedom Train, a project whose timeliness never seemed to wane. The idea came up in 1957 but was put aside.

In the 1960s, the suggestion received renewed consideration. Media moguls endorsed the idea, for which they saw a manifest need. One publisher thought the Train would be especially useful if directed to campuses crawling with "troublemakers." Some saw obstacles. A respondent cautioned that the young of the 1960s were worldlier and less susceptible to "chauvinistic" or "D.A.R." messages. A magazine editor feared that a people attuned to television were more jaded than their 1947 counterparts. One man warned of the decay of railroad facilities. The Boston passenger station where the train stopped in 1947 might not, it was feared, exist by 1966. A second Freedom Train proved impracticable.[14]

The 1960s proved inhospitable to the AHF. The Left spoke often of "participatory democracy," but theirs was not the civic activism which the foundation preached. The absence of order and deference put the New Left beyond the pale. A proposed AHF radio-TV campaign for 1968 restated that group's orientation with the slogan "Participation in the political Process—Work—Contribute—Vote":

> Although vital measures are being undertaken in private and public sectors to get at the root causes of some of our complex problems, it is clear that we cannot resolve them quickly. But we can move speedily to rebuild faith in the means of resolving them, especially in the basic efficacy of our political process. . . . Violence is not the answer. Civil disobedience is not an answer. Dissent, protest—yes. But the country cannot long endure the inherent anarchy of either violence or civil disobedience.

With the Vietnam debate become a "diatribe," cities erupting, and "alienated youth" scorning "the political process," a crisis that compared to the Civil War impended. "If ever there was a time to restore faith in the system," the AHF sensed, "it is now."[15]

As problems mounted in the 1960s, the AHF elaborated a program based on its tested premises of encouraging a sense of political efficacy and opening up the system. Yet the AHF did not get enough contributions to carry on the program the times called for, and without a program in being, it would not get the contributions. That conundrum proved insoluble. The fundraising shortfall that curtailed its programs was aggravated by 1968's turmoil and "dramatic events." Its chairman suggested that "the political events of 1968 underscore the need" for the AHF's activities, but "they drastically affected our ability to finance our program." Faced with a deficit, AHF quietly closed its doors just after that stormy year.[16]

It was high irony that consumerism and leisure, features of capitalism so celebrated by Americanists, should undo their efforts. The Nixon-Khrushchev "kitchen debate" amid shiny appliances in a model home at the Moscow trade fair was a moment of drama in cold-war pageantry. "Frankly," confessed the United States Information Agency, "we do not really understand why the Soviets agreed to an exchange of exhibitions of this kind." The U.S. display seemed likely to "have a tremendous impact among a people who are still far short of consumer goods." [17]

Yet if American living standards tended to subvert the USSR, so too they may have unstrung the U.S. Given goods and freedom to enjoy them, Americans did so with such gusto that in alarming numbers they stayed away from the rites of citizenship. Patriots sometimes identified individualism as the culprit. A rationale for the Lubbock Plan for anti-communist civic education warned that "too many Americans, by pursuing selfish interests, sacrifice the common good." Similarly, a state VFW spokesman warned of "excessive individualism," which he termed "another name for selfish personal gains at the expense of many." [18]

Some civic activists sensed that the private drained the public sphere of ranks and energy. Though individualism and material plenty were touted virtues of the American system, they could be mixed blessings. Thomas D'Arcy Brophy of the American Heritage Foundation declared that "our material ab[u]ndance has to some extent sapped the spiritual strength of many of us." A Sons of the American Revolution officer deplored the trend "which has downgraded a number of our national holidays into 'bargain days'" with little patriotic content. "Washington's Birthday is a horrible example, and the Fourth of July is rapidly slipping into the same category." In his 1970 Loyalty Day summons, the national VFW loyalty director declared: "The main problem today is that too many fine Americans, leading the 'good life,' are not inclined to become involved. . . ." [19]

A changing culture also figured heavily in the decline of cold-war pageantry. Mid-fifties America was home to rock and roll—a sort of stand-in for an attendant mingling of racial and ethnic cultures—plus action painting, new styles of dress, greater informality, changing attitudes toward sexual morality, an explosion of gaudy visuality, and rising gratification through consumption. Boundaries were being crossed or disappearing. Technological advances like TV, portable radios, and LP and 45 rpm records hastened that culture's spread. In comparison, much of the cold-war pageantry was old-fashioned and earth-bound.[20]

There was the related matter of age cohorts. The notion of the "generation gap" gave concern to those who safeguarded the nation's moral and civic fiber. A political consultant informed the AHF that "not only today's students, but their teachers as well, are the products of a completely different environment than that of those who have been exposed to the depression, economic insecurity and involvement in a world war."[21]

Several types of cold-war pageantry proved to be time-sensitive. The day of the Freedom Train—as of railroads—had passed. Mosinee's "Day Under Communism" worked once, but only once. Commemorations tended to succeed to the extent they had tourist and entertainment value. Loyalty Day parades had to compete with the lure of new pursuits made possible by growing leisure and mobility. They also experienced a loss of centrality. Fifth Avenue residents griped at the interruption of their beauty sleep; too, more parochial parades like those for Puerto Rican or Israeli Independence Day came to compete with Loyalty Day. Asked why Loyalty Day parades had died out in New York City, one VFW leader cited these circumstances and stated with asperity, "there *is* no loyalty anymore."[22]

A waning sense of emergency also eroded public dutifulness. In the shadow of the crises of the Cold War's first eight or ten years, it was possible to turn out marchers and spectators. The pivotal foreign-policy decisions of 1947–48 and the events that triggered them; such further jolts as the Berlin Blockade, the fall of Nationalist China, the end of America's atom monopoly and the coincident spy scare; Joe McCarthy's run in the public eye; and the Korean War—all these produced a sense of alarm to be tapped by civic and patriotic activists.

By 1954, however, gloom receded. The nation resisted immediate involvement in the beckoning Indochina crisis, McCarthy was done in, and in a year the "Spirit of Geneva" would awaken a glimmer of hope that

Cold War hostilities might be made more manageable. With the American Communist movement so weakened that its public presence was negligible, a patriotic counterpresence proved harder to sustain. There would be new crises—over Berlin again, the Straits of Taiwan, Soviet advances in space, Laos, Vietnam and Cuba. They would not elicit updated equivalents of earlier innovations like Loyalty or Armed Forces Day. The response would more often be technocratic (the National Defense Education Act of 1958, the space program), bureaucratic, professional[23] or conventionally political. The streets were not empty, but different folk would soon be amarch.

Populist anti-communism seemed to retreat indoors. By the early 1960s, its face was seen less in Loyalty Day parades than in seminars like the Navy League-initiated "Operation Alert" in Lubbock and other cities; in "Strategy for Survival" conferences promoted by Army officers and such rightist groups as Freedom Forum, Harding College; in John Birch Society study groups; or in revivalist groups like the Christian Anti-Communist Crusade. These activities were more distant from the center of public life than the civic efforts of past years; their identification with "extremism" helped discredit anti-communism generally.[24]

Increasingly, Americans seemed to eschew the repetitive and merely rhetorical aspects of cold-war pageantry. One, two, or three times—if that—was enough for most. Entertainment and celebrities would draw them, as with some aspects of Armed Forces Day and some anniversary celebrations. They would come for the show and sometimes stay for the speeches.

Public-spirited, amateur, grassroots efforts to attract attention faced growing competition from profit-oriented, professional, and national counterparts. Television helped empty the public square. History, memory and patriotism could, of course, be packaged and commoditized. Disneyland, opened in 1955, trumped a lot of local entertainment.[25] The amateur in Mosinee yielded to the professional—journalists in Rushville, the Army in Lampasas, and filmmakers as in the 1951 movie *The Whip Hand* (in which, outside "Wissaukee," Reds improbably seized a compound where they carry on mind-altering medical procedures which will enable them to take over the country).

Pluralism, individualism, freedom of choice, abundance, leisure: these were cherished aspects of American life, but they complicated the task of those who sought to organize and publicize occasions on which these blessings were to be acknowledged. It remained a sometimes cruel paradox that what required defense through patriotic and civic activism also generated competition for the time and energies the guardians of coldwar civic virtue demanded of their fellow-Americans.

Notes

Introduction

1. *New York Times*, July 5, 1918, p. 1.

2. See Mark C. Carnes's excellent *Secret Ritual and Manhood in Victorian America* (New Haven, Conn., 1989).

3. American patriotism is a remarkably unstudied topic. For a valuable collection of recent work, see John Bodnar, ed., *Bonds of Affection: Americans Define Their Patriotism* (Princeton, 1996). For an earlier effort, see Merle Curti, *The Roots of American Loyalty* (New York, 1946).

4. *Chicago Sun-Times*, June 16, 1992, p. 26; *New York Times*, June 1, 1989, p. 18; *Chicago Tribune*, Oct. 16, 1988, sec. 3, p. 6.

5. The galaxy of literature on ceremony and display is expanding. It often relies on sociology and anthropology and has inspired fascinating work in the history of early modern Europe and the French Revolution. For an introduction to the interplay of elite and plebeian cultures in American history, see John Bodnar, *Remaking America: Public Memory, Commemoration, and Patriotism in the Twentieth Century* (Princeton, N.J., 1992). For pageantry in general, see David I. Kertzer, *Ritual, Politics, and Power* (New Haven, Conn., 1988).

6. David Glassberg, *American Historical Pageantry: The Uses of Tradition in the Early Twentieth Century* (Chapel Hill, N.C., 1990), p. 43. The following discussion depends shamelessly on Glassberg.

7. Ibid., pp. 63, 78, 80, 159ff., and passim.

8. Ibid., pp. 106–8, 237, 248, 257 and passim; brochure, John B. Rogers Producing Company, n.d. [1947], "A Complete Service...," State Historical Society, Project Files, Series 1658, Box 3, State Historical Society of Wisconsin (hereafter SHSW).

9. See Len Travers, *Celebrating the Fourth: Independence Day and the Rites of Nationalism in the Early Republic* (Amherst, Mass.: 1997).

10. *New York Times*, July 5, 1945, p. 4.

11. Jane M. Hatch, comp. and ed., *The American Book of Days*, 3d ed., (New York, 1978), p. 502; Wilbur Zelinsky, *Nation Into State: The Shifting Symbolic Foundations of American Nationalism* (Chapel Hill, N.C., 1988), pp. 70, 74.

12. For an important treatment of this phenomenon, see Stuart McConnell, "Reading the Flag: A Reconsideration of the Patriotic Cults of the 1890s," in Bodnar, ed., *Bonds of Affection*, pp. 102–19.

13. *Century* (July, 1910) quoted in Glassberg, *American Historical Pageantry*, p. 41.

14. Karal Ann Marling, *George Washington Slept Here: Colonial Revivals and American Culture, 1876–1986* (Cambridge, Mass., 1988), p. 19; Hatch, ed., *American Book of Days*, pp. 553–54. Flag Day has had a contested parentage. The strongest claims are those of Bernard J. Cigrand and Laura B. Prisk. Radio script, "Bernard J. Cigrand," WKOW, June 10, 1948, Box 8, Series 1762, State Historical Society Project Files, SHSW; *New York Times*, June 14, 1938, p. 21.

15. *New York Times*, June 14, 1918, p. 22.

16. Edward George Hartmann, *The Movement to Americanize the Immigrant* (New York, 1948 [1967]), pp. 110–11 and passim; Department of Labor, *Proceedings of the Naturalization Reception held at Philadelphia, Pa., May 10, 1915* (Washington, D.C., 1915), pp. 15–17.

17. Hartman, *Movement to Americanize*, pp. 112–21, 207–08, and passim; Bureau of Naturalization, Department of Labor, *The Work of the Public Schools with the Bureau of Naturalization* (Washington, D.C., 1917), p. 8, Immigration and Naturalization Service Library; "Address of President Wilson to the Citizenship Convention," July 13, 1916, ibid.; John Higham, *Strangers in the Land: Patterns of American Nativism, 1860–1925* (New Brunswick, N.J., 1955), p. 243.

18. *New York Times*, May 25, 1918, p. 7, June 5, 1918, p. 8, June 7, 1918, pp. 12, 13, June 26, 1918, p. 7, June 27, 1918, p. 9, June 28, 1918, p. 11, June 30, 1918, p. 14, July 1, 1918, p. 7, July 2, 1918, p. 13, July 3, 1918, p. 7, July 4, 1918, p. 1, July 5, 1918, pp. 1, 6; Hartman, *Movement to Americanize*, p. 208.

19. Hartman, *Movement to Americanize*, pp. 233–37, 265.

20. Hatch, ed., *American Book of Days*, pp. 850–51; Hartman, *Movement to Americanize*, p. 219; Michael Kammen, *A Machine That Would Go of Itself: The Constitution in American Culture* (New York, 1986), pp. 219–24, 278, and ch. 10. Also see Kammen's magisterial treatment of the development of the American culture of memory: *Mystic Chords of Memory: The Transformation of Tradition in American Culture* (New York, 1991).

21. William Pencak, *For God and Country: The American Legion, 1919–1941* (Boston, 1989), pp. 289–90; Bodnar, *Remaking America*, p. 41 and ch. 2 passim.

22. Barry D. Karl, *The Uneasy State: The United States from 1915 to 1945* (Chicago, 1983), p. 65 and passim. Yet as Michael Kammen notes, in the 1930s the federal government assumed a growing role in commemorating the nation's past. *Mystic Chords of Memory*, pp. 458–59, 465 and *passim*.

23. Karal Ann Marling, *George Washington Slept Here*, pp. 329, 332, and ch. 11 passim.

24. Marvin H. McIntyre to Laura B. Prisk, June 5, 1934, Official File (OF) 282A, Franklin D. Roosevelt Library (FDRL); Stephen Early to William F. Clarke, April 9, 1941, ibid.

25. On the persistence of power located in states and localities, see James T. Patterson, *The New Deal and the States: Federalism in Transition* (Princeton, 1969); Bruce Stave, *The New Deal and the Last Hurrah: Pittsburgh Machine Politics* (Pittsburgh, 1970).

Chapter 1

1. See, e.g., *New York Times*, Sept. 18, 1940, p. 15, Sept. 18, 1941, p. 12.

2. Ibid., June 6, 1938, p. 10, June 30, 1940, III, 7, July 5, 1940, p. 28.

3. Ibid., March 9, 1937, p. 25, March 10, 1937, p. 25, Sept. 20, 1939, p. 3, Oct. 3, 1941, p. 18, Oct. 18, 1941, p. 21, Feb. 2, 1942, p. 17, Jan. 27, 1943, p. 16; *Milwaukee Journal*, June 14, 1939, II, 1.

4. Paul L. Murphy, *The Constitution in Crisis Times, 1918–1969* (New York, 1972), pp. 197, 200; Samuel Walker, *In Defense of American Liberties: A History of the ACLU* (New York, 1990), p. 109; *New York Times*, Sept. 21, 1942, p. 16; David R. Manwaring, *Render Unto Caesar: The Flag Salute Controversy* (Chicago, 1962).

5. *New York Times*, Feb. 13, 1941, p. 10, Feb. 15, 1941, p. 32, Feb. 18, 1941, p. 12, March 18, 1941, p. 15, July 13, 1941, p. 22.

6. New York was especially needful; Moss termed it "the greatest hot-bed of foreign isms in the United States." Ibid., June 10, 1938, p. 16, June 12, 1938, II, 4, June 13, 1938, p. 7, June 14, 1938, pp. 18, 21, June 15, 1938, pp. 16, 25, May 15, 1941, p. 15.

7. William Pencak, *For God & Country: The American Legion, 1919–1941* (Boston, 1989), pp. 288–90.

8. William F. Russell, "Course of Study for Members of the Service," (Jan. 1, 1943), p. 3, INS Historical Reference Library; Victor P. Morey, "Present Objectives of Citizenship Education," INS, *Monthly Review*, III (Dec., 1945): 234–37. Cf. Richard Weiss, "Ethnicity and Reform: Minorities and the Ambience of the Depression Years," *Journal of American History* 66 (Dec., 1979): 566–85.

9. Carl B. Hyatt, *Gateway to Citizenship*, rev. ed. (Washington, D.C., 1948), pp. 40–41, 43; Memo, "I Am An American Day," n.d., Box 101, Records of the National Conference on Citizenship, National Archives, Suitland, Md. Cited hereafter as NCC Records.

10. *Congressional Record*, 86 (May 7, 1940), A2754; Edward Arnold to Edwin M. Watson, March 30, 1942, OF 282, FDRL; Statement by Benjamin Edwards Neal, May 15, 1945, OF 320-A, Harry S. Truman Library (HSTL); Neal to John Anson Ford, Feb. 25, 1939; "'I Am An American' Panegyric," n.d. [1939], both Box 71, Ford MSS, Henry E. Huntington Library.

11. Richard W. Hawkins to Truman, May 1, 1952, OF 320-A, HSTL; Mrs. Seghers to Dwight D. Eisenhower, May 26, 1953, OF 102-F-l, Eisenhower Library (DDEL); *New York Times*, May 18, 1947, p. 53.

12. "I Am An American Day: 1943," INS, *Monthly Review*, 1 (July, 1943): 3; invitation, "The Thirty-Sixth Annual 'I Am An American Day' Celebration" [1961], INS Library.

13. Clippings, *Milwaukee Journal*, n.d. [Oct. 4, 1931]; *Milwaukee Sentinel*, Sept. 25, 1955, Aug 19, 1956; *Milwaukee Evening Post*, Oct. 2, 1939, all in Elly Vajda Seng scrapbook (Washington, D.C.).

14. Henry C. Gardiner, "The Origin of 'I Am An American' Day," n.d., Box 99, NCC Records.

15. *Milwaukee Journal*, May 9, 1939, p. 13, May 21, 1939, p. 6; *Congressional Record*, 86 (May 15, 1940), 2958–59; *New York Times*, Jan. 8, 1939, II, 10, May 15, 1939, p. 16; Robert U. Brown, "Shop Talk at Thirty," *Editor and Publisher* (June 12, 1948), 72.

16. *New York Times*, May 30, 1939, p. 15, May 31, 1939, p. 8, June 2, 1939, p. 11, June 3, 1939, p. 7; *Washington Post*, June 2, 1939, p. 13; INS, Department of Labor, *Report of New Citizens Day Ceremonies Held in 1939* (Washington, D.C., 1940), pp. 3, 5, 11, Box 1, INS Library; Burritt C. Harrington, *Community Recognition of Citizenship: A Handbook for "I Am An American Day" Committees* (Washington, D.C.,1944), p. 2, ibid.

17. Harrington, *Community Recognition*, p. 3; *Cong. Record*, 86, pp. 539, 3010, 4275–77, 4281–82, 4675, 4693, 5115–16; "I Am An

American Day: 1943," INS *Monthly Review* 1 (July, 1943): 2.

18. William Gellermann, *Martin Dies* (New York, 1944), p. 52.

19. For several years the term "New Citizens Day" was also used. *Washington Post*, May 18, 1940, p. 8, May 19, 1940, p. 3, May 20, 1940, p. 6; *New York Times*, May 20, 1940, p. 6, April 16, 1941, p. 12, May 18, 1945, p. 16; INS, *Report of New Citizens Day Ceremonies Held in 1940* (Washington, D.C., 1941), pp. 9–10.

20. *New York Times*, April 27, 1941, p. 27, May 4, 1941, p. 20, May 5, 1941, p. 12, May 6, 1941, p. 22, May 14, 1941, p. 14, May 16, 1941, p. 13, May 19, 1941, pp. 1, 3, 4.

21. Ibid., April 9, 1942, p. 16, May 18, 1942, pp. 1, 8.

22. Ibid., May 16, 1943, p. 44, May 17, 1943, pp. 1, 3, May 22, 1944, p. 1, May 21, 1945, pp. 1, 11.

23. INS (with NEA), *Program Aids for Citizenship Recognition Ceremonies*, rev. ed., (Washington, D.C., n.d. [1945]), 3; "I Am An American Day: 1943," INS *Monthly Review*, 1 (July, 1943): 2–5; Ugo Carusi, "I Am An American Day, 1945," ibid., II (April, 1945): 123; Burritt C. Harrington, "The Observance of Citizenship Day, 1945," ibid., II (Aug., 1945): 184–85; Harrington, *Community Recognition of Citizenship*, 13; memorandum, T. B. Shoemaker to Tom C. Clark, Feb. 13, 1946, OF 320-A, HSTL.

24. *New York Times*, May 19, 1946, IV, 8.

25. The police penchant for inflating attendance figures makes all estimates suspect. *New York Times*, May 20, 1946, p. 4, June 9, 1946, VI, 46, May 12, 1947, p. 27, May 19, 1947, p. 1, May 17, 1948, p. 11, May 16, 1949, p. 3, May 22, 1950, p. 10, May 21, 1951, p. 3.

26. *New York Times*, May 20, 1946, p. 4, April 20, 1947, p. 4, May 19, 1947, p. 23; *Chicago Tribune*, May 17, 1948, p. 19.

27. Ugo Carusi, "Honoring American Citizenship," INS *Monthly Review*, III (April, 1946): 287; Carl B. Hyatt to J. Albert Woll, Nov. 25, 1964, Box 98, NCC Records; NEA, *Report of the First National Conference on Citizenship*, n.d. [1946], p. 8; Watson B. Miller, "Foreign-Born Citizen's Day at the Fifth National Conference on Citizenship," INS *Monthly Review*, 7 (April, 1950): 128.

28. NEA, *Report of the First National Conference on Citizenship* [1946], pp. 27, 46–47; *New York Times*, May 18, 1946, p. 11.

29. See Athan Theoharis, *Spying on Americans: Political Surveillance from Hoover to the Huston Plan* (Philadelphia, 1978), pp. 45–46, 76, 199, 206; Peter L. Steinberg, *The Great "Red Menace": United States Prosecution of American Communists, 1947–1952* (Westport, Conn., 1984); James Gilbert, *A Cycle of Outrage: America's Reaction to the Juvenile Delinquent in the 1950s* (New York, 1986), p. 37 and passim.

30. Truman to John E. Swift, Aug. 4, 1949, President's Personal File (PPF) 211; *I & N Reporter*, 1 (Oct., 1952): 18.

31. Theoharis, *Spying on Americans*, pp. 133–34; Peter H. Irons, "American Business and the Origins of McCarthyism: The Cold War Crusade of the United States Chamber of Commerce," in Robert Griffith and Theoharis, eds., *The Specter: Original Essays on the Cold War and the Origins of McCarthyism* (New York, 1974); House Un-American Activities Committee, 80th Cong., 1st Sess., *Hearings Regarding the Communist Infiltration of the Motion Picture Industry* (1947), p. 453; Seattle *Post-Intelligencer*, Aug. 8, 1948, p. 1.

32. Francis P. Matthews speech, May 1, 1951, Box 49, Matthews Papers, HSTL; NEA, *Report of the First National Conference on Citizenship* (NEA, [1946]), p. 101; Paul H. Griffith to Truman, July 11, 1947, PPF 350, HSTL; Dies to Charles A. Schrade, April 30, 1954, Box 136, Dies MSS, Sam Houston Regional Library & Research Center, Liberty, Tex.

33. Howard Pew and F. C. Crawford, "What Is NAM's 1947 Public Relations Program?" Box 4, Paul H. Griffith Papers, HSTL.

34. Carl B. Hyatt, draft, "National Conference on Citizenship," 1958, Box 23, NCC Records; *Cong. Record*, 95 (Feb. 14, 1949), 1192; Earle T. Hawkins, "The Origin and Progress of the National Conferences on Citizenship," *Citizenship USA*, 1 (Oct., 1948): 4, in Box 102, NCC Records.

35. See Elizabeth A. Fones-Wolf, *Selling Free Enterprise: The Business Assault on Labor and Liberalism, 1945–1960* (Urbana, Ill., 1994).

36. Chester La Roche to Harry S. Truman, July 11, 1947, PPF 2151, HSTL; James W. Young speech, "What Advertising Learned from the War," Dec. 11, 1945, Folder 3–5, Thomas D'Arcy Brophy MSS, SHSW; Mark Leff, "The Politics of Sacrifice on the American Home Front in World War II," *Journal of American History*, 77 (March, 1991): 1307–12; Robert Griffith, "The Selling of America: The Advertising Council and American Politics, 1942–1960," *Business History Review*, 57 (Autumn, 1983): 388–412.

37. "Autobiography—Kenneth Dale Wells," 1983, pp. 71–72, 82–83, and passim, Folder 4, Box 1, Series I, Kenneth D. Wells Collection, Brigham Young University; Wells biography, "1949(?)" Folder 3, ibid.; "Four Years Work for Freedom, 1949–1953" (Aug. 31, 1953), p. 9, Folder 1, Box 1, Series 3, ibid.; untitled ms., n.d. [1953?], ibid.

38. "The Objective of Freedoms Foundation of Valley Forge," n.d. [1950], OF 320, HSTL; Freedoms Foundation nomination form, "General Awards Program for 1950," [1950], ibid.

39. Winthrop W. Aldrich, "Statement of Principles, The American Heritage Foundation," in "The American Heritage Program for Your

Community," n.d. [1947], Pamphlet File (OF 320), HSTL.

40. Bert Cochran quoted in Fones-Wolf, *Selling Free Enterprise*, p. 285.

41. On this topic, see T. J. Jackson Lears, "The Concept of Cultural Hegemony: Problems and Possibilities," *American Historical Review*. 90 (June, 1985): 567–93. One might so define "corporate America" as to leave nothing "outside" it, but that then makes it a less than useful historical construct.

42. J. Howard Pew and F. C. Crawford, "What is NAM's 1947 Public Relations Program?" n.d., Box 4, Paul H. Griffith Papers, HSTL; U.S. Chamber of Commerce, "A Program for Community Anti-Communist Action," 1948, Box 13, Francis P. Matthews Papers, HSTL.

43. Harold M. Dudley to Col. Paul Griffith, Dec. 15, 1953, and Jan. 23, 1954; "America the Beautiful," n.d. [ca. Dec. 15, 1953], all in Box 1, Griffith Papers.

44. Such motives had, of course, underlain Progressive-era civic pageantry. See Glassberg, *American Historical Pageantry*; and Paul Boyer, *Urban Masses and Moral Order in America, 1820–1920* (Cambridge, Mass., 1978), pp. 256–60.

45. Bowron to William H. McReynolds, Jan. 26, 1945, Box 1, Bowron Collection, Huntington Library; Bowron to DeWitt Wallace, Sept. 13, 1946, Box 2, ibid. Cf. Arthur C. Verge, "The Impact of the Second World War on Los Angeles," *Pacific Historical Review* 63 (Aug., 1994): 289–314.

46. Bowron to Stettinius, March 6, 1945, Box 1; Bowron to Los Angeles City Council, April 18, 1945, ibid.; Souvenir Program, April 23, 1945, Box 34; clipping, *Los Angeles Times*, April 24, 1945, Box 6, all in Bowron Coll.

47. *New York Times*, June 10, 1945, p. 20; *Los Angeles Times*, Oct. 17, 1945, p. 2.

48. Bowron to Marshall F. McComb, Sept. 13, 1945, Box 2; Bowron remarks, Oct. 27, 1945, Box 34, both in Bowron Coll.; *New York Times*, Oct. 28, 1945, p. 30; *Los Angeles Times*, Oct. 25, 1945, p. 2, Oct. 27, 1945, II, 1 & 8, Oct. 28, 1945, p. 1.

49. Bowron to J. K. Wallace, Sept. 7, 1946; Fact sheets, "Los Angeles Centennial Week—August 7–13, 1946," n.d., both Box 2, Bowron Coll.; *Los Angeles Times*, Aug. 9, 1946, p. 1, Aug. 11, 1946, II, 1, Aug. 14, 1946, II, 1; *New York Times*, Sept. 5, 1947, p. 42.

50. Speech, Sept 9, 1945; remarks, Aug. 26, 1945, both in Box 34, Bowron Coll. The group's charges of Ku Klux Klan activity in LA led Bowron to suspect the "Communist-inspired" MFD wanted to stir up minorities and "distrust of established government." Bowron to Foreman, Los Angeles County Grand Jury; Bowron to Dewitt Wallace,

both Sept. 13, 1946, Box 2, ibid.

51. "Remarks by Mayor Fletcher Bowron, Los Angeles Centennial Celebration," Aug. 13, 1946, Box 35; "Remarks by Mayor Fletcher Bowron at Americanization Rally," Nov. 2, 1946, ibid.; clipping, *Los Angeles Times*, Nov. 3, 1946, Box 82, all in Bowron Coll.

52. Bowron to William Randolph Hearst, May 19, 1947, Box 2, ibid.

53. Interview with Clinton W. Kanaga, Jr., April 12, 1989; memorandum, "Kansas City Junior Chamber of Commerce Democracy Beats Communism Program," n.d., Kanaga Files, Kansas City, Mo. Ronald Wayne Johnson, "The Communist Issue in Missouri: 1946–1956," (dissertation, University of Missouri, 1973), pp. 60–62, alerted me to this episode.

54. Clipping, "Today's Moderns: An Ex-Marine Leads Kansas City Fight on Reds," *New York Herald-Tribune*, Oct. 25, 1948, Kanaga Files; Speaker's Manual, "Democracy Beats Communism!" Kansas City Junior Chamber of Commerce [1948], Box 18, Phil M. Donnelly MSS, University of Missouri—Western Historical Manuscript Collection, State Historical Society of Missouri, Columbia, Mo.; Kanaga interview.

55. Clipping, "Today's Moderns"; *Swing* (Nov., 1948), 7; Cliff C. Jones, Jr., to "Dear Jaycee," n.d. [Sept., 1948], all in Kanaga Files.

56. Clipping, "Communism's Flaws to Be Examined Here This Month," *Kansas City Star*, n.d.; "Democracy Beats Communism," suggested speech for high schools, n.d. [1948], both ibid.

57. Three clippings, n.d., ibid.; Kanaga interview; *Cong. Record*, 96 (81st Cong., 2d Sess.), A1618.

58. A Texas Congressman credited Shepperd with the idea, but two Missouri solons answered for Kansas City. Club President's Round Table, "Notice of Meeting on Monday, August 2, 1948"; clipping, *Kansas City Star*, June 8, 1948, both in Kanaga Files; *Cong. Record*, 95 (Oct. 11, 1949), A6209–11; ibid., 96 (March 3, 1950), A1618; (March 10, 1950), 3169; Kanaga interview.

59. It resembled the Rededication Weeks connected with the 1947–48 Freedom Train. See Ch. 2.

60. Sheppard had political ambitions. As Jaycee president, he had made a 24,000-mile "Flight for Freedom" to "mobilize" young men to better appreciate "democracy and the 'fifth freedom'—the free enterprise system." In the 1950s, as state Attorney General, he augmented Texas's red scare. Clipping, *Washington Evening Star*, Nov. 2, 1947, President's Personal File (PPF) 2337, HSTL; *Cong. Record*, 95 (Oct. 11, 1949), A6209–10; Don E. Carleton, *Red Scare! Right-wing Hysteria, Fifties Fanaticism and Their Legacy in Texas* (Austin, Tex., 1985), pp. 258–61.

61. Claire O'Neil to Truman, March 11, 1952, PPF 87, HSTL; Angelo

Menendez to Truman, Jan. 25, March 2, 1949, Official File (OF) 200, HSTL; memo, n.d., "Americanism-Day"; clipping, *Uniontown Morning Herald*, May 2, 1955, both Box 2, Paul H. Griffith Papers, HSTL.

62. "The Weirton Plan" was based on the Credo of Freedoms Foundation. Weirton Chamber of Commerce, "How to Conduct an Americanism Week," n.d. [1951], Box 16, Records of the American Heritage Foundation, R.G. 200, National Archives.

63. Dr. James D. Weaver to "Fellow Erieites," April 9, 1951; "Loyalty Day Program," May 1, 1951, both in Box 49, Francis P. Matthews Papers, HSTL. On Loyalty Day, see Ch. 3.

64. *Milwaukee Journal*, Dec. 3, 1951, p. 3, Dec. 9, 1951, p. 6, Dec. 11, 1951, pp. 5, 11, Dec. 12, 1951, p. 16, Dec. 14, 1951, II, 1. Organizers sought help from the American Heritage Foundation. Robert W. Hansen to AHF, Oct. 10, 1951, Box 14, AHF Records.

65. H. R. Jesson to Harry S. Truman, April 29, 1952; Program, "Greater Muskegon Freedom Week, May 10–16, 1952," both in OF 1125, HSTL; summary, Freedoms Foundation at Valley Forge 1952 Awards Program, Feb. 22, 1953, Folder 4, Box 7, Series 3, Wells Coll.

66. H. Epstein to Truman, Feb. 4, 1948, OF 186, HSTL; *New York Times*, Feb. 29, 1949, p. 15; *Honolulu Advertiser*, May 20, 1950, p. 3. Cf. Thomas Michael Holmes, "The Specter of Communism in Hawaii, 1947–1953," (dissertation, University of Hawaii, 1975), p. 239.

67. *American Legion Magazine* (July, 1950): 29; see annual lists of Freedoms Foundation awards in boxes 7–8, Series 3, Wells Coll.

Chapter 2

1. "Address by Honorable Tom C. Clark At Bill of Rights Luncheon," Dec. 10, 1946, Official File (OF) 320-C, HSTL; *New York Times*, Dec. 11, 1946, p. 2; clipping, *Waterbury Republican*, Dec. 15, 1946, Box 5, Freedom Train, Educational Programs Division, Records of the National Archives and Records Service (Record Group 64). Cited herafter as FT Records.

2. Clark speech, Federal Bar Association, Nov. 20, 1945, Box 1, Clark Papers, University of Texas Law Library (courtesy of Debra Beil); *New York Times*, Sept. 17, 1947, p. 23.

3. Coblenz, "The Freedom Train and the Story of Its Origin: Our Civil Liberties on Wheels," *Manuscripts*, 10 (Winter, 1957): 31–34, 59; James Gregory Bradsher, "Taking America's Heritage to the People: The Freedom Train Story," *Prologue*, 17 (Winter, 1985): 230; "Prospectus for A Public Tour of a train containing original documents pertaining to American Government as contrasted to original Nazi documents," n.d. [1946], Box 199, American Heritage Foundation Papers, RG

200, NARA. (Cited hereafter as AHF Papers.)

4. Truman to Clark, n.d. [April 20, 1946], OF 320-C, HSTL; memorandum, "Bill" [Hassett] to [Charles G.] Ross, Jan. 23, 1947, ibid; memorandum, Coblenz to Colonel McInerny, Sept. 9, 1946, Box 37, Clark Papers, HSTL; EEH [Elizabeth E. Hamer], memorandum, Sept. 17, 1946; Clark to Solon J. Buck, Dec. 24, 1946, both in Box 2, FT Records.

5. "Timetable of Events Leading to Freedom Train Visit in Seattle," April 13, 1948, Box 198, AHF Papers; "Background for the Seattle Story," n.d. [1948], ibid.; *New York Times*, Nov. 8, 1945, p. 36; Clark speech, Bill of Rights Luncheon, Dec. 10, 1946, OF 320-C, HSTL; press release, n.d. [Oct. 29, 1945], Box 6, Records of Savings Bond Division (War Finance Division), Motion Pictures and Special Events Section, Treasury Department, Record Group 56, NARA; J. Edward Shugrue, press release, Nov. 9, 1945, ibid.

6. The Library of Congress had even pondered a tour of documents by armored car. Thad Page to A. S. Arnold, April 12, 1950, Box 1, FT Records; Hugh Russell Fraser, "America's Heritage on Wheels," *Pathfinder* 54 (Sept. 24, 1947): 20; testimony of Verner W. Clapp in *Freedom Train*, Hearings on H.J.Res 84, House Committee on Post Office and Civil Service (81st Cong., lst Sess.), p. 25.

7. Department of Justice, Press Release, Dec. 11, 1946, OF 320-C, HSTL; Clark speech, Bill of Rights Luncheon, Dec. 10, 1946, ibid. Louis Novins claimed the meeting was planned (and Clark's remarks written) in Barney Balaban's office. Novins to Brophy, July 19, 1948, Box 212, AHF Records.

8. "Background for the Seattle Story," n.d. [1948], Box 198, AHF Records; "Addresses Delivered at the White House Conference," May 22, 1947, ibid.

9. Novins to Thomas D'Arcy Brophy, July 19, 1948, Box 212, ibid.

10. *New York Times*, May 16, 1947, p. 11; "Addresses Delivered at the White House Conference," May 22, 1947, Box 198, AHF Papers.

11. Memoranda, Coblenz to Attorney General, May 26 and June 19, 1947, Box 37, Clark Papers, HSTL; AHF, "Information for Fraternal, Veteran's and Service Organizations on The American Heritage Program and the Freedom Train," n.d., Box 3, FT Records.

12. Stuart J. Little, "The Freedom Train: Citizenship and Postwar Political Culture, 1946–1949," *American Studies*, 34 (Spring 1993), 38, 46, 48.

13. "TCC" [Clark] to "Matt" [Connelly], April 16, [1946], OF 320-C, HSTL; Clark to Truman, June 2, 1947, Box 37, Clark Papers, HSTL.

14. "Prospectus for A Public Tour of a train . . . ," [1946], Box 198,

AHF Papers; annotation by Elizabeth E. Hamer on "Address by Honorable Tom C. Clark ... At Bill of Rights Luncheon," Dec. 10, 1946, Box 2, FT Records.

15. Memorandum, "EEH" [Hamer] to SJB [Solon J. Buck], Jan. 29, 1947; memorandum, Hamer to Bess Glenn, Aug. 27, 1946, both in Box 2, FT Records.

16. Ralph W. Gwinn to Tom C. Clark, Feb. 5, 1947; Clark to Gwinn, Feb. 7, 1947, both in Box 37, Clark Papers, HSTL.

17. Clipping, *New York World-Telegram*, Sept. 12, 1947 (Lyle C. Wilson), Box 11, AHF Records; Louis Wirth to Louis A. Novins, Dec. 4, 1947; Novins to Wirth, Dec. 16, 1947, both Box 198, ibid.

18. Richard Condon, press release, "Freedom Train Documents Expanded to 128," Sept. 16, 1947, Box 200, AHF Records; AHF, "Information for Fraternal, Veteran's and Service Organizations on The American Heritage Program and the Freedom Train," n.d. [1947], Box 3, FT Records.

19. Truman did visit the Train twice, once in Washington in November 1947 and while campaigning in September 1948. In both cases his rhetoric was general and nonpartisan. Governor Thomas E. Dewey, the GOP candidate, offered equally ecumenical remarks when the train visited Albany. *New York Times*, Nov. 12, 1947, p. 34, Nov. 29, 1947, p. 15, Sept. 18, 1948, p. 9.

20. Hoffman to Clark, May 29, 1947; Clark, "Statement . . . concerning the Freedom Train," June 18, 1947, both in Box 37, Clark Papers, HSTL; clippings, *Washington Daily News*, May 28, 1947, Box 2, FT Records; *Chicago Tribune*, May 27, 1947; Ruth Montgomery, "'Freedom Train' to Tour U.S. in Fight on Crime," n.d. [June 18, 1947]; *Dallas News*, June 19, 1947, all Box 5, ibid.

21. *Chicago Tribune*, May 22, 1947, p. 12, May 26, 1947, p. 22. The *Trib* had reportedly said it would "'go all the way'" to promote the train if it came to Chicago for the *Tribune*'s centennial and halted next to the Tribune Tower. Unsigned memo, "Status of Attorney General's Project," Dec. 30, 1946, Box 212, AHF Records.

22. *New York Times*, June 26, 1947, p. 27 clipping, *New York Sun*, Sept 29, 1947, Box 11, AHF Records; clipping, *New York Daily News*, May 15, 1947, Folder 497, Box 50, Cultural Interests Series, Office of the Messrs. Rockefeller, Record Group 2, Rockefeller Family Archives, Rockefeller Archive Center.

23. National Blue Star Mothers of America to Hoover, Sept. 13, 1947, Freedom Train folder #2, Box 37, Clark Papers, HSTL; Blue Star Mothers, handbill, "Americans, Attention!" n.d., Box 38, ibid.

24. Clipping, *People's Voice*, Sept. 20, 1947, Box 5, FT Records. New

Deal luminaries Thurman Arnold, Abe Fortas and Paul A. Porter found incongruous the government's sponsoring a Freedom Train even as it dismissed State Department employees on vague disloyalty charges. *New York Times*, Nov. 3, 1947, p. 5.

25. *New York Times*, Sept. 14, 1947, p. 18, Sept. 26, 1947, p. 25; memoranda, Hoover to Clark, Sept. 25 and 26, 1947, Box 37, Clark Papers, HSTL; clipping, *New York Daily News*, Sept. 26, 1947, Box 11, AHF Records.

26. Clipping, *Brooklyn Eagle*, Sept. 11, 1947, Box 11, AHF Records. *Pravda* called the train "hypocrisy on wheels." *New York Times*, Dec. 5, 1947, p. 9.

27. Louis A. Novins to Leo Burnett, July 28, 1947; Burnett to Novins, July 30, 1947, both in Box 213, AHF Records.

28. *Good Citizen*, pp. 51, 58; radio spots in Box 10, AHF Records. On the tensions pulling at American domesticity during the Cold War, see Elaine Tyler May, *Homeward Bound: American Families in the Cold War Era* (New York, 1988).

29. *New York Times*, Sept. 14, 1947, p. 18, Nov. 10, 1947, p. 5, Nov. 28, 1947, p. 22. Richard M. Freeland has posited an "intimate" link between the Freedom Train and "the campaign for Cold War foreign policy." *The Truman Doctrine and the Origins of McCarthyism: Foreign Policy, Domestic Politics, and Internal Security, 1946–1948* (New York, 1972), p. 233.

30. *New York Times*, Sept. 17, 1947, p. 23.

31. Clipping, *Chicago Defender*, Aug. 23, 1947, Box 11; Novins to Arthur M. Johnson, Feb. 29, 1968, Box 33; "Addresses Delivered at the White House Conference," May 22, 1947, Box 198; Edward Stanley to Novins, July 24, 1947, Box 208, all in AHF Records.

32. Hughes, "Freedom Train," *New Republic*, 117 (Sept. 15, 1947): 27; Robeson column, *People's Voice*, Sept. 27, 1947, clipping, in Freedom Train folder #3, Box 38, Clark Papers, HSTL.

33. Clipping, *New York Sun*, Sept. 28, 1947, Box 11; home office communication, dated Oct. 3, 1947, Box 219; minutes, Board of Trustees, Oct. 6, 1947, Box 214; Brophy, memorandum to Aldrich, Nov. 17, 1947, Box 219; Press release, Dec. 24, 1947, Box 220, all in AHF Records; *New York Times*, Dec. 25, 1947, p. 8.

34. Novins, "Memorandum on Memphis Incident," Nov. 18, 1947, Box 200, AHF Records; AHF press release, n.d. [Dec., 1947], ibid.; clipping, *New Orleans Times-Picayune*, Dec. 28, 1947, Box 5, FT Records; *Washington Post*, Jan. 16, 1949, p. 4B; clipping, *Roanoke World-News*, Nov. 20, 1947, Thad Page Records, NARA; Eric Friedheim, Progress Report, week ending Nov. 22, 1947, Box 207, AHF Records.

35. Memorandum, William Coblenz to Attorney General, May 13, 1948, Freedom Train folder #4, Box 38, Clark Papers. *Chicago Tribune,* July 1, 1948, III, 9, July 2, 1948, p. 6, July 4, 1948, p. 8, July 6, 1948, p. 1, July 7, 1948, p. 8.

36. Brendan Byrne to Howard Mayer, June 5, 1959, Box 202, AHF Records; Draft report, n.d. [1949?], Box 199, ibid.; *Washington Post,* Dec. 19, 1948, p. 6B; Herman F. Schaden, "The Freedom Train," *Washington Evening Star,* Nov. 3, 1947, Box 4, FT Records; excerpt, letter of Courtenay Monsen, Feb. 17, 1948, Freedom Train Folder, Box 1, ibid.

37. Address by Brophy, May 22, 1947, Box 7, AHF Records; *The First Two Years,* pp 12–13, Box 12, ibid.

38. Clipping, *Kansas City Times,* June 1, 1948, Thad Page Records; *Washington Post,* Jan. 21, 1949, ibid. On the railroad's romantic allure, see John R. Stilgoe, *Metropolitan Corridor: Railroads and the American Scene* (New Haven, Conn., 1983).

39. Irving Berlin, "Freedom Train," c. 1947, Box 200, AHF Records; Press release, "Freedom Train," n.d., Box 4, FT Records; "Statement by Fox Case 5-17-49 . . . ," Planning and Control Cases (NARA), RG 64; Gilbert Bailey, "Why They Throng to the Freedom Train," *New York Times Magazine* (Jan. 25, 1948), p. 52; *New York Times,* Jan. 25, 1948, p. 52; Murrow, "Statement re Freedom Train—Columbia Broadcasting System," April 7, 1949, Page Records, NARA: Herman S. Hettinger, "The American Heritage Program (Evaluation and Recommendations)," Oct. 16, 1948, Box 210, AHF Records.

40. *Washington Post,* Dec. 19, 1948, p. 6B; clipping, *Rocky Mountain News,* Sept. 2, 1947, p. 33, in Box 4, FT Records; Clark to Ramsey Clark, March 31, 1948, Box 38, Clark Papers.

41. *The First Two Years,* p. 91; Brophy, *Highlights of the First Year;* Brophy to Irving Berlin, Aug. 26, 1948, Box 210, AHF Records; *Pathfinder* 54 (Sept. 24, 1947): 21.

42. Brophy, *The Freedom Train: Highlights of the First Year of the American Heritage Foundation,* Nov. 4, 1948, Box 19, Scott W. Lucas MSS, Illinois State Historical Library; Schaden, "The Freedom Train," *Washington Evening Star,* Nov 3, 1947, clipping, Box 4, FT Records; *New York Times,* Sept. 23, 1947, p. 20, Sept. 27, 1947, p. 17, Dec. 22, 1948, p. 28; *Los Angeles Times,* Feb. 25, 1948, p. 2.

43. Clipping, *New York Post,* Sept. 25, 1947, Box 5, FT Records; *Washington Post,* Dec. 19, 1948, p. 6B, Jan. 21, 1949, p. 1C; *New York Times,* Sept. 26, 1947, p. 25.

44. New York State Library, *Official Document Book New York State Freedom Train* (Albany, N.Y., 1950), p. 65 and passim; Memorandum, Arthur Wild to John Murphy, Aug. 19, 1948, Box 198, AHF Records;

clipping, *Washington Daily News*, Feb. 6, 1948, Box 5, FT Records.

45. Brophy, *Highlights of the First Year*; Brophy, "Memorandum Report" to AHF Trustees, Jan. 19, 1948, Folder 497, Box 50, Cultural Interests Series, Office of the Messrs. Rockefeller, Record Group 2, Rockefeller Family Archives.

46. Freedom Train Souvenir Section, *Iowa City Press-Citizen*, June 15, 1948, Box 5, FT Records; clipping, *Baton Rouge Morning Advocate*, Jan. 14, 1948, ibid.; Michael Spatz, Activities Report, Feb. 16, 1948, Box 207, AHF Records; memorandum, Arthur Wild to John Murphy, Aug. 25, 1948, Box 198, ibid.

47. Frank Crane, report, April 26, 1948, Box 207, AHF Records; Crane, "Activity Report," [ca. Aug. 3, 1948], Box 198, ibid.; memoranda, Arthur Wild to John Murphy, June 7 & 21, 1948, ibid.

48. *Washington Post*, Nov. 30, 1947, p. 4B; Clipping, *Freedom & Union* (Jan., 1949), Box 4, FT Records; Brophy, *Highlights of the First Year*; Memorandum, Arthur Wild to John Murphy, July 9, 1948, Box 198, AHF Records; Crossley, Inc., "Freedom Train Campaign Test Study," Provo, Utah, March-April, 1948, Box 199, ibid.

49. Brophy to Edward R. Murrow, Nov. 19, 1948, Box 212, AHF Records; "Statement on Freedom Train Appropriation Estimates," n.d. [May 13, 1949], Planning and Control Cases (NARA).

50. Coblenz to Clark, Nov. 17, 1948, Planning and Control Cases; Coblenz to Thad Page, ibid.; stenographic transcript, Hearings before the Subcommittee of the Senate Committee on the Post Office and Civil Service, Jan. 28, 1949, pp. 18, 57, Box 19, Lucas MSS.

51. Copy, Wayne C. Grover to Sen. Olin D. Johnston, Jan. 24, 1949, Box 19, Lucas MSS; memorandum, William A. Coblenz, Nov. 30, 1948, Planning and Control Cases; memorandum, Thad Page, Feb. 4, 1949, ibid.; draft, Grover to Brophy, April 7, 1949, ibid.; memorandum, Collas G. Harris to Archivist, Jan. 10, 1949, Thad Page Records, NARA; *Congressional Record*, 95 (Feb. 14, 1949), 1192, 1194, 1197.

52. Copy, Frank Pace, Jr., to Sen. Johnston, Feb. 1, 1949; Robert Bahmer to Brophy, June 6, 1949; NARA press release, Sept. 16, 1949, all in Page Records; Grover to J. Edward Shugrue, April 7, 1950, Planning and Control Cases; *New York Times*, April 15, 1949, p. 5.

53. *Philadelphia Inquirer*, Sept. 18, 1947, p. 1; Novins to John Foster Dulles, July 14, 1948, Box 212; Byrne to Charles L. Parkin, Dec. 30, 1958, Box 202, all in AHF Records.

54. Pat Frank, "Main Street on a Flattop," *Collier's*, 122 (Nov. 27, 1948): 16–17, 62. Frank's *Alas, Babylon* (1959), a tale of the aftermath of nuclear war, became a cult novel.

55. Policy Planning Staff, minutes of Dec. 7, 1948; memoranda, Ken-

nan to Robert Lovett, Dec. 15 and 16, 1948; memorandum, Howland H. Sargeant to George Butler, Dec. 15, 1948; Sargeant, "Memorandum on Proposal for Main Street on a Flat-top," Dec. 14, 1948, all in Box 11A, Records of Policy Planning Staff, 1947–1953, RG 59, NARA; Memorandm, LAL to Sargeant, March 22, 1949; George V. Allen, memorandum for the files, April 18, 1949; memorandum, Sargeant to Carlisle Humelsine, March 23, 1949, all in State Department Decimal File 1945–1949, 811.20200 (D), Box 4562, RG 59, NARA.

56. Earl Newsom to John C. Cornelius, March 2, 1956; Abbott Washburn to Newsom, March 1, 1956, and attached memoranda, n.d., all Box 2, AHF Records; Cornelius to Newsom, March 12, 1956, Box 19, ibid.

57. Walter Bedell Smith to Novins, July 21, 1955, Box 19, AHF Records; [Brendan Byrne?] to Cornelius, Dec. 20, 1957, Box 1, ibid.; Wayne C. Grover to Rep. Tom Murray, n.d. [1962], Planning and Control Cases (NARA).

58. Copy, Tom C. Clark to Charles E. Wilson, Sept. 7, 1965, Box 6; Louis A. Novins to Clark, April 11, 1967, Box 30; AHF, "The Freedom Train: A Timely Program for 1965–1966," n.d. [1965], Box 199, all in AHF Records.

59. In 1949, Rochester, N.Y., weighed using model railroads to fight juvenile delinquency. The police commissioner termed it "the latest technique in combating the frustration complexes of children and parents" who lacked access to such toys. *New York Times*, Dec. 29, 1949, p. 29.

60. "A Mouthpiece for CD," *Stet* (April, 1952), p. 2, Box 5, Files of Spencer Quick, HSTL; *Civil Defense Alert*, v. 1, n. 9 (Feb.–March, 1952): 5, ibid.; *Washington Post*, Jan. 7, 1952, p. B1.

61. Draft, Wells to W. C. Doherty, n.d. [1952], Folder 6, Box 11; "Valley Forge Foundation Report on 'Alert America' Convoys," Feb. 10, 1953, Folder 1, Box 3; "The Alert America Campaign for Your Community," n.d. [1951], ibid.; Freedoms Foundation, "Public Relations Report," n.d. [1952], Folder 6, Box 1, all in Series 3, Wells Collection, Brigham Young University.

62. In 1951, the AHF added "Civil Defense preparations" to its list of the attributes of good citizenship. Memorandum, Allan M. Wilson to staff (Advertising Council), May 3, 1951, Files of Charles W. Jackson, Papers of Harry S. Truman, HSTL.

63. *Public Papers of the Presidents of the United States. Harry S. Truman, 1951–53* (Washington, 1966), pp. 25–27; press release, address by Millard Caldwell, Jacksonville, Florida, June 30, 1952, Box 5, Quick Files, HSTL.

64. Novins, "Recommendations for Future Program," Sept. 27, 1951, Box 14, AHF Records; Brophy, "Memorandum on the Future Opera-

tions of the American Heritage Foundation," Jan. 1, 1949, OF 320-C, HSTL; *The First Two Years*, pp. 17, 25.

65. C. M. Vandeburg to Avery McBee, Nov. 9, 1951, Box 14, AHF Records.

66. "Organizations Cooperating with . . . This Campaign—as of 3/15/52," Box 15, ibid.; Byrne to John C. Cornelius, Oct. 27, 1960, Box 1, ibid.; John D. Rockefeller, Jr. to Thomas M. Debevoise, April 18, 1952, Folder 498, Box 50, Cultural Interests Series, Rockefeller Family Archives, RAC.

67. AHF press release, Nov. 5, [1960], Box 1, AHF Records; Jack Cornelius article, "Two Years in Search of Huckster," n.d. [1958], ibid.; AHF, "1956 Non-Partisan 'Register, Inform Yourself, and Vote' Program," n.d., Box 4, ibid.

68. C. M. Vandeburg to Brophy, Oct. 3 and July 16, 1951; "Suggestions for a new program Presented by LAN [Novins] at 11/4/48 AHF Board of Trustees meeting"; "A Program to Promote National Unity and Morale," n.d. [ca. Feb., 1951], all Box 14, ibid.; memorandum, Walter Bedell Smith and John C. Cornelius to Executive Committee, Oct. 17, 1956, Box 19, ibid.

69. Vandeburg to Brophy, "Interim Report with Suggestions," July 16, 1951, Box 14, ibid.; Kershaw Burbank, memorandum "KB—Thomas D'Arcy Brophy," April 7, 1950, Folder 1409A, Box 162, Cultural Interests Series, Rockefeller Family Papers, RAC.

70. *New York Times*, Aug. 19, 1950, p. 15 (Allentown). See Ch. 1 for Freedom Week and Ch. 6 for the anniversary of Independence.

71. Copy, Eisenhower to Brophy, May 7, 1953; Clipping, *New York Times*, May 15, 1953, "Ford Named Head of Freedom Drive"; Minutes, AHF Board of Trustees, March 31, 1953, all Box 17, AHF Records.

72. AHF, "30-second spot announcement #2," April, 1954, Box 20, AHF Records; Crusade for Freedom press release, Feb. 1, 1954, ibid.; *New York Times*, Jan. 28, 1954, p. 31, Jan. 29, 1954, p. 24, Feb. 20, 1954, p. 17.

Chapter 3

1. For a tiny sampling of the vast literature on parades and their rowdy kin, riots, see Susan G. Davis, *Parades and Power: Street Theatre in Nineteenth-Century Philadelphia* (Philadelphia, Pa., 1986); Peter Shaw, *American Patriots and the Rituals of Revolution* (Cambridge, Mass., 1981); Paul A. Gilje, *The Road to Mobocracy: Popular Disorder in New York City, 1763–1834* (Chapel Hill, N.C., 1987); Sean Wilentz, *Chants Democratic: New York City & the Rise of the American Working Class, 1788–1850* (New York, 1984).

2. Elon H. Hooker to W. Dwight Morrow, Aug. 19, 1926; reprint, "Reds Train Children of Strikers at Passaic to Riot, Boo America," *New York Herald-Tribune*, Aug. 4, 1926, both in "American Defense Society (1) folder, Dwight Morrow MSS, Amherst College.

3. Robert K. Murray, *Red Scare: A Study in National Hysteria, 1919–1920* (New York, 1964 [1955]), pp. 74–76.; *Daily Worker*, April 1, 1948, p. 1, April 11, 1948, p. 3, April 13, 1948, p. 7.

4. "Defend Your Home: A Program for Local Activities Against Communism," n.d. [1948], p. 16, Box 10, Francis P. Matthews Papers, HSTL.

5. Form letter, Joseph M. Aimee and James J. Mackin to Matthew J. Connelly, n.d. [April, 1948], Official File, Invitations, Brooklyn, NY, HSTL. For a rare reference to Loyalty Day, see Wilbur Zelinsky, *Nation into State: The Shifting Symbolic Foundations of American Nationalism* (Chapel Hill, N.C., 1988), p. 75.

6. "Americanization," *Foreign Service*, 12 (May, 1924): 27; Capt. Walter I. Joyce, "A Red Letter Day in the V.F.W.," ibid., 16 (April, 1928): 8–9; *V.F.W. Magazine*, 40 (March, 1953): 22; cf. ibid., 42 (Feb., 1955): 46.

7. *New York Times*, March 12, 1930, p. 3, March 28, 1930, p. 16, April 6, 1930, p. 19, April 22, 1930, p. 1, May 1, 1930, p. 5, May 2, 1930, pp. 1, 20. For Boston, see p. 26. On the 1930 rallies as precedents for Loyalty Day, see VFW pamphlet, "Loyalty Day," n.d. [1990], in author's possession.

8. *New York Times*, April 25, 1950, p. 21; Joel L. Schlesinger to Brig. Gen. Frank Mullaney, Feb. 21, 1952, OF 1285-B, HSTL.

9. The parade was under the auspices of an umbrella Loyalty Day Parade Committee. The New York County Council of the VFW established a "cooperating committee" headed by Major General Julius Ochs Adler, general manager of the *New York Times*. *New York Times*, April 19, 1948, p. 24.

10. Mary Adele Whalen, memorandum, n.d. [1950], OF 84, HSTL. Philadelphia also held a parade in 1948. Telegram, Colbert C. McClain to Maj. Gen. Harry H. Vaughan, April 24, 1948, ibid.

11. *New York Times*, May 3, 1953, p. 24, April 30, 1954, p. 4; program, "Loyalty Day Celebration, Brooklyn, N.Y.," May 1, 1948, Tom Clark Papers, HSTL; clipping, *Brooklyn Eagle*, March 13, 1948, OF 84, HSTL; James. J. Mackin to Matthew J. Connelly, March 23, 1948, ibid.

12. The *Daily Worker* surmised that the "thousands" of veterans expected to march with the Left were what most irked Loyalty Day's backers. *New York Times*, April 13, 1948, p. 22, April 30, 1948, p. 25; *Daily Worker*, April 14, 1948, p. 5, April 18, 1948, p. 5.

13. *New York Times*, April 19, 1948, p. 24, April 22, 1948, p. 56, May 1,

1948, p. 1, May 2, 1948, p. 1; *Daily Worker*, April 20, 1948, pp. 3, 6, May 2, 1948, p. 2.

14. Dewey forces also worked to freeze out Stassen. Mackin to Connelly, March 23 and April 14, 1948; Joseph M. Aimee and Mackin to Tom Clark, April 13, 1948; telegram, Connelly to Mackin, April 26, 1948, all OF 84, HSTL; Clark to Mackin, March 12 and April 20, 1948, Clark Papers, HSTL.

15. The Roman Catholic Christophers devoted the day to prayers for Russia's deliverance. *New York Times*, April 13, 1948, p. 22, April 19, 1948, p. 24, April 29, 1948, p. 10, April 30, 1948, p. 25, May 2, 1948, p. 3; Mackin to Clark, April 13, 1948, OF 84, HSTL.

16. *Daily Worker*, April 20, 1948, p. 8.

17. *New York Times*, April 19, 1948, p. 24, April 30, 1948, p. 1, May 2, 1948, p. 1, March 27, 1949, p. 30; *Daily Worker*, May 2, 1948, p. 2, May 3, 1948, p. 4, May 4, 1948, p. 5.

18. *New York Times*, March 12, 1949, p. 3, April 10, 1949, p. 37, April 23, 1949, p. 3, April 27, 1949, p. 29, April 29, 1949, p. 46, April 30, 1949, p. 6, May 1, 1949, p. 1.

19. *New York Times*, March 12, 1949, p. 3, March 27, 1949, p. 30.

20. Dick Roffman to James C. Hagerty, April 14, 1949, Loyalty Day folder #1, Thomas E. Dewey MSS, Rush Rhees Library, University of Rochester; *Foreign Service*, v. 36 (May, 1949): 24; *New York Times*, May 1, 1949, pp. 1, 3.

21. *Foreign Service*, 37 (March, 1950): 18; ibid., (June, 1950): 13, 32; *V.F.W. Magazine*, 38 (June, 1951): 13; *Chicago Tribune*, April 30, 1950, p. 5; *New York Times*, April 10, 1950, p. 35, April 17, 1951, p. 10; State of New York, Assembly resolution of March 10, 1949, Loyalty Day folder #1, Dewey MSS.

22. *V.F.W. Magazine*, 39 (June, 1952): 19; *New York Times*, April 22, 1950, p. 5, April 30, 1950, p. 3; *Daily Worker*, May 1, 1950, pp. 3, 14.

23. John Bodnar, *Remaking America: Public Memory, Commemoration, and Patriotism in the Twentieth Century* (Princeton, N.J., 1992), pp. 13–16 and passim.

24. *Daily Worker*, April 14, 1948, April 16, 1948, p. 9, April 20, 1948, pp. 8, 9; *New York Times*, April 16, 1949, p. 6, April 20, 1950, p. 4.

25. Profs. David M. Oshinsky and Allen Weinstein caution me not to exaggerate the cultural hegemonizing implicit in these events. Though dragooned as New York City school students into Loyalty Day parades, they preferred that fate to a day in the classroom—a reminder that youthful realities may preempt Gramscian social criticism.

26. Kurt Lang and Gladys Engel Lang, "The Unique Perspective of Television and its Effect: A Pilot Study," *American Sociological Review*,

18 (Feb., 1953): 3–12.

27. *New York Times*, April 16, 1951, p. 3, April 28, 1951, pp. 1, 16, April 29, 1951, pp. 1, 40.

28. Louis G. Feldmann, "The Reds Are on the Run," *V.F.W. Magazine*, 42 (June, 1955): 23, 26; idem., "Why Loyalty Day?" ibid., 43 (March, 1956): 38; *New York Times*, April 27, 1958, p. 46.

29. Maj. Gen. Harry H. Vaughn to Colbert C. McClain, April 29, 1948, OF 84, HSTL; telegram, McClain to Vaughn, April 24, 1948, ibid.; Joel L. Schlesinger to Brig. Gen. Frank Mullaney, Feb. 21, 1952, OF 1285-B, HSTL; *New York Times*, April 26, 1952, p. 12, April 27, 1952, pp. 1, 55.

30. *New York Times*, April 22, 1953, p. 18, April 24, 1953, p. 13, April 29, 1953, pp. 1, 11, May 2, 1953, p. 3.

31. Ibid., March 14, 1954, p. 58, May 1, 1954, p. 10, May 1, 1955, p. 75; *V.F.W. Magazine*, 43 (July, 1955); 23, 26; ibid. (March, 1956): 38.

32. *New York Times*, March 30, 1955, p. 14, April 21, 1955, p. 31; Feldmann, "The Reds Are on the Run," *V.F.W. Magazine*, 43 (June, 1955): 23; Omar B. Ketchum to Bernard M. Shanley, April 21, 1955; memo, "Barbara" to Shanley, April 25, 1955; Richard L. Roudebush to Eisenhower, July 9, 1958; Gerald D. Morgan to Roudebush, July 10, 1958, all in GF l-F-3, DDEL; *Public Papers of the Presidents: Dwight D. Eisenhower, 1958* (Washington, 1959), p. 558.

33. *New York Times*, May 3, 1953, p. 1, May 2, 1954, pp. 1, 50, May 1, 1955, p. 1, May 29, 1956, p. 56, April 28, 1957, p. 1; cf. ibid., April 29, 1962, p. 64.

34. Ibid., April 28, 1957, p. 70, April 11, 1958, p. 24, April 16, 1958, p. 27, April 17, 1958, p. 38, April 24, 1958, p. 33, April 25, 1958, p. 33, April 27, 1958, pp. 1, 46, May 19, 1958, p. 27.

35. Ibid., April 25, 1959, p. 5, April 26, 1959, p. 43, May 3, 1959, p. 60, May 27, 1959, p. 28, April 23, 1965, p. 39.

36. Ibid., Feb. 12, 1960, p. 12, May 1, 1960, p. 1, April 29, 1962, p. 64, April 28, 1963, p. 45, April 13, 1965, p. 39, April 14, 1965, p. 40, April 16, 1965, p. 31.

37. John C. Cornelius, "Progress Report—June 2, 1958, Box 20, AHF Records; AHF and ABA, "Law Day Program Fact Sheet," n.d. [1959], ibid.; *New York Times*, Feb. 5, 1958, p. 8; *Cong. Record*, 104 (85th Cong., 2d Sess.), pp. 7690–91, 8237; Paul W. Steer to William A. Geoghegan, April 11, 1963, HO 20 Law Day #l, White House Central Files, John F. Kennedy Library; "Facts in Brief About Law Day U. S. A.," n.d., ibid.

38. Some locales, often law schools, had held Law Days before this first national one. The University of Alabama Law School had done so since prior to 1949. S. R. Starnes to John R. Steelman, March 14, 1949, OF 761-S, HSTL.

39. *Time*, 71 (May 5, 1958), 1, 14–18; *New York Times*, April 27, 1958, p. 54, May 2, 1958, pp. 1, 16; Cornelius, "Highlights and Pre-View of Report," Dec. 2, 1958, Box 1, AHF Records.

40. "Facts in Brief About Law Day U. S. A.," loc. cit.; Telegram, K.J. Kelly to Eisenhower, April 29, 1959, GF 1-F-3, DDEL; Ted C. Connell to JFK, April 3, 1961; Lee C. White to Connell, April 12, 1961, both HO 22 Loyalty Day #1, White House Central Files (WHCF), JFKL.

41. The speaker was historian Staughton Lynd, just back from North Vietnam. Thomas Dinan and Domenick Volpe to JFK, Feb. 5, 1963, HO 22 Loyalty Day #2, WHCF, JFKL; *New York Times*, May 1, 1966, p. 3.

42. Robert E. Hansen, "Let's Not Let Up On Loyalty Day," *VFW Magazine*, 45 (March, 1958): 4; Christenberry, "In Defiance of Dictators," ibid., 46 (April, 1959): 34.

43. After the VFW's Americanism chairman chided the post, the invitation was reinstated. *New York Times*, May 2, 1955, p. 2, April 24, 1956, p. 56, April 30, 1965, p. 19, May 3, 1965, p. 25.

44. Feldmann, "What Loyalty Day Means to America's Future," *V.F.W. Magazine*, 43 (April, 1956): 31. On the demise of the anti-communist persuasion, see Richard Gid Powers, *Not Without Honor: The History of American Anticommunism* (New York, 1995).

45. *V.F.W. Magazine*, 43 (April, 1956), 22; *New York Times*, April 28, 1963, p. 45. The presence of civil defense workers in parades also signified an obligation to accept the premises of nuclear deterrence.

46. *New York Times*, April 30, 1967, p. 2.

47. James J. Mackin to Matthew Connelly, July 16, 1948, OF 299-D, HSTL; Joseph M. Aimee to Connelly, Nov. 17, 1948, PPF 200, HSTL.

Chapter 4

1. Interview with Judge John Decker, Feb. 14, 1988; "Background Information on American Legion 'Communist Day' Project," n.d. [April 1950], Box 30, Wisconsin Department American Legion Papers (hereafter WDAL Papers), State Historical Society of Wisconsin; Paul Thielen to Jack Cejnar, March 8, 1950, ibid.

2. No competition with Loyalty Day was intended. Decker interview; phone interview with Brig. Gen. Francis Schweinler, Feb. 4, 1988; Paul F. Thielen to Schweinler, Feb. 2, 1950, Box 30, WDAL; *Mosinee Times*, April 19, 1950, p. 1, May 10, 1950, p. 5. For the anti-communist tenor of the region's political culture, see Howard R. Klueter and James J. Lorence, *Woodlot and Ballot Box: Marathon County in the Twentieth Century* (Wausau, Wis., 1977), pp. 364–67.

3. Thielen to Schweinler, Feb., 17, 1950; Schweinler to Thielen, Feb. 17, 1950; Thielen, memorandum to Public Relations Commission,

March 2, 1950; "Background Information . . . ," n.d. [April 1950], all Box 30, WDAL Papers; Decker interview.

4. Thielen to Schweinler, Feb. 2, 1950; Kenneth Greenquist to Thielen, Feb. 21, 1950; Cejnar to Thielen, March 6, 1950; William B. Arthur to Thielen, March 10, 1950; Boyd B. Stutler to Thielen, March 8, 1950; Thielen to Arthur, March 15, 1950; Thielen to Cejnar, March 7 and April 5, 1950; Thielen to Greenquist, March 2, 1950, all in ibid.

5. Cejnar to Thielen, April 7, 1950; Schweinler to "Dear Sir or Madam," April 8, 1950; Thielen to G. E. Sipple, April 13, 1950, all in Box 30, WDAL Papers; *Mosinee Times*, April 12, 1950, p. 1.

6. The *Daily Worker* claimed Kronenwetter "viewed the whole vicious project with disgust and distaste," but Carl Gewiss, Mosinee Chief of Police, recalled no such opposition by his friend. Background Information . . . ," n.d. [April 1950], Box 30, WDAL Papers; telephone interview with Irene Kronenwetter, Aug. 18, 1977; *Mosinee Times*, May 3, 1950, p. 6; *Daily Worker*, May 7, 1950, p. 7; interview with Gewiss, Aug. 17, 1977.

7. Schweinler to author, Feb. 29, 1988; *Mosinee Times*, April 19, 1950, p. 1; "Background Information . . . ," Box 30, WDAL Papers.

8. Thielen to Schweinler, April 3, 1950, Box 30, WDAL Papers. On Kornfeder, see *Hearings before the Internal Security Subcommittee of the Committee on the Judiciary*, U. S. Senate, 82d Cong., 2d Sess., *Institute of Pacific Relations* (Sept. 20, 1952), pp. 865–68, 884; Herbert L. Packer, *Ex-Communist Witnesses* (Stanford, 1962), p. 202; Kornfeder to Robert Humphreys, Feb. 15, 1954, Nov. 27, 1961, Box 3, Humphreys Papers, DDEL.

9. See Theodore Draper, *The Roots of American Communism* (New York, 1957); and Benjamin Gitlow, *The Whole of Their Lives* (New York, 1948).

10. *Madison Capital-Times*, May 1, 1950, p. 6; Decker interview.

11. Thielen to Ralph Alderson, April 17, 1950; Thielen to Schweinler, April 3, 1950; Thielen to Kornfeder, April 13, 1950, all in Box 30, WDAL Papers; *Harvester World* (June 1950), 11; *Mosinee Times*, April 26, 1950, p. 1.

12. *Mosinee Times*, April 19, 1950, p. 1, April 26, pp. 1, 4, 6; *Milwaukee Journal*, April 30, 1950, p. 1.

13. "Press Registration for Mosinee's May Day," n.d., Box 30, WDAL Papers; *Badger Legionnaire* (May, 1950), p. 4; ibid., (June 1950), p. 1; *Milwaukee Journal*, April 30, 1950, p. 2; *Wausau Daily Record-Herald*, May 1, 1950, p. 1; Mosinee *Times*, May 3, 1950, pp. 3, 6.

14. *Milwaukee Journal*, April 30, 1950, p. 1; John F. O'Melia to Thielen, March 21, 1950; Cejnar to Thielen, April 7 and 17, 1950; Thielen to

Cejnar, March 9, 1950; Cejnar to William B. Arthur, March 8, 1950; Thielen to Schweinler, April 18, 1950, all Box 30, WDAL Papers.

15. *Mosinee Times*, April 12, 1950, p. 10, April 19, 1950, p. 1, April 26, 1950, p. 1; *Milwaukee Journal*, May 11, 1950, p. 20; *Life Magazine*, 28 (May 15, 1950), 47.

16. Fliers, Communist Party of Wisconsin, "So This Is Supposed to be Communism" and "For Peace—May Day 1950," Dessert Library, Mosinee; *Chicago Sun-Times*, May 1, 1950, clipping, ibid.; *Des Moines Register*, May 1, 1950, p. 1; *New York Times*, May 1, 1950, p. 1.

17. *Chicago Sun-Times*, May 1, 1950, p. 8; Gewiss interview; *Minneapolis Tribune*, May 1, 1950, p. 1; *Mosinee Times*, May 10, 1950, p. 5; *Milwaukee Journal*, May 1, 1950, p. 3; *Wausau Daily Record-Herald*, May 1, 1950, p. 1.

18. *Mosinee Times*, May 3, 1950, p. 1; *Harvester World* (June, 1950), 11; Gitlow, "Report on the Plan of Armed Insurrection," n.d. [April 30, 1950], Folder 5, Box 5, Gitlow Papers, Hoover Institution; Carl Cederburg broadcast for WWJ (Detroit), copy courtesy of Grace O'Connor, Mosinee Senior High Librarian.

19. The other Lutheran and the Catholic church did not participate. "They just didn't like the idea," said Rev. Bennett. Chronology, "It Happened One Day in Mosinee," n.d. [April 1950], Folder 5, Box 5, Gitlow MSS; Cederburg radio broadcast, WWJ; *Milwaukee Journal*, May 1, 1950, pp. 1–2, May 1, 1983, p. 10; clipping, May 1, 1950, at Dessert Library, Mosinee.

20. *Milwaukee Journal*, May 1, 1950, p. 3, May 2, 1950, p. 3; Cederburg broadcast; *Washington Post*, May 1, 1950, p. 1, May 2, 1950, p. 4; *Catholic Digest*, 19 (July 1950): 73; *Chicago Sun-Times* clipping, Dessert Library, Mosinee.

21. Whence these Reds had come was never made clear. One man greeted first news of the pageant with an epic poem suggesting "giant aircraft" whose landing "woke the citizens, with great alarm." But Schweinler said: "In theory they are our own people. They have fallen under Communistic influence and now they have risen up in insurrection." In the pre-coup dramatics, Kornfeder had reported "compliance with the orders of the military organization" of the CPUSA, but the point received little emphasis. *Mosinee Times*, May 3, 1950, p. 3; *Chicago Sun-Times*, May 2, 1950, p. 3; Carl Cederburg broadcast, May 1, 1950, WWJ.

22. Cederburg broadcast; "It Happened One Day in Mosinee," Gitlow MSS; *Milwaukee Journal*, April 30, 1950, p. 1, May 1, 1950, p. 2; *Madison Capital-Times*, May 1, 1950, p. 6.

23. Handwritten speech, n.d., "The Young Communist League is the

Mass Organization of the Youth," Folder 5, Box 5, Gitlow Papers; "It Happened One Day in Mosinee," ibid.; *Harvester World* (June, 1950), 8; *Mosinee Times*, May 3, 1950, p. 10; *Wausau Daily Record-Herald*, May 1, 1950, p. 1.

24. *Mosinee Times*, May 3, 1950, pp. 6, 10; Wausau *Daily Record-Herald*, May 2, 1950, p. 1; "It Happened One Day in Mosinee," *American Legion Magazine*, 48 (June, 1950): 32; "Address Delivered by Charles L. Larson," May 1, 1950, Box 30, WDAL Papers; *Milwaukee Journal*, May 1, 1983, p. 10; Schweinler to author, Feb. 29, 1988.

25. *Wausau Daily Record-Herald*, May 2, 1950, p. 1, May 8, 1950, p. 1; *Milwaukee Sentinel*, May 2, 1950, p. 1; Decker interview.

26. *Wausau Daily Record-Herald*, May 2, 1950, p. 1; *Mosinee Times*, May 3, 1950, pp. 1, 6, May 10, 1950, p. 10; *Daily Worker*, May 8, 1950, p. 9, May 9, 1950, p. 7. The *Times* reported both the fishing accident and "a couple of slight heart attacks previously."

27. *Mosinee Times*, May 3, 1950, pp. 1, 4; *Daily Worker*, May 1, 1950, p. 7, May 2, 1950, p. 7, May 3, 1950, p. 1, May 4, 1950, p. 5, May 7, 1950, p. 7, May 8, 1950, pp. 1, 8, May 9, 1950, p. 9, May 14, 1950, p. 2.

28. *Madison Capital-Times*, May 5, 1950, pp. 1, 8; *New York Post*, May 2, 1950, p. 28, May 3, 1950, p. 49; *Mosinee Times*, May 17, 1950, p. 2, Sept. 27, 1950, p. 1; *Commonweal*, 52 (May 12, 1950): 116–17.

29. *Minneapolis Morning Tribune*, May 3, 1950, p. 6; *Des Moines Register*, June 16, 1950, p. 8.

30. *Wausau Daily Record-Herald*, May 1, 1950, p. 1; American Legion National Public Relations Division, press release, n.d. [ca. May 2, 1950], "Legion One-Day Publicity Smash," Mosinee file, American Legion headquarters, Indianapolis; *Mosinee Times*, April 19, 1950, p. 10, April 26, 1950, pp. 5, 6, May 3, 1950, pp 1, 3, 6.

31. Edward F. McGinnis to Thielen, March 14, 1950, Box 30, WDAL Papers; *Mosinee Times*, April 19, 1950, pp. 2, 8, April 26, 1950, pp. 1, 4.

32. Decker interview; Cejnar to Thielen, March 6, 1950, WDAL Papers. Cf. *Life Magazine*, 28 (May 15, 1950), 46–47; *Chicago Tribune*, April 30, 1950, p. 13. In Mosinee the term "program" was more common. See Schweinler to "Dear Sir or Madam," April 8, 1950, WDAL Papers.

33. Detroit had a strong theoretical susceptibility to Red takeover. In May 1948 *Look* had carried an article, "Could the Reds Seize Detroit?" Carl Cederburg radio broadcast, May 1, 1950, WWJ.; interview with Edwin Morgan, *Detroit News*, May 7, 1950, reprinted in *Mosinee Times*, May 10, 1950, p. 5; "It Happened One Day in Mosinee," *American Legion Magazine*, 48 (June, 1950): 32.

34. Interview with Win Freund, Aug. 19, 1977; *Mosinee Times*, May 3,

1950, p. 6; *Wausau Daily Record-Herald*, March 18, 1977, p. 13.

35. *Wausau Daily Record-Herald*, May 1, 1950, p. 1; *Milwaukee Journal*, May 1, 1950, p. 1; *New York Times*, May 2, 1950, p. 3; *Washington Post*, May 1, 1950, p. 1.

36. *Wausau Daily Record-Herald*, May 2, 1950, p. 1; *Milwaukee Journal*, May 1, 1950, p. 2; *Life Magazine*, 28 (May 15, 1950), 46.

37. *Milwaukee Sentinel*, May 2, 1950, pp. 1, 2. American films did dwell on how Communist poison might enter the American system. Often women—vixens and bad mothers—were to blame. Michael Rogin, "Kiss Me Deadly: Communism, Motherhood, and Cold War Movies," *Representations*, 6 (Spring 1984): 1–36.

38. *Milwaukee Journal*, April 30, 1950, p. 1; *Chicago Sun-Times*, May 2, 1950, p. 3; "The Town That Saw Red," *Catholic Digest*, 19 (July 1950): 73; *Wausau Daily Record-Herald*, May 1, 1950, p. 1.

39. The literature on carnival and societal role reversals is vast. E.g., David I. Kertzer, *Ritual, Politics, and Power* (New Haven, Conn., 1988), pp. 144–50; Michael Bakhtin, *Rabelais and His World*, Helene Iswolsky trans. (Bloomington, Ind., 1984). For an extreme instance when Carnival's social play became deadly serious, see Emmanuel LeRoy Ladurie, *Carnival in Romans* (New York, 1979).

40. *Milwaukee Journal*, May 2, 1950 p. 3; *Mosinee Times*, May 3, 1950, p. 3.

41. *Mosinee Times*, May 3, 1950, p. 1; *Milwaukee Journal*, May 1, 1950, p. 2, May 11, 1950, p. 20; *Minneapolis Morning Tribune*, May 2, 1950, p. 1. The *Daily Worker* (May 7, 1950, p. 7) said pageant planners "had been inciting anti-Communist and war hysteria to a higher pitch throughout the country, and the vast corps of news and radio men were solicited and came here on that basis."

42. *Wausau Daily Record-Herald*, May 2, 1950, p. 14. On the other hand, a local merchant said it was "the bunk." To the *Daily Worker* (May 7, 1950, p. 7), the millworker showed that the pageant was a media event, not a folk product; it neglected to publish the comment after the semicolon.

43. *Mosinee Times*, April 26, 1950, p. 4, May 10, 1950, p. 5, May 17, 1950, p. 2; clipping, May 1, 1950, Dessert Library, Mosinee; *New York Times*, May 15, 1960, p. 11.

44. *Hartley Sentinel*, May 25, 1950, p. 1, June 1, 1950, p. 1, June 8, 1950, p. 1, June 15, 1950, p. 1, June 22, 1950, pp. 1, 12; *Omaha World-Herald*, June 11, 1950, p. 21, June 15, 1950, p. 1; phone interviews with W. R. Vezina and Ingwer Hansen, Jan. 9, 1996; *Des Moines Register*, June 15, 1950, p. 3, June 16, 1950, p. 8.

45. *Indianapolis Star*, Dec. 2, 1951, p. 1 and II, 1; interview with A.

Hartwell Coons, Jan. 21, 1991. That Coons, manager of the *Rushville Republican*, was a friend of the *Star*'s photographer might explain the selection of Rushville. That no other resident whom I interviewed remembered the event—several were quite incredulous—suggests its local invisibility.

46. *Indianapolis Star*, Dec. 2, 1951, p. 1 and II, p. 1.

47. *Binghamton Press*, Feb. 1, 1953, p. 2; *Troy, N.Y., Times Record*, Jan. 22, 1953, p. 16, Jan. 26, 1953, pp. 13, 17, Jan. 29, 1953, p. 37, Jan. 30, 1953, p. 13, Jan. 31, 1953, p. 7. Cf. David Caute, *The Great Fear: The Anti-Communist Purge Under Truman and Eisenhower* (New York, 1978), p. 351. On the Crusade for Freedom, see ch. 2.

48. AKALH-DC 354.25, "Final Report on Exercise LONG HORN," June 18, 1952, pp. 2–4, Box 505; Record Group 319, NA, Washington, D.C.; "General Plan, Exercise Long Horn," Dec. 15, 1951, Box 506, ibid.; *New York Times*, March 23, 1952, p. 27, March 27, 1952, p. 13, April 4, 1952, p. 10.

49. Provost Marshal, Final Report, Annex I, *Military Government Operations in Exercise Long Horn*, April 18, 1952 (hereafter cited as *MGOELH*); press release LH-19, March 5, 1951; "Lampasas High School Talk," March 5, 1952; Headquarters, 82nd Airborne Division, "Command Report on Military Government activities for Exercise Long Horn," n.d., all in Box 434, RG 337, NA; leaflet, "The U.S. Will Return"; Capt. Eugene T. Newhall to Commanding General, Fourth U.S. Field Army, April 9, 1952, Box 440, ibid.

50. *Life*'s brief item mentioned only a parachute drop bedeviled by a death and many injuries and a fistfight between two units over the roughing-up of a "prisoner." *Military Government Operations*; HQ, 82nd Airborne Division, "Command Report"; Press Release LH-19, March 5, 1952; *Lampasas Dispatch*, special issue, Juvember 33, 1969, all Box 434, RG 337; *Life* (April 7, 1952), 53.

51. Headquarters Maneuver Director, Exercise Long Horn, Office of the Assistant Chief of Staff, J-1, "Final Report," n.d., pp. 7–8, Box 431, RG 337; AKALH-DC 354.25, "Final Report on Exercise LONG HORN," June 18, 1952, Box 505, RG 319; Jean R. Moenk, *A History of Large-Scale Army Maneuvers in the United States, 1934–1964* (Fort Monroe, U.S. Continental Army Command, 1969), pp. 173, 176, 178; *New York Times*, March 17, 1952, p. 39, March 23, 1952, p. 27, April 4, 1952, p. 10; *Fairmont (WVA) Times*, April 4, 1952, p. 10 (courtesy of Prof. Charles H. McCormick).

52. *New York Times*, March 22, 1938, p. 23, July 12, 1941, p. 5; *Milwaukee Journal*, May 31, 1939, p. 4. Several West Coast cities witnessed military displays such as mock bombings in these years. Roger Lotchin,

Fortress California, 1910–1961: From Warfare to Welfare (New York, 1992), pp. 77–78, 126–27.

53. *New York Times*, May 17, 1941, p. 8, May 18, 1941, p. 8, July 12, 1941, p. 5, Sept. 19, 1941, p. 13.

54. Ibid., May 17, 1947, p. 1.

55. *Omaha World-Herald*, June 11, 1950, p. 11; *New York Times*, July 27, 1956, p. 23.

56. "A Program to Promote National Unity and Morale," n.d. [1951], Box 14, AHF Records; memorandum, Brendan Byrne to C. M. Vandeburg, June 2, 1953, Box 18, ibid.

57. For those with a taste for counterfactual play and a fear of the Red menace there remained an outlet: civil defense activities, including the Ground Observer Corps.

58. Foes of such hearings often charged that their purpose was theatrical, not legislative. One trenchant critique of the House Un-American Activities Committee was compiled by Eric Bentley, a scholar of drama.

59. This is a broader paradox that affects liberal democracies. Robert Westbrook acutely depicts its impact on federal efforts to mobilize Americans during World War II. See "Private Interests and Public Obligations in World War II," in Richard Wightman Fox and T.J. Jackson Lears, eds., *The Power of Culture: Critical Essays in American History* (Chicago, 1993), pp. 195–222.

Chapter 5

1. *Congressional Record*, 95 (1949), A2848, 5432, 7166, 10208, 11106; Senate Judiciary Committee, 81st Cong., 1st Sess, *Designating June 14 of Each Year as Flag Day*, Report to accompany S. J. Res. 103.

2. "Address for Flag Day, 1950," n.d. National Public Relations Division, American Legion, Box 12, Wisconsin Department American Legion Papers, SHSW.

3. T. B. Shoemaker to Tom C. Clark, Feb. 13, 1946, OF 320-A, HSTL; Edward Arnold to Truman, April 29, 1952, ibid.

4. Daniel Yergin, *Shattered Peace: The Origins of the Cold War and the National Security State* (Boston, 1977).

5. Jane M. Hatch, comp. and ed., *The American Book of Days*, 3d ed., (New York, 1978), p. 454; *New York Times*, May 19, 1945, p. 18, May 20, 1950, p. 2; *Cong. Record*, 91 (May 4, 1945), A2067. The new day preempted but never fully eliminated separate service days.

6. Louis Johnson to Truman, Aug. 30, 1949; Philip B. Perlman to Truman, Feb. 3(?), 1950; Truman proclamation, "Armed Forces Day, 1950," Feb. 28, 1950, all OF 1285-X, HSTL.

7. Louis Johnson to John R. Steelman, March 6, 1950; "br," memo-

randum, March 7, 1950; "Program, National Armed Forces Day Dinner," May 19, 1950; clipping, May 20, 1950, all ibid.

8. Clipping, May 20, 1950, ibid.; *New York Times*, May 20, 1950, p. 2, May 16, 1954, p. 85; *Washington Post*, May 20, 1950, p. 1B, May 21, 1950, p. 1.

9. *Ibid.*, May 17, 1951, p. 35, May 20, 1951, p. 1, April 24, 1952, p. 16, May 16, 1952, p. 8, May 18, 1952, p. 21.

10. Ibid., May 13, 1956, p. 13, May 16, 1951, p. 71, May 11, 1953, p. 3, May 11, 1954, p. 31, May 12, 1957, p. 13, May 17, 1957, p. 50; *Washington Post*, May 19, 1951, p. 2.

11. *New York Times*, May 19, 1951, p. 4, May 18, 1959, p. 18, May 15, 1955, p. 85, May 18, 1958, p. 33, May 21, 1955, p. 19, April 15, 1958, p. 41.

12. Ibid., May 14, 1952, p. 24, May 8, 1954, p. 19, May 15, 1955, p. 85, May 10, 1959, p. 4.

13. *Washington Post*, May 21, 1950, p. 17; Truman Proclamation, "Armed Forces Day, 1952," March 21, 1952, OF 1285-X, HSTL; *New York Times*, May 16, 1951, p. 71, May 17, 1951, p. 35.

14. But not entirely. In 1951 the *New York Times* noted that goal, and the Defense Secretary's announcement of Armed Forces Day was reported to have "scotched . . . any private hope the individual services might have for a return to their own separate anniversary 'days.'" On Armed Forces Days after 1955 a ceremony was held at the grave of James Forrestal, the first Secretary of Defense. *New York Times*, Jan. 30, 1951, p. 49, May 14, 1951, p. 24, May 20, 1956, p. 41, May 19, 1957, p. 3; Proclamation, "Armed Forces Day, 1951," April 2, 1951, OF 1285-X, HSTL.

15. *New York Times*, May 14, 1951, p. 24, May 13, 1951, p. 15, May 3, 1953, p. 19, May 18, 1958, p. 32; Gen. A. C. Wedemeyer speech, "The American Citizen—Defender of Freedom," May 15, 1951, OF 1285-X, HSTL.

16. *New York Times*, May 20, 1951, p. 4, May 17, 1953, p. 31, May 21, 1961, p. 38. Coincident with planning for the first Armed Forces Day, under Paul Nitze's leadership, State and Defense Department officials were drafting NSC-68, a document that called for broad and long-term mobilization for a deepening Cold War.

17. The phrase "They are 'our' Armed Forces . . ." also crept into the *Times*' 1958 editorial. *New York Times*, May 18, 1952, p. 14, May 15, 1954, p. 14, May 13, 1957, p. 30, May 12, 1958, p. 28, May 20, 1961, p. 22.

18. Ibid., May 5, 1954, p. 38, May 18, 1955, p. 21, May 21, 1960, p. 22.

19. Ibid., May 20, 1950, p. 1, May 19, 1951, p. 4, May 15, 1954, p. 1,

May 19, 1954, p. 1, May 17, 1959, p. 46.

20. Wedemeyer speech, May 15, 1951, OF 1285-X, HSTL; *Washington Post*, May 16, 1953, p. 1; *New York Times*, May 22, 1955, p. 84.

21. *New York Times*, May 14, 1951, p. 16, April 24, 1952, p. 16, May 17, 1953, p. 31.

22. In 1957 New York's congressional delegation did propose that the Coney Island air show be designated a national event to "serve as our answer to the annual Soviet May Day flyover in Moscow." Ibid., March 28, 1957, p. 10.

23. Ibid., May 20, 1951, p. 3, May 15, 1954, p. 5, May 21, 1955, p. 7, May 22, 1955, p. 84.

24. Ibid., May 19, 1956, p. 21, May 21, 1956, p. 7, May 20, 1956, p. 1, May 17, 1959, p. 1, May 13, 1960, p. 6, May 14, 1960, p. 1.

25. Ibid., May 16, 1954, p. 84, May 20, 1956, p. 41, May 17, 1959, pp. 1, 46; *Washington Post*, May 18, 1951, p. 1.

26. *Washington Post*, May 16, 1953, p. 1, May 17, 1953, p. 2; *New York Times*, May 17, 1953, p. 31, May 19, 1954, p. 1. For Ike's characteristically dispeptic response to the dedication of the Marine Corps Iwo Jima monument in Washington, see Karal Ann Marling and John Wetenhall, *Iwo Jima: Monuments, Memories, and the American Hero* (Cambridge, Mass., 1991), ch. 1.

27. In Manhattan's parade, 35,000 marched in 1951, 20,000 in 1952, 25,000 in 1953 (with a crowd estimated at 1,250,000), 25,000 in 1954 (with a million onlookers), 30,000 in 1955 and 1956 (before crowds of 150,000), 26,000 in 1957 (150,000 viewers), 28,000 in 1958 (250,000 viewers). *New York Times*, May 20, 1951, p. 1, May 18, 1952, p. 1, May 17, 1953, p. 1, May 16, 1954, p. 1, May 22, 1955, p. 1, May 20, 1956, p. 1, May 19, 1957, pp. 1, 3, May 18, 1958, p. 1, May 17, 1959, p. 1, May 22, 1960, p. 1.

28. *Washington Post*, May 20, 1950, p. 1B, May 19, 1951, p. 2, May 16, 1953, p. 6, May 16, 1954, p. 17M; *New York Times*, May 10, 1954, p. 9, May 15, 1955, p. 85.

29. In 1940 Congress guaranteed ambiguity by labeling it both Citizenship and I Am An American Day. [ABA], *Citizenship Quarterly Bulletin* (Dec., 1951): 6; Roger W. Jones to Attorney General, March 5, 1951, OF 1285-X, HSTL; memorandum, Jones to Steelman, Jan. 25, 1951, ibid.; William D. Hassett to Lee A. Yates, March 13, 1952, OF 320-A, HSTL; Peyton Ford to Sen. Pat McCarran, Aug. 3, 1951, Box 99, Records of Citizenship Day, National Conference on Citizenship, RG 200, NA. (Cited hereafter as NCC Records.)

30. "Department of Justice Statement On House Joint Resolution 314 Before Sub-Committee No. 4, House Judiciary Committee," Oct. 10,

[1951], OF 320-A, HSTL; *Cong. Record*, 98 (Feb. 20, 1952), 1174–75.

31. R. J. Colbert to J. Howard McGrath, April 2, 1952, Box 100, NCC Records; Edward Arnold to Truman, May 11, 1952; Richard W. Hawkins to Truman, May 1, 1952; Nell M. Putnam to Truman, March 2, 1952, all in OF 320-A, HSTL; Clipping, *Los Angeles Evening Herald-Express*, March 1, 1952, OF 102-F-1, DDEL.

32. SAR Resolution, "Patriotic Anniversaries," [May, 1952], enclosed in William S. Bennet to Truman, Sept. 18, 1952, Box 100, NCC Records; J. Lee Rankin to John R. Hill, n.d. [Dec., 1953], Box 99, ibid.; *New York Times*, Sept. 15, 1952, p. 22, April 24, 1953, p. 5.

33. Copy, Edward G. Riekert to Rep. Albert H. Bosch, Jan. 15, 1954, GF 1-F-1, DDEL; Judge Paul P. Rao to James C. Hagerty, Nov. 8, 1954, ibid.; Mrs. Paul d'Otrenge Seghers to Eisenhower, May 26, 1953, OF 102-F-1, ibid.; Hagerty to Gerald D. Morgan, March 9, 1955, ibid.; *New York Times*, May 17, 1953, p. 30, Sept. 14, 1953, p. 13, Sept. 21, 1953, p. 3; *American Legion Magazine*, 53 (Aug., 1952): 30.

34. Newsletter, *The Minute Women of the U.S.A., Inc.,* (Sept., 1953), File 45, Box 135, Martin Dies MSS; Frederic Fox to Mrs. Robert L. Yates, Aug. 10, 1956, "Patriotic Celebration," Box 27, Frederic Fox Records, DDEL.

35. Fox memoranda, "'Day of Prayer' Proclamation," Aug. 6, 1957; "The National Day of Prayer," Oct. 8, 1957; "For the Record: National Day of Prayer," Jan. 31, 1971, all in Box 34, Fox Papers.

36. J. Ronald Oakley, *God's Country: America in the Fifties* New York, 1986), p. 320; Stephen J. Whitfield, *The Culture of the Cold War* (Baltimore, Md., 1991), pp. 88–89; Arthur E. Summerfield to Sen. Mike Mansfield, April 2, 1954, Box 3, Series 8, Mansfield MSS, University of Montana; *Congressional Record*, 100 (1954), 4591; *New York Times*, March 20, 1947, p. 29, June 15, 1954, p. 31.

37. M. L. Brown to Mansfield, July 2, 1953, Box 3, Series VIII, Mansfield MSS; *American Legion Magazine*, 52 (May, 1952): 31; ibid., 53 (March, 1953): 29; *Congressional Record*, 99 (Aug. 1, 1953), A4963.

38. Edward H. Nelson to Eisenhower, Oct. 23, 1953, GF l-F, DDEL; *The Sertoman* (Nov., 1952): 3, ibid.; *New York Times*, Feb. 20, 1955, V, 5; John C. Cornelius, AHF Annual Report to the Board of Trustees, Dec. 2, 1958, Box 1, AHF Records.

39. Gwen King to Kenneth O'Donnell, April 28, 1961; [JFK] to John S. Gleason, April 19, 1963, both HO 23, WHCF, JFKL.

40. Clifton to Col. Gordon L. Barclay, June 16, 1962; Clifton to William I. Nichols, March 25, 1963; Clifton, Memorandum for the Record, May 24, 1963; ". . . day of glory," n.d.; Nichols to Pierre Salinger, May 10, 1963, all HO 18, ibid.; *This Week Magazine* (June 30, 1963).

Kennedy edited the story himself.

41. Bowron to Los Angeles City Council, June 12, 1946, Box 2, Bowron Coll., Huntington Library.

42. Loyalty Day itself obscured Child Health Day, which Congress had assigned to May 1 in 1928. James C. Hagerty, "Statement by the President," July 18, 1958, OF 102-F-1, DDEL.

43. *New York Times*, May 18, 1952, p. 19.

Chapter 6

1. See Michael Kammen, *Mystic Chords of Memory: The Transformation of Tradition in American Culture* (New York, 1991), pp. 587–89.

2. Stanley Coben, "A Study in Nativism: The American Red Scare of 1919–1920," *Political Science Quarterly*, 79 (March, 1964): 70; Robert K. Murray, *Red Scare: A Study in National Hysteria, 1919–1920* (Minneapolis, Minn., 1955), p. 86; *New York Times*, July 3, 1951, p. 9; *Public Papers of the Presidents, Harry S. Truman, 1951* (Washington, D.C., 1965), pp. 520–23; Charles B. Hosmer, Jr., *Preservation Comes of Age: From Williamsburg to the National Trust, 1926–1949* (Charlottesville, N.C., 1981), ch. 1.

3. John D. Rockefeller, Jr., "The Genesis of the Williamsburg Restoration," *National Geographic*, 71 (April 1937): 401; remarks of JDR, Jr., Nov. 29, 1940, Folder 182, Box 4, Papers of John D. Rockefeller, Personal, Rockefeller Archives Center, Pocantico Hills, N.Y. (hereafter RAC).

4. Cf. Kenneth Chorley, "Notes for talk at Laurenceville School on Thursday, January 25, 1951," Colonial Williamsburg Foundation Archives, Williamsburg, Va.; William R. Traum speech, May 5, 1960, "The Civil War Centennial Travel Picture," Box 14, Records of the Civil War Centennial Commission, R.G. 79, NA.

5. Hosmer, *Preservation*, pp. 187–88, 897, chs. 7–8, and passim.

6. The Liberty Bell was the symbolic focus of a national savings bond drive in 1950. A mallet tap on the original bell opened the drive, which continued as fifty-two uncracked replicas went on tour. Hosmer, *Preservation*, p. 721; *Milwaukee Journal*, May 11, 1950, p. 20 (Peattie), May 14, 1950, II, 7.

7. Clipping, *Colonial Williamsburg News* (May 1955), Folder 1456, Box 167, Cultural Interests Series, Rockefeller Family Archives (hereafter CIS, RFA), RAC; "Interim Report, Special Survey Committee," Nov. 3, 1950, Folder 1409A; John D. Rockefeller, 3d, to Malcolm MacDonald, May 26, 1950, Folder 1409C, both Box 162, ibid. Cf. Kammen, *Mystic Chords of Memory*, pp. 581–87.

8. The Special Survey remained aware of more liberal goals such as

"racial equality" and "civil liberties." See generally Folders 1409A and 1409B, CIS, RFA; "Eighteenth-Century American Concepts Particularly Appropriate to Williamsburg," n.d. [ca. 1950], Folder 1254, Box 143, ibid.

9. John D. Rockefeller, Jr., made contributions to this and other AHF projects. Chorley to Winthrop W. Aldrich, Jan. 23, 1947, and attachments, folder 1312, Box 150, ibid.; John D. Rockefeller, Jr., to Aldrich, Sept. 26, 1947, Folder 499, Box 50, ibid.

10. A national winner in 1949 was Charles Kuralt. Justice Tom Clark served briefly as National Chairman. Colonial Williamsburg unsuccessfully lobbied to take over the entire program. Chorley to John D. Rockefeller (Jr. and 3rd), Feb. 19, 1951; Robert K. Richards to John D. Rockefeller, 3rd, June 23, 1952, both Folder 1422, Box 164, ibid.; Memorandum, Chorley to E. P. Alexander, Sept. 6, 1951, Voice of Democracy program, microfilm records, Colonial Williamsburg (CW) Foundation Archives, Williamsburg, Va.

11. "Summary Report on the First Williamsburg International Assembly, June 9–12, 1957," Williamsburg International Assembly folder, Publications; "The Tenth Anniversary Banquet," Williamsburg Student Burgesses, Feb. 13, 1967, Williamsburg Student Burgesses Folder, both in Publications, CW Foundation Archives.

12. Press release, Colonial Williamsburg, June 30, 1949; 12 #9 Magazine—Opening, January June 1949"; clipping, *Newport News Daily Press*, June 26, 1949; Kershaw Burbank to Carleton Young, Aug. 12, 1949; clipping, July 5, 1949; Smith, "Address," July 4, 1949, all in two folders "Block 12 #9 Magazine—Opening," Block and Building Records, CW Foundation Archives; Memorandum, Burbank to Kenneth Chorley, July 11, 1949, Folder 1312, Box 150, CIS, RFA.

13. *Public Papers of the Presidents of the United States. Dwight D. Eisenhower, 1953* (Washington, D.C., 1960), pp. 296–97; *New York Times*, May 16, 1954, p. 1, June 15, 1958, II, part 2, p. 5; "Heads of State and Guest Dignitaries Who Have Visited Colonial Williamsburg, 1953–1986," CW Foundation Archives.

14. Chorley, "The New Commonwealth of the Intellect," speech before English-Speaking Union, at the Royal Institution of Great Britain, Feb. 27, 1958, Folder 1443, Box 167, CIS, RFA.

15. It was hoped the award might earn comparison with the Nobel or Pulitzer prizes, but Churchill's was the only one given. "Background Memorandum: The Williamsburg Award," (Oct., 1955); Kenneth Chorley to Richard Nixon, Oct. 12, 1955, both in Box 822, General Correspondence, Nixon Papers, National Archives—Southwest Pacific Region, Laguna Niguel, California.

16. "Remarks by Mr. Rockefeller following toasts to the Queen and to the President," April 27, 1956, microfilm records of dignitaries' visits to Williamsburg, CW Foundation Archives; Chorley, "The New Commonwealth of the Intellect," Feb. 27, 1958, Folder 1443, Box 167, CIS, RFA.

17. Robert N. Bellah, "Civil Religion in America," *Daedalus*, 96 (Winter 1967), 9–10. Bellah leaves us bereft of terminology for the centenaries of Theodore Roosevelt, Woodrow Wilson and the Republican Party, also in this period.

18. Malone cited projects to publish works of Hamilton, Jefferson, Franklin, Lincoln, Madison and the Adamses. *New York Times Magazine*, May 27, 1956, VI, 32. For the many celebrations in the 1930s, see Michael Kammen, *Mystic Chords of Memory*, pp. 422–24, 439, 452–53, 456–58, 494; Bodnar, *Remaking America*, pp. 126–35.

19. *New York Times*, Jan. 20, 1946, p. 36, July 5, 1946, p. 6, June 4, 1950, p. 74, Sept. 5, 1950, p. 27, July 2, 1954, p. 21; "National Public Relations-Publicity Program for Minnesota Centennial," Feb. 14, 1957, Box 1, AHF Records.

20. *New York Times*, Dec. 2, 1956, X, 15, July 2, 1959, p. 4.

21. J. Harvie Williams to Alexander Hamilton Bicentennial Commission, July 29, 1955, Box 537, Gen. Corres., Nixon Papers; Memorandum, "mb" [Mary Broder] to Brendan Byrne, Oct. 8, 1958, Box 6, AHF Papers; clipping, "Civil War Exhibit Caravan May Travel Across U.S.," n.d. [ca. Nov. 2, 1958], ibid.

22. "Preview of the Plans of the National Capital Sesquicentennial Commission 1800–1950," n.d. [ca. April, 1949], OF 51-y, HSTL; Minutes of Meeting of National Capital Sesquicentennial Commission (NCSC), June 28 [1949], ibid.; *New York Times*, April 16, 1949, p. 28, Oct. 16, 1949, II, 15.

23. *Congressional Record*, 95 (June 9, 1949), A3630; ibid., 96 (May 8, 1950), 3674.

24. *New York Times*, Dec. 25, 1949, p. 13, Dec. 27, 1949, p. 8, Dec. 28, 1949, p. 32, Dec. 31, 1949, p. 17, March 16, 1950, p. 34, May 28, 1950, IV, 7, June 4, 1950, p. 63; John L. Handy to Truman, May 18, 1950; Statement of Jerome B. McKee, n.d. [May, 1950]; J. A. Kamerow et al. to Truman, May 24, 1950, all OF 51-y, HSTL.

25. *New York Times*, April 16, 1950, p. 87; *Cong. Record*, 96 (April 21, 1950), A2863–64. Barkley also warned of the "sharpest threat" to freedom, from those who would curb it at home in the face of threats from abroad. Were Paine alive, "he might be charged with being subversive."

26. Press release, "Nation Invited to Washington . . . ," n.d. [1950], OF 51-y, HSTL; *New York Times*, March 10, 1950, p. 32, June 11, 1950, II, 10, July 7, 1950, p. 23, July 13, 1950, p. 30, Aug. 18, 1950, p. 16; *Washington*

, p. 1B, May 23, 1950, p. 1, June 15, 1950, p. 2B.
nes, Aug. 5, 1950, p. 8, Aug. 6, 1950, p. 72; "Official
" for "Faith of Our Fathers," n.d. [1951], p. 2, OF 51-y,

mes, Dec 3, 1950, p. 65; "New Properties, Costumes and Scenery for 1951 Production," [1951]; "Faith of Our Fathers: Tentative Revised Outline 1951"; Melvin D. Hildreth to Truman, May 5, 1952; Truman to Hildreth, May 9, 1952, all OF 51-y, HSTL.

29. *Washington Post*, May 22, 1950, pp. 1, 9.

30. C. M. Vandeburg to Harold Brightman, Nov. 5, 1951; Vandeburg to Thomas D'Arcy Brophy, "Interim Report With Suggestions," July 16, 1951, ibid.; Vandeburg to Independence Homecoming Committee, March 27, 1951, all in Box 14, AHF Records.

31. Washington provided $42,000. "Report to the Board of Trustees of the American Heritage Foundation," [1951]; memorandum, Byrne to Brophy, June 30, 1950; Vandeburg to Brophy, "Interim Report With Suggestions," July 16, 1951; Matthew J. Connelly to Byrne, March 26, 1951, all Box 14, AHF Papers; *New York Times*, March 20, 1951, p. 8, May 18, 1951, p. 12; press release, May 17, 1951, OF 215, HSTL.

32. *New York Times*, July 1, 1951, p. 31, July 3, 1951, p. 9, July 5, 1951, p. 8; *Public Papers of the Presidents. Harry S. Truman, 1951*, pp. 370–72; "Report to Trustees," [1951], Folder: AHF—Meeting (1951), Box 14, AHF Papers; *Life*, 31 (July 2, 1951).

33. This effort was seconded by the Committee to Proclaim Liberty, which sought to restore the day's "spiritual emphasis" with church bell ringing and suitable services. Backers, many oriented to the right, included Douglas MacArthur and Herbert Hoover. The bells impressed some auditors, but others misconstrued them as a signal the Korean War had ended. Committee to Proclaim Liberty, press release, June 11, 1951, Box 9, Marquis Childs MSS, SHSW; *Chicago Tribune*, July 5, 1951, p. 6.

34. "Report to the Trustees," [1951], Box 14, AHF Records; Vandeburg to Harold Brightman, Nov. 5, 1951, ibid.; *New York Times*, July 5, 1951, pp. 1, 8.

35. July 4, 1953, was designated that year's National Day of Prayer. Special church services took place and the vice president spoke at ceremonies in Philadelphia. *Washington Post*, July 5, 1953, pp. 1, 6.

36. "Report to Trustees," [1951], Folder: AHF—Meeting (1951), Box 14; Vandeburg to Brophy, "Interim Report with Suggestions," July 16, 1951, ibid, AHF Records.

37. The context for Dewey's remarks was the rancorous McCarthy-Army hearings. *New York Times*, June 6, 1954, II, 19, June 20, 1954, II,

16, June 22, 1954, p. 8; *Albany Knickerbocker News,* June 2, 1954, p. ⅃ June 5, 1954, p. B2, June 9, 1954, p. B3, June 16, 1954, p. 1, June 18, 1954, pp. 1, B3, June 23, 1954, p. 1.

38. Other members included Thomas E. Dewey, the President's brother Edgar Eisenhower, Judge Arthur T. Vanderbilt (no admirer of the Warren Court), and conservative Senators Harry F. Byrd, A. Willis Robertson, John Marshall Butler and Edward Martin. Two members represented the American Bar Association.

39. *New York Times,* Sept. 26, 1954, p. 74, Oct. 12, 1954, p. 26, Nov. 1, 1954, p. 31, Jan. 12, 1955, p. 25; Leo Katcher, *Earl Warren: A Political Biography* (New York, 1967), p. 326.

40. *New York Times,* April 6, 1955, p. 24; *John Marshall Bicentennial Celebration 1955. Final Report of the U.S. Commission for the Celebration of the Two Hundredth Anniversary of the Birth of John Marshall* (Washington, D.C., [1956]), pp. 17–21; Edward K. Moss to J. Vaughan Gary, Sept. 30, 1955, Box 5, Entry 325, RG 79 (John Marshall Bicentennial Commission), NA. Cited hereafter as JMBC.

41. Conrad L. Wirth, Director of NPS, was Executive Director of the Commission; Herbert E. Kahler, Chief Historian of NPS, took part in its affairs; and former government historian Edmund C. Gass was its Administrative Assistant. Press release, NPS, June 23, 1955, Box 5, JMBC.

42. Transcript, meeting of JMBC Executive Committee, June 23, 1955, Box 1; Summary Minutes, First Meeting of the JMBC, April 5, 1953, ibid.; Summary Minutes, Meeting of JMBC, Aug. 16, 1955, Box 2; J. Vaughan Gary to A.K. Missimer, April 21, 1955, Box 1; Conrad Wirth to Edward S. Corwin, Dec. 2, 1955, Box 3; Memorandum, Rogers W. Young to Herbert E. Kahler, ibid., all in JMBC Papers.

43. *New York Times,* Aug. 25, 1955, pp. 1, 10.

44. Ibid., Aug 21, 1955, VI, 49, Aug. 24, 1955, p. 26.

45. *Cong. Record,* 101 (June 22, 1955), 9029–30; *New York Times,* Sept. 11, 1955, II, 34, Jan. 17, 1956, p.22, Oct. 25, 1956, p. 35.

46. *Cong. Record,* 102 (Jan. 18, 1956), 857; *New York Times,* June 15, 1955, p. 4, Jan. 18, 1956, p. 17, Jan. 22, 1956, p. 56, March 11, 1956, p. 123, June 14, 1956, p. 47.

47. *New York Times,* May 2, 1957, p. 22; Minutes, Hamilton Bicentennial Commission, Feb. 1, 1955, Box 25, Gen. Corres. Nixon Papers; *Cong. Record,* 100, 83d Cong, 2d Sess. (Aug. 3, 1954), 13079–80; "Establishment of a Commission to Celebrate the Two Hundredth Anniversary of the Birth of Alexander Hamilton," Hearing, Subcommittee of Senate Committee on the Judiciary, 83d Cong., 2d Sess., on S. J. Res. 140, p. 7.

48. *Cong. Record,* 100 (March 16, 1954), 3331; *New York Times,* Jan. 11,

1957, pp. 17, 22, Jan. 12, 1957, p. 22; Bower Aly to Sponsors, July 8, 1957, Box 25, Gen. Corres., Nixon Papers; Minutes, Hamilton Bicentennial Commission, Feb. 1, 1955, ibid.

49. *New York Times*, Sept. 17, 1956, p. 16. The uncertainties surrounding his birth made it hard for celebrants to settle on a date. A second set of ceremonies took place August 4, 1957. Ibid., Dec. 19, 1954, VI, 25, Aug. 5, 1957, p. 22.

50. Ibid., Jan. 10, 1957, p. 34, Jan. 12, 1957, p. 22.

51. *The Jamestown Festival: Plans for a National Celebration in 1957* (Richmond, [1955]); Richard Nixon to Harry F. Byrd, Sept. 18, 1953, Box 169, Gen. Corres., Nixon Papers; *New York Times*, Aug. 14, 1955, p. 84, Jan. 22, 1956, II, 21, March 3, 1956, p. 36, March 17, 1956, p, 38, July 29, 1956, II, 23, Aug 24, 1956, p. 14, Feb. 10, 1957, II, 31, March 31, 1957, VI, 44, Dec. 8, 1957, p. 142.

52. *New York Times*, Dec. 21, 1956, p. 3, March 24, 1957, II, 25, April 1, 1957, p. 27, April 7, 1957, p. 9, April 2, 1957, p. 36, June 14. 1957, p. 12.

53. Ibid., April 11, 1957, p. 33, April 12, 1957, p. 27, April 13, 1957, p. 21, April 17, 1957, p. 33, April 20, 1957, p. 32, May 18, 1957, p. 40.

54. Ibid., May 13, 1957, p. 11, May 14, 1957, p. 38, June 10, 1957, p. 7.

55. In 1958, the Polish Embassy celebrated the 350th anniversary of the arrival of Polish artisans in Jamestown. The USSR apparently pressed no claim based on Russian settlements on the Pacific Coast. Ibid., Aug. 27, 1958, p. 60.

56. Ibid., May 12, 1957, X, 3, June 9, 1957, p. 52, June 13, 1957, p. 1, June 25, 1957, p. 16, Oct. 15, 1957, p. 8.

57. Ibid., Sept. 24, 1956, p. 19, Sept. 28, 1956, p. 54, Oct. 27, 1956, p. 27, Aug. 11, 1957, II, 14, Oct. 17, 1957, p. 1, Oct. 18, 1957, pp. 1, 4, Oct. 21, 1957, p. 9, Oct. 22, 1957, p. 1; Robert V. Hatcher to Eisenhower, April 8, 1955, OF 154-B-1, DDEL.

58. "The Hudson-Champlain 350th Anniversary Celebrations of 1959," Final Report (New York, 1960), pp. 4–5; *New York Times*. Sept. 29, 1957, II, 21, July 29, 1958, p. 25, Nov. 5, 1958, p. 121, Oct. 10, 1958, p. 62, Nov. 2, 1958, p. 56, Jan. 28, 1959, p. 18, Feb. 26, 1959, p. 63, April 12, 1959, XI, 31. Definitive on 1909 is Karal Ann Marling, *George Washington Slept Here: Colonial Revivals and American Culture, 1876–1986* (Cambridge, Mass., 1988), pp. 201–2.

59. *New York Times*, Sept. 6, 1957, p. 23, Sept. 29, 1957, II, 21, Jan. 22, 1958, p. 9, Dec. 11, 1958, p. 30, Jan 11, 1959, p. 81, April 16, 1959, p. 5, Sept. 20, 1959, XII, 9.

60. Ibid., Feb. 15, 1959, p. 54, April 12, 1959, XI, 31, May 1, 1959, p. 31, May 10, 1959, X, 9, 10, July 10, 1959, p. 27.

61. Ibid., March 7, 1959, p. 42, April 3, 1959, p. 11, April 4, 1959, p. 2,

June 7, 1959, XII, 9, June 12, 1959, p. 1; Leon Michael, press release, "The Hudson-Champlain 350th Anniversary Celebrations," March 27, 1959, Box 169, Gen. Corres., Nixon Papers.

62. *New York Times,* Sept. 12, 1959, pp. 1, 10, Sept. 14, 1959, p. 2, Sept. 15, 1959, p. 3, Sept. 18, 1959, p. 40, Sept. 19, 1959, p. 4, Sept. 20, 1959, p. 67.

63. Ibid., May 10, 1959, X, 9, June 7, 1959, XII, 9, June 11, 1959, p. 31, June 12, 1959, pp. 1, 19, June 13, 1959, pp. 1, 19, June 24, 1959, p. 48, June 29, 1959, p. 31.

64. See, e.g., ibid., June 16, 1959, p. 4, June 17, 1959, p. 18.

65. Ibid., June 11, 1959, p. 31, June 12, 1959, p. 19. Michael Kammen notes the persistence of a "peculiar concatenation of tradition and progress" as a theme in other contexts. *Mystic Chords of Memory,* p. 514.

66. *Cong. Record,* 101 (June 22, 1955), 9030; *New York Times,* May 27, 1956, VI, 25, 34, April 2, 1957, p. 36.

Chapter 7

1. Bellah, "Civil Religion in America," *Daedalus,* 96 (Winter, 1967: 9–10, 16.

2. See John W. Jeffries, "The 'Quest for National Purpose' of 1960," *American Quarterly* 30 (Fall, 1978): 451–70.

3. John E. Allen, undated memorandum [1957]; C.J. Corliss to Schwengel, April 19, 1957; Corliss to Sen. William F. Knowland, April 27, 1958, all Box 38, Lincoln Sesquicentennial Commission Papers, LC (hereafter LSC Papers). Also see Kammen, *Mystic Chords of Memory,* pp. 589–90; Merrill D. Peterson, *Lincoln in American Memory* (New York, 1994), pp. 362–71.

4. Minutes, LSC meetings, Jan. 10 and May 17, 1958, Box 36, LSC Papers; "Lincoln Commission Seems Bogged Down," *Indianapolis Star,* April 16, 1958, in *Congressional Record,* 104 (April 29, 1958), A3878; *Lincoln Sesquicentennial Intelligencer,* (Jan., 1959); ibid. (Sept., 1959); *New York Times,* April 17, 1958, p. 20.

5. Clippings, *Washington Post,* May 21, June 23, and July 27, 1958, all Box 35, LSC Papers; *New York Times,* July 26, 1958, p. 15.

6. There was money to hire a public relations firm. "Report of Subcommittee on Special Projects," May 7, 1958, Box 36; Baringer, Executive Director's Report, Jan. 24, 1959; Minutes, Executive Committee meeting, April 24, 1959, all Box 36, LSC Papers; *Lincoln Sesquicentennial Intelligencer* [hereafter *LSI*] (Jan., 1959).

7. *LSI* (Jan., 1959); *New York Times,* Feb. 12, 1959, p. 22.

8. *LSI* (March, 1959); ibid. (June, 1959); clipping, n.d. [1959], "Voice of America Sets Lincoln Tribute," Box 35, LSC Papers.

9. *New York Times*, Sept. 14, 1959, p. 13, Sept. 17, 1959, p. 19.

10. GOP aides occupied some seats. Ibid., Feb. 1, 1959, II, 1, Feb. 13, 1959, p. 21; *LSI*, (Jan., 1959); *Washington Post*, Jan. 25, 1959, p. E5.

11. On this event, see Kammen, *Mystic Chords*, pp. 590–610; Bodnar, *Remaking America*, pp. 206–26.

12. Virgil Carrington Jones speech, April 16, 1959, Box 12, Civil War Centennial Commission Papers, Record Group 79, National Archives (hereafter CWCCP); Bell Wiley, Transcript, "National Assembly, Civil War Centennial Commission," Jan. 14, 1958, Box 11, ibid.; *New York Times*, June 9, 1957, X, 15.

13. Such qualms abated by 1958, when Congress passed a measure to give federal pensions to over a thousand widows of Confederates. *Southern Advertising and Publishing*, 36 (July, 1961): 10; *New York Times*, Feb. 4, 1956, p. 40, Feb. 5, 1956, p. 7, March 2, 1958, p. 36, May 14, 1958, p. 33.

14. U.S. Grant 3rd to Eisenhower, July 27, 1954, President's Personal File 47, DDEL; *New York Times*, May 17, 1959, p. 46.

15. Williams claimed he would turn 117 in 1959. Albert Woolson, the last Union veteran, died in 1956. *New York Times*, May 30, 1959, p. 2. Sept. 4, 1959, p. 6, Dec. 20, 1959, p. 1, Dec. 21, 1959, p. 27, Dec. 24, 1959, p. 20.

16. *Cong. Record*, 104 (Aug. 20, 1958), 18631; 85th Cong., 1st Sess., *H. J. Res. 253* (Report No. 1076).

17. William B. Hesseltine, "The Civil War Industry," *Michigan History* 42 (Dec., 1958): 427; Victor Gondos, Jr., "Karl S. Betts and the War Centennial Commission," *Military Affairs* 27 (Summer, 1963): 51–70. Chicago's Civil War Round Table dated from 1940. *The Civil War Round Table* [Chicago], XXVI (Nov., 1965), Box 1, CWCCP.

18. *100 Years After* (May, 1958); ibid., (June, 1960). This was the monthly newsletter of the National Civil War Centennial Commission.

19. Edmund C. Gass of the NPS was the CWCC's assistant executive director (and briefly its executive director). Memorandum, Roy E. Appleman to Chief Historian, June 12, 1956, Box 32, CWCCP; Memorandum, W.G. Carnes to Conrad Wirth, June 12, 1956, ibid.; *100 Years After*, (Feb., 1959); ibid., (June 1965).

20. *New York Times*, March 30, 1959, p. 50; transcript, "National Assembly, Civil War Centennial Commission," Jan. 14, 1958, pp. 68–69, Box 11, CWCCP.

21. *Congressional Record*, 103 (Feb. 27, 1957), 2754, (Aug. 19, 1957), 15185–86, (Aug. 30, 1957), 16675; ibid., 104 (Aug. 20, 1958), 18631–32; Gondos, "Karl S. Betts," 53–55; *New York Times*, Jan. 30, 1957, p. 60, May 21, 1957, p. 37, June 9, 1957, X, 15, Sept. 8, 1957, p. 46; CWCC, *100*

Years After, (Sept., 1958), 1.

22. *New York Times,* Dec. 8, 1957, p. 37, Dec. 25, 1957, p. 34. The largely northern membership drew comment.

23. *New York Times,* Dec. 21, 1957, p. 20; "Current Biography of Major General U. S. Grant, 3rd, Ret'd," (Feb., 1959), Box 25, CWCCP; Marling, *Washington Slept Here,* p. 324.

24. "Biographical Sketch—Karl S. Betts," (Feb., 1959), Box 25, CWCCP; Herbert E. Kahler to Bradley Nash, March 22, 1957, Box 32, ibid; Betts speech, May 7, 1960, Box 31, ibid; Grant to Betts, May 15, 1961, Box 65, ibid.; *New York Times,* April 6, 1958, p. 50.

25. Betts speech, May 5, 1960, Box 14; Betts press release, Dec. 28, 1958, Box 31; Betts to Col. Robert S. Henry, July 30, 1958, Box 39, all CWCCP; Edmund C. Gass to Mary Broder, Oct. 13, 1958, Box 6, AHF Papers.

26. Minutes of Fifth Meeting of the Civil War Centennial Commission, Jan. 6, 1959, Box 20, CWCCP.

27. National Better Business Bureau, "The Civil War Centennial Commission," May 25, 1961, Box 8; Betts to Short, Aug. 31, 1960, Box 32; CWCC press release, March 1, 1961, Box 31, all CWCCP.

28. *Cong. Record,* 103 (Aug. 19, 1957), 15185; Virginia Civil War Commission news release, Aug. 20, 1962, Box 92; telegram, Eisenhower to Grant, April 15, 1959, Box 12 both in CWCCP.

29. Transcript, "National Assembly, Civil War Centennial Commission," Jan. 14, 1958; "Statement of Objectives and Suggestions for Civil War Centennial Commemorations," Jan. 15, 1958, both Box 11, ibid.

30. Marshall W. Rissman, resolution, n.d.; unsigned memorandum, n.d. [both Jan. 14, 1958], both in Box 12, CWCCP; "Mississippi's Greatest Hour: A Manual for Local Observances of the Centennial of the War Between the States, 1961–1965," (Jackson, Miss., [c. 1960]); J. Duane Squires, "Some Thoughts on New Hampshire and the Civil War Centennial," *Historical New Hampshire,* 16 (Dec., 1961): 3, both in Box 35, CWCCP. Other states employed similar language.

31. Betts to Dr. Ross Livingston, May 26, 1958; Betts, Statement at Second National Assembly, April 16–17, 1959, both Box 12, CWCCP. Congress had mandated annual national assemblies.

32. "Statement of Objectives and Suggestions for Civil War Centennial Commemorations," in *Digest of Action Taken by the National Assembly Convened by the Civil War Centennial Commission,* Jan. 14–15, 1958, Box 11; Introduction of Hon. Dewey Short, drafted by Betts, "Civil War Centennial Commission, 2nd National Assembly," [March 24, 1959], Box 12; Betts speech, May 5, 1960, Box 14; Betts speech, press release, May 7, 1960, Box 31, all in CWCCP.

33. Address by Dewey Short, April 16, 1959, Box 12, ibid.

34. National advertising manager of the *San Francisco Chronicle*, Lee made numerous Centennial appearances. Grant speech, May 5, 1960, Box 14; Betts, "Outline of speech for Mr. Dewey Short," Aug. 31, 1960, Box 32; Robert E. Lee, IV, speech, April 11, 1961, Box 15, all CWCCP; *New York Times*, March 15, 1961, p. 33.

35. Kentucky Civil War Centennial Commission, *Kentucky Remembers the Civil War Centennial* (Lexington, 1961), Box 33; "Centennial Commemoration July 22–23, 1961," Box 36 (#2), both in CWCCP.

36. "General Grant's Opening Remarks" at conference at DuPont Company, Aug. 27, 1959, Box 27; Grant to Harold Lambert, July 20, 1959, Box 93; "Report on Observance of The Centennial of the Civil War," Jan. 5, 1960, Box 20, all ibid.

37. It was reprinted in the newsletter of John Kasper's Seaboard White Citizens Council. On Kasper's agitations against racial integration, see Anthony Lewis, *Portrait of a Decade: The Second American Revolution*, Bantam edition (New York, 1965), pp. 33–37.

38. Clippings, *Washington Post*, Sept. 10, 1959, and *Washington Daily News*, June 25, 1959; Herman Edelsberg to Grant, June 19, 1959; Grant to Joseph F. Barr, July 29, 1959; Betts to Gerald D. Morgan, July 14, 1959; Grant to Edelsberg, July 15, 1959; Emanuel Celler to Eisenhower, July 10, 1959, all in OF 154-A, DDEL.

39. *New York Times*, Dec. 8, 1960, p. 22, Jan. 8, 1961, p. 1, Jan. 9, 1961, p. 1; note, "F" [Frederic Fox] to John Eisenhower, Dec. 30, [1960], OF 154-A, DDEL.

40. Nevins to Robertson, Feb. 16, 1963, Box 97, CWCCP; Howard N. Meyer, "Rally Round What Flag?" *Commonweal*, 74 (June 9, 1961): 271.

41. Betts to Cong. Wint Smith, Feb. 6, 1959, Box 32, CWCCP; CWCC press release, Aug. 19, 1958, Box 71, ibid.

42. *New York Times*, March 10, 1961, p. 29, March 15, 1961, p. 1, March 18, 1961, pp. 1, 8, March 22, 1961, p. 1, March 23, 1961, p. 23, March 24, 1961, pp. 1, 18, March 26, 1961, pp. 1, 72, April 2, 1961, p. 41; Statement by Cong. Tuck, March 21, 1961, Box 15; Betts to Carl Haverlin, April 28, 1961, Box 83; Grant to Sen. Ralph Yarborough, June 7, 1961, Box 23, all CWCCP; JFK to Grant, March 14, 1961; Memorandum, Harris Wofford to Kenneth O'Donnell, "Re: The New Civil War," n.d. [ca. March 24, 1961] and "A Report on the Civil War," March 24, 1961, all in Folder FG 633, White House Central File (WHCF), John F. Kennedy Library.

43. Speech by Ashley Halsey, Jr., April 11, 1961, Box 15; Carl Haverlin, Report, Fourth National Assembly of the National Civil War Centennial Commission, April 11–12, 1961, Box 83; statement by Donald Flamm,

April 12, 1961, Box 15, all in CWCCP; *Newsweek,* 57 (Apr. 21, 1961): 40.

44. Craven to Betts, July 23 and Aug. 2, 1958; Betts to Craven, July 28, 1958, all in Box 28, CWCCP. The terms of the warning emerged from Craven's own Civil War scholarship.

45. *New York Times,* Sept. 19, 1961, p. 32; Meyer, "Rally Round What Flag?": 273; Grant to Olive Ann Pixley, Jan. 25, 1961, Box 32, CWCCP; Press release, Feb. 22, 1959, Box 31, ibid.

46. Wilbur W. Nusbaum for the Committee for First Manassas, "First Manassas (A Prospectus)," April 7, 1960, Box 36 (#l); Betts to R. U. Darby, March 30, 1960, Box 78; "Second Annual Report of the Executive Director," Jan. 5, 1960, Box 20; Betts to Grant, March 19, 1959, Box 32; press release, Dec. 28, 1958, Box 31, all CWCCP; *New York Times,* April 6, 1961, p. 34.

47. Hambleton Tapp to Betts, Aug. 31, 1961, Box 69; Ira L. West to Grant, April 19, 1959, Box 32; A. B. Moore to Betts, Aug. 8, 1961, Box 69, all CWCCP; *New York Times,* April 16, 1961, p. 72, May 1, 1961, p. 29. For extremist views, see Box 32, CWCCP.

48. Malcolm R. Hebert, press release, "The Civil War has come to the appliance industry!" n.d., Box 56, CWCCP; *New York Times,* May 30, 1961, p. 16, June 4, 1961, p. 22 ; Don Gerlinger to Betts, Aug. 29, 1961, Box 69, CWCCP; Cartoon, n.d., Box 32, ibid.

49. Some advertisers apparently so feared offending either side that they avoided Civil War themes. Grant to Mrs. Pierre S. Du Pont, III, Sept. 27, 1959, Box 32; Kermit V. Sloan speech, "Advertising and the Civil War Centennial," April 11, 1961, Box 15, both CWCCP; *100 Years After* (Aug. 1958); *New York Times,* Dec. 12, 1960, p. 46.

50. *New York Times,* April 19, 1961, p. 27, Sept. 7, 1961, p. 31, Sept. 16, 1961, p. 44; Schwengel et al. to Grant, Aug. 21, 1961, and memorandum, n.d. [Aug. 21, 1961?]; transcript, Special Meeting of CWCC, Aug. 30, 1961; Schwengel to Grant, Aug. 22 & 23, 1961, all in Box 20, CWCCP; Grant to JFK, Aug. 30, 1961, folder FG 633/A, WHCF, JFKL; Betts press release, Sept. 15, 1961, Box 94, CWCCP.

51. Schwengel to JFK, Sept. 30, 1961, Folder FG 633, WHCF, JFKL; *New York Times,* Oct. 14, 1961, p. 10, Dec. 5, 1961, p. 31; CWCC Executive Committee, Minutes, Dec. 3, 1961, Box 97, CWCCP; Nevins statement, Dec. 4, 1961, Box 20, ibid.

52. Statement by Nevins, Dec. 4, 1961, Box 97, CWCCP; *100 Years After* (Feb., 1962); Robertson to Marshall Moore, April 17, 1962, Box 32, CWCCP; "Suggested specifications for the Impact Series," n.d., Box 97, ibid.

53. Reportedly JFK's enthusiasm for reenactments caused Nevins to reconsider, but Robertson denied the story. Robertson to George A.

Riek, May 15, 1962, Box 59; Robertson to Everett J. Landers, May 9, 1962, Box 82; James V. Murfin speech, "Antietam and Maryland in the Centennial," May 23, 1963, Box 15, all CWCCP; *New York Times*, May 7, 1962, p. 22, May 14, 1962, p. 14.

54. *New York Times*, Sept. 16, 1962, p. 86; press release, Feb. 19, 1965, Box 73, CWCCP; Adam G. Adams, "Activities and Accomplishments, Florida Civil War Centennial Commission," April 8, 1963, Box 74, ibid.

55. Scott Candler to Betts, Aug. 1, 1960, Box 32, CWCCP; Schwengel to Nevins, Feb. 23, 1962; A. B. Moore to Robertson, March 6, 1962; Robertson to Nevins, Feb. 28, 1962, all in Box 43, CWCCP. And see Scott A. Sandage, "A Marble House Divided: The Lincoln Memorial, the Civil Rights Movement, and the Politics of Memory, 1939–1963," *Journal of American History*, 80 (June, 1993), 135–78.

56. T.J. Reardon, Jr., memorandum to heads of executive departments and agencies, Aug. 15, 1962, Folder FG 610, WHCF, JFKL; Robertson to Rep. Morris K. Udall, Oct. 30, 1962, Box 43, CWCCP.

57. Schwengel to Kenneth O'Donnell, Aug. 24, 1962, Folder FG 633, WHCF, JFKL; Memorandum, Arthur Schlesinger, Jr., to Pierre Salinger, April 20, 1962, ibid.; "Correspondence with the White House Relative to Emancipation Proclamation Centennial Ceremony, Sept. 22, 1962," n.d. [Aug., 1962], Box 43, CWCCP; Robertson to Nevins, Aug. 3 & 27, 1962, Box 97, ibid.; Memorandum, Gass to Nevins et al., July 27, 1962, Box 43, ibid.

58. Nevins to Stevenson, Aug. 24, 1962, Box 97; Robertson to James V. Murfin, Sept. 27, 1962, Box 25; Schwengel, press release, Sept. 17, 1962, Box 64; Jack Jurey, WTOP editorial, Sept. 18, 1963, Box 43, all in CWCCP.

59. *100 Years After* (Oct., 1962); *Washington Post*, Sept. 23, 1962, p. 1; Nevins to Senate Appropriations Committee, Feb. 9, 1963, Box 97, CWCCP.

60. Minutes, 12th Meeting, CWCC, Sept. 22, 1962, Box 21; Minutes, Executive Committee, CWCC, May 23, 1963, Box 23; Robertson to Julian Vaughan, Sept. 5, 1963, Box 18; minutes, 14th meeting of CWCC, Jan. 14, 1964, Box 21; Virgil Carrington Jones to Bruce Catton, Nov. 28, 1962, Box 17, all in CWCCP.

61. The liberals were Father Theodore M. Hesburgh, member of the U.S. Civil Rights Commission and President of Notre Dame, and New Jersey Governor Richard J. Hughes. *New York Times*, June 30, 1963, p. 39, July 1, 1963, p. 17, July 2, 1963, p. 14, Feb. 13, 1965, p. 7.

62. Program, "Seventh National Assembly Sponsored by the U. S. Civil War Centennial Commission," Atlanta, June 10–12, 1964, Box 18, CWCCP.

63. Virginia Civil War Commission, *Centennial News Letter* (April, 1965), Box 92, CWCCP; *New York Times*, April 9, 1965, p. 35, April 10, 1965, p. 30.

64. *Cong. Record*, 111 (89th Cong., lst Sess.), 10535–36; *New York Times*, April 26, 1965, p. 34. His opaque terms probably did not embrace critics of the Vietnam War; the first teach-in had occurred only a month before. Criticism of "extremists" was a staple in the historical lesson-drawing stimulated by the Centennial.

65. The resolution creating the American Revolutionary Bicentennial Commission was enacted in 1966.

Chapter 8

1. Protestors in 1954 included Rev. A. J. Muste, Bayard Rustin, and Dorothy Day and represented the War Resisters League, the Forum of Reconciliation and the *Catholic Worker*. *New York Times*, April 25, 1954, p. 62, June 15, 1954, pp. 1, 32, June 16, 1955, p. 19, June 18, 1955, p. 8, July 21, 1956, p. 6, July 21, 1957, p. 35.

2. Todd Gitlin, *The Sixties: Years of Hope, Days of Rage* (New York, 1987), pp. 82–83. For tactical considerations underlying Selma's civil rights demonstrations, see David J. Garrow, *Protest at Selma: Martin Luther King, Jr., and the Voting Rights Act of 1965* (New Haven, Conn., 1978).

3. Amy Swerdlow, "Ladies' Day at the Capitol: Women Strike for Peace Versus HUAC," *Feminist Studies*, 8 (Fall, 1982), 493–520.

4. A harbinger of later protests appeared at a 1962 parachute demonstration at New York's Governors Island when twelve pickets displayed signs contending "war is not a game." *New York Times*, May 21, 1961, p. 38, May 13, 1962, p. 79, May 20, 1962, p. 1, May 19, 1963, p. 75, May 17, 1964, p. 40, May 16, 1965, pp. 1, 4, May 22, 1966, pp. 1, 82, May 21, 1967, p. 1, May 19, 1968, p. 45.

5. Ibid., May 19, 1968, p. 45, May 17, 1970, p. 62; *Toledo Blade*, May 21, 1970, p. 4.

6. *New York Times*, May 14, 1968, p. 49, May 16, 1970, p. 7, May 16, 1971, p. 1.

7. Ibid., April 14, 1968, p. 78, April 28, 1968, p. 72, May 1, 1970, p. 42, May 3, 1970, p. 92, May 4, 1975, p. 60.

8. *New York Herald Tribune*, Jan. 12, 1953, p. 3.

9. On actions by conservative youth, including support of student loyalty oaths, see Gregory L. Schneider, "The Other Sixties: Young Americans for Freedom and the Politics of Conservatism," (dissertation, University of Illinois at Chicago, 1996), chs. 1–2.

10. *New York Times*. Aug. 24, 1959, p. 2; Matthews, "Off My Chest,"

American Opinion (Sept., 1959) Box 483, Gen. Corres., Nixon Papers; Fulton Lewis, Jr., column, *Los Angeles Examiner*, Aug. 21, 1959; Josephine Ripley column, *Christian Science Monitor*, Aug. 21, 1959; David Lawrence, "'Enter, Czar Nikita!'" *US News* (Aug. 10, 1959), all in Box 1, Series 330 (Khrushchev Visit), Nixon Papers.

11. *New York Times*, Aug. 26, 1959, p. 15, Aug. 27, 1959, p. 1, Sept. 1, 1959, p. 3, Sept. 4, 1959, p. 4; Matt Cvetic to Nixon, Sept. 1, 1959, Box 198; Victor Lasky to Nixon, [Aug. 22, 1959], Box 439; memorandum, de Toledano to Nixon, "Speeches on the Khruschev Visit," n.d. [1959], Box 213, all in Gen. Corres., Nixon Papers.

12. Clipping, *Baltimore Sun*, Sept. 13, 1959, Box 1, Series 330, Nixon Papers; *New York Times*, Aug. 19, 1959, p. 44, Sept. 9, 1959, p. 13. Security problems necessitated eliminating the Disneyland tour—to Khrushchev's disgust.

13. *New York Times*, Aug. 7, 1959, p. 2, Aug. 13, 1959, p. 11, Sept. 1, 1959, p. 3, Sept. 4, 1959, p. 4, Sept. 6, 1959, pp. 1, 7, Sept. 11, 1959, p. 8.

14. Ibid., Aug. 12, 1959, p. 17, Aug. 21, 1959, pp. 1, 3, Aug. 24, 1959, p. 2.

15. Kenneth W. Ingwalson, "Generalized Comments Resulting from an Informal Meeting . . . on 'What to do about the Contemplated Visit of Mr. Khrushchev' Held August 14, 1959," Box 101; Ben Moreel to "All Bishops of the Catholic Church," Aug. 26, 1959, ibid.; handbill, Committee against U.S.A. Surrender, "Cry, Oh Beloved Country!" (San Marino, Calif., n.d. [1959]), Box 172, all in Gen. Corres., Nixon Papers.

16. *New York Times*, Sept. 6, 1959, p. 20, Sept. 11, 1959, p. 8, Sept. 14, 1959, p. 19, Sept. 19, 1959, pp. 1, 11, Sept. 24, 1959, p. 22.

17. Ibid., Sept. 10, 1959, pp. 14, 41, Sept. 13, 1959, p. 20, Sept. 15, 1959, p. 35, Sept. 18, 1959, p. 18, Sept. 21, 1959, p. 19.

18. Ibid., Sept. 16, 1959, pp. 1, 18, 19, 20, Sept. 18, 1959, p. 1; notes on phone call from Nora De Tole[dano], Sept. 15, 1959, Box 213, Gen. Corres., Nixon Papers.

19. *New York Times*, Sept. 18, 1959, p. 17, Sept. 20, 1959, p. 1, Sept. 21, 1959, p. 1, Sept. 25, 1959, pp. 1, 15; Kenneth D. Wells speech, Feb. 13, 1960, Folder 1, Box 14, Series 3, Wells MSS.

20. Wells speech, April 23, 1959, Folder 7, Box 13, Series 3, ibid.

21. *New York Times*, Sept. 19, 1960, pp. 1, 18, 19, Sept. 20, 1960, pp. 1, 15, Sept. 21, 1960, pp. 1, 17.

22. VFW, Department of Alabama, booklet, "Loyalty Day 1960," [March, 1960]. GF l-F-3, DDEL; News release, Civitan Club of Saint Louis, Sept. 14, 1961; Mayor Robert King High to JFK, Oct. 13, 1961; Ben Hill Griffin, Jr., to JFK, Nov. 6, 1962, all in Folder HU 6, Box 376, WHCF, JFKL; *Group Research Report*, 2 (April 10, 1963), p. 26, Series 4,

National Farmers Union MSS, Western Historical Collections, University of Colorado.

23. *Toledo Blade,* May 21, 1970, p. 4; *New York Times,* July 4, 1969, pp. 23, 44, Nov. 7, 1969, p. 10, Nov. 11, 1969, p. 1; Freedoms Foundation, "Foundation Family News," May, 1970, Folder 1, Box 2, Series 3, Wells Collection; Freedoms Foundation, "Eighteenth Annual National and School Awards," Feb. 22, 1967, Folder 9, Box 8, ibid.; "America Speaks Out," *V.F.W. Magazine,* 57 (Feb., 1970): 26.

24. Ironically, "1776" won a Freedoms Foundation award for 1969. *New York Times,* July 4, 1969, pp. 23, 44, June 24, 1970, p. 37.

25. ARBA, *The Bicentennial of the United States of America: A Final Report to the People* (Washington, D.C.,1977), pp. 208, 263.

26. *New York Times,* Feb. 9, 1973, p. 16, Dec. 17, 1973, p. 26; Peoples Bicentennial Commission, *Birthday: A Planning and Activity Guide for Citizens' Participation During the Bicentennial Years* (New York, 1974); W.S. McBirnie, "Warning to All Americans. . . . ," Series XI, Box 94, Mike Mansfield MSS.

27. ARBA, *Final Report,* preface and pp. 225, 257, 291.

28. Ibid., pp. 4, 47; *New York Times,* July 5, 1976, pp. 1, 18.

Conclusion

1. Much of it stemmed, the latter said, from "the newness of our population, which has no appreciation or knowledge" of LA's "distinct" heritage. Bowron to City Council, June 12, 1946, Box 2, Bowron Collection; *Los Angeles Times,* Feb. 4, 1948, p. 15.

2. "Eight Weekends with Politics: Mr. Bryce Harlow speaking on 'Compromise and Democracy: Legislative Action,'" n.d. [1963?], Box 320, Gen. Corres., Nixon Papers.

3. Booklet, "Loyalty Day 1960," VFW, Department of Alabama, n.d. [March, 1960], General File 1-F-3, DDEL. Cf. the VFW's National Commander in 1969, on the need to counter radical demonstrations: "Don't keep silent while the street mob takes control. . . . Let us not stand aside as this country goes the way of ancient Greece and Rome because its citizens were too indifferent, too apathetic, too slovenly to act." *V.F.W. Magazine,* 57 (Dec., 1969): 3.

4. Navy League of the United States in association with Freedoms Foundation of Valley Forge, "Project Alert: A Call for Community Education. . . ," 3d ed. (New Orleans: E. S. Upton Printing Co., 1961), p. iv; Navy League, *Alert! The Lubbock Plan* (Washington, D.C., 1960), p. 6, both in Folder 1, Box 5, Series 3, Kenneth D. Wells MSS. Other communities undertook similar programs.

5. Allen C. Gottschaldt to Sherman Adams, Nov. 3, 1954, GF 1-G;

Gerald D. Persons to Joyce Chesney, April 10, 1959, GF 1-F-3, ibid.; "Ronnie" to President Eisenhower, June 1, 1960, GF 1-G, all in DDEL.

6. Frederick G. Dutton to Brendan Byrne, Aug. 28, 1961; *Challenge to Americans: The struggle we face and how to help with it* (Advertising Council, 1962), p. 25, both in HU 6 Ideologies, WHCF—Subject Files, JFKL.

7. Press release, "Loyalty Day, 1963," April 19, 1963, HO 22 Loyalty Day (#1), WHCF, JFKL. JFK's 1962 Loyalty Day proclamation hinted at the balance it sought by repudiating "totalitarian concepts of either the left or the right." Proclamation, "Loyalty Day, 1962," ibid.

8. *Christopher News Notes*, no. 96 (March, 1959), Box 4, AHF Records; Noe P. Jimenez to *Corpus Christi Caller*, n.d. [May, 1959], GF 1-F-3, DDEL.

9. Walter Bedell Smith and John C. Cornelius to AHF Executive Committee, Oct. 17, 1956, Box 19, AHF Records; memorandum, Brendan Byrne to Thomas D'A. Brophy, March 30, 1951, Box 14, ibid. On this broad problem in another context, see Robert Westbrook, "Private Interests and Public Obligations in World War II," in Richard Wightman Fox and T. J. Jackson Lears, eds., *The Power of Culture: Critical Essays in American History* (Chicago, 1993), pp. 195–222.

10. Cornelius, "For the Rexall Reporter: Let's All Register! Let's All Vote!" n.d. [1960], Box 1, AHF Records; Brophy to Thomas M. De-Bevois, April 15, 1952, Folder 497, Box 50, CIS, RFA; Memorandum, Yorke Allen, Jr., to Dana S. Creel, March 11, 1957, Folder 498, ibid.

11. Memorandum, Daniel W. Montenegro to [Roger] Tubby, Aug. 22, 1961, HU 6, Subject Files, WHCF, JFKL.

12. See file HU6 Ideologies, WHCF, JFKL.

13. Louis A. Novins, "Recommendations for Future Program," Sept. 27, 1951, Box 14, AHF Records.

14. See letters to George Gallup, July–August, 1965, Box 202, AHF Records.

15. Advertising Council, "Radio-TV Bulletin," Sept.–Oct., 1968, Box 28; unsigned, draft of letter [by Samuel C. Brightman], n.d. [ca. Nov. 24, 1967], Box 29; Donald H. McGannon and Charles E. Wilson to Robert P. Keim, July 9, 1968, Box 28, all in AHF Records.

16. Leo Burnett to Novins, Feb. 27, 1968; Brophy to Henry Ford II, May 2, 1967, both Box 29; Novins to Lee Howard, Oct. 30, 1968, Box 33; McGannon to "Fellow Trustees," Nov. 11, 1968, Box 28, all in AHF Records. The 1970 *Encyclopedia of Associations* (6th edition, Margaret Fisk, ed. [Detroit: Gale Research Co.]: 752) listed the AHF as "address unknown."

17. Memorandum, Abbott Washburn to Robert E. Cushman, July 20,

1959, Series 407, Nixon Papers. On the Kitchen Debate, see Karal Ann Marling, *As Seen on TV: The Visual Culture of Everyday Life in the 1950s* (Cambridge, Mass., 1994), ch. 7.

18. Navy League, *Alert! The Lubbock Plan*, p. 4; "Loyalty Day 1960," VFW, Department of Alabama, n.d. [March, 1960], General File 1-F-3, DDEL.

19. Brophy to Admiral Arleigh K. Burke, Sept. 24, 1962, Box 3, AHF Records; Col. Gordon L. Barclay to Maj. Gen. Chester V. Clifton, June 5, 1962, Folder HO18, White House Central Files, JFKL; Raymond B. Edwards, "Loyalty Day Is For All Americans," *V.F.W. Magazine* 57 (March, 1970): 16.

20. See W. T. Lahmon, Jr., *Deliberate Speed: The Origins of a Cultural Style in the American 1950s* (Washington, D.C., 1990); Marling, *As Seen on TV*; George Lipsitz, *Rainbow at Midnight: Labor and Culture in the 1940s* (Urbana, Ill., 1994). For a different political take on 1950s culture, see Jeffrey Hart, *When the Going Was Good! American Life in the Fifties* (New York, 1982).

21. Samuel C. Brightman, "Some Thoughts on the Current Political Scene," n.d. [ca. March 1, 1968], Box 29, AHF Records.

22. Interview, confidential source. Loyalty Day persists mostly in small towns and suburbs. See *Chicago Tribune*, May 3, 1996, II, 3.

23. The intrusion of Law Day—conducted by lawyers—upon the ceremonial time once commandeered by veterans and politicos for Loyalty Day hints at this trend.

24. On Strategy for Survival, see Randall Bennet Woods, *Fulbright: A Biography* (Cambridge, England, 1995), pp. 279ff. On this and the general discrediting of anticommunist "extremism," see Richard Gid Powers, *Not Without Honor: The History of American Anticommunism* (New York, 1995), ch. 10.

25. See John M. Findlay, *Magic Lands: Western Cityscapes and American Culture After 1940* (Berkeley, Calif., 1992), ch. 2.

John Marshall Bicentennial Commission, Records (R.G. 79). Cited as JMBC.

Records of the National Archives and Records Service (R.G. 64). Freedom Train, Educational Programs Division (cited as FT Records).
  Thad Page Records.
  Planning and Control Cases (NARA).
State Department (R.G. 59).
  Decimal File 1945-1949.
  Records of the Policy Planning Staff.
Treasury Department (R.G. 56).
  Records of Savings Bond Division (War Finan...

Manuscript Sources

Abilene, Kans., Dwight David Eisenhower Library.
  Papers of Dwight D. Eisenhower.
    General File.
    Official File.
    President's Personal File.
    Frederic Fox Records.
  Frederic Fox Papers.
  Robert Humphreys Papers.

Amherst, Mass., Amherst College, Robert Frost Library.
  Dwight Morrow MSS.

Boston, Mass., John F. Kennedy Library.
  Papers of John F. Kennedy.
    White House Central File (WHCF).
    White House Staff Files.

Boulder, Co., University of Colorado, Western Historical Collections.
  National Farmers Union Mss.

Columbia, Mo., State Historical Society of Missouri, University of Missouri-Western Historical Manuscript Collection.
  Phil M. Donnelly MSS.

Hyde Park, N.Y., Franklin D. Roosevelt Library.
  Papers of Franklin D. Roosevelt.
    Official File.

Independence, Mo., Harry S. Truman Library.
    Papers of Harry S. Truman.
        Official File.
        Pamphlet File.
        President's Personal File.
        Files of Charles W. Jackson.
        Files of Spencer Quick.
    Tom S. Clark Papers.
    Paul. H. Griffith Papers.
    Francis P. Matthews Papers.

Kansas City, Kans.,
    Clinton W. Kanaga, Jr., Files (privately held).

Kansas City, Mo., Veterans of Foreign Wars National Headquarters.
    Americanism Files.

Laguna Niguel, Calif., National Archives–Southwest Pacific Region
    Richard M. Nixon Papers.
        General Correspondence.
        Series 330 (Khrushchev Visit).
        Series 407.

Liberty, Tex., Sam Houston Regional Library & Research Center.
    Martin Dies MSS.

Madison, Wis., State Historical Society of Wisconsin.
    Fred Bassett Blair MSS.
    Thomas D'Arcy Brophy MSS.
    Marquis Childs MSS.
    Wisconsin Department American Legion Papers (WDAL).
    State Historical Society, Project Files.

Missoula, Minn., University of Montana.
    Mike Mansfield MSS.

Mosinee, Wis., Dessert Library.
    Misc. Clippings.

Palo Alto, Calif., Hoover Institution.
    Benjamin Gitlow Papers.

Pocantico Hills, N.Y., Rockefeller Archive Center (RAC).
    Rockefeller Family Archives, Office of the Messrs. Rockefeller.
        Cultural Interests Series.
        Papers of John D. Rockefeller, Personal.

Provo, Utah, Brigham Young University.
    Kenneth D. Wells Collection.
    Kenneth D. and Ruth E. Wells Autobiographical Files.

Rochester, N.Y., University of Rochester, Rush Rhees Library.
    Thomas E. Dewey MSS.

        alif., Henry E. Huntington Library.
        Collection.

San Marino, C~~~~
    Fletcher Bowron ⌣~~~~
    John Anson Ford Collection.

Springfield, Ill., Illinois State Historical Library.
    Scott W. Lucas MSS.

Suitland, Md., National Archives and Records Administration.
    Records of the American Heritage Foundation (R.G. 200). Cited as
        AHF Papers.
    Records of the National Conference on Citizenship (R.G. 200). Cited
        as NCC Records.

**Tempe, Ariz., Arizona State University, Hayden Library, Arizona
    Historical Foundation.**
    Barry Goldwater MSS.

**Washington, D.C., Immigration and Naturalization Service Historical
    Reference Library** *(misc. collections).*

————, **Library of Congress (LC).**
    Clinton P. Anderson MSS.
    Lincoln Sesquicentennial Commission Papers (LSC).

————, **National Archives and Records Administration.**
    Army–Operations General Decimal Files 1952, 354.2
    Long Horn (R.G. 319)
    Headquarters Army Ground Forces (R.G. 337).
    General Staff, G-3 (Exercise Long Horn).
    Civil War Centennial Commission, Records (R.G. 79). Cited as
        CWCCP.

(Wa... ...ice Division).

————, Ehy Vajda Seng Scrapbook (privately held).

Williamsburg, Va., Colonial Williamsburg Foundation Archives.
  Block and Building Records.
  Dignitiaries' Visits.
  Publications–Williamsburg Student Burgesses.
  Voice of Democracy Program.

Index